# RADICAL SOCIALISM IN CZECHOSLOVAKIA
Bohumír Šmeral, the Czech Road to Socialism and the Origins of the Czechoslovak Communist Party (1917-1921)

BERNARD WHEATON

East European Monographs, Boulder
Distributed by Columbia University Press, New York
1986

EAST EUROPEAN MONOGRAPHS, NO. CCXIII

Copyright © 1986 by Bernard Wheaton
Library of Congress Card Catalog Number 86-80729
ISBN 0-88033-110-0

Printed in the United States of America

# CONTENTS

List of Tables     v
Key to Abbreviations     vii
Introduction     xi

## Part One

Šmeralism .................................................... 3

## Part Two

Chapter One    Nationalism in the Czech Lands ................... 29
Chapter Two    The Challenge from the
                     Political Environment ............................ 57
Chapter Three   The Challenge of the Radical
                     Socialists ......................................... 75
Chapter Four    The Economic Demands ....................... 103
Chapter Five    The Social Problem—Town and Country ........ 125

## Part Three

The External Environment ...................................... 149

Conclusion     165
Notes     173
List of Works Consulted     191
Name Index     201
Subject Index     203

Frontispiece.  Dr. Bohumír Šmeral.

## LIST OF TABLES

1. Ownership of Property .......................................... 107
2. Retail Prices in Prague .......................................... 109
3. Cost of Goods ................................................. 111
4. Average Wages Earned ......................................... 112
5. Relationship Between Wages and Prices ......................... 113
6. Strikes 1919–1923 .............................................. 118
7. Number of Agricultural Concerns ............................... 133
8. Pattern of Ownership/Renting .................................. 134
9. Composition of Labour Force ................................... 134

# KEY TO ABBREVIATIONS IN NOTES AND TEXT

| | |
|---|---|
| AMV | Archiv Ministerstva vnitra |
| AMZV | Archiv Ministerstva zahranicnich veci |
| AÚD KSČ | Archiv Ústavu dějin Komunisticke strany Československa |
| AÚ ML | Archiv Ústavu Marsismu-Leninismu |
| AÚV KSČ | Archiv Ústředního výboru Koministické strany Československa |
| | |
| COD | Ceskoslovenska obec delnicka |
| CNSP | Czech National Socialist Party |
| CPC | Czechoslovak Communist Party |
| | |
| DSP | Communist Socialist Party |
| | |
| KPR | Kancelář presidenta republiky |
| | |
| MP | Marxist Party |
| | |
| NSP | National Socialist Party |
| | |
| OSC | Odborove sdruzeni Ceskoslovenske |
| | |
| SAB | Státní archiv, Brno |
| SÚA MSP | Státní ústřední archiv, Ministerstvo sociální péče |
| SÚA MVP | Státní ústřední archiv, Ministerstvo veřejných práci |
| SÚA NV | Státní ústřední archiv, Národní výbor |
| SÚA PM | Státní ústřední archiv, Presidium Mistodržitelství |
| SÚA PMV | Státní ústřední archiv, Presidium Ministerstva vnitra |
| SD | Social Democrats |

KEY TO ABBREVIATIONS IN NOTES AND TEXT

SD MP      Social Democratic—Marxist Party
SDP        Social Democratic Party

TZ NS"R"    Těsnopisecké zprávy Národniho shromáždění "revoluční"

VÚA MNO   Vojenský ústřední archiv, Ministerstvo Národní obrany

# ACKNOWLEDGEMENTS

This book grew out of a disaster, more academic than unnatural, and nearly did not see the light of day either in this or any other form. The fact that it has I owe to a great many people of whom a few in particular must carry the can for my completing it at all, if not for its final appearance. Zdeněk Kavan, Lecturer in International Relations at the University of Sussex, kicked me back from the intellectual and psychological abyss more times than anyone reasonably should, while Beryl Williams, Senior Lecturer in Russian History also at Sussex, was an unfailing source of encouragement. Professor Zbyněk Zeman is also to be warmly thanked for making a number of suggestions at an early stage and for reading the manuscript.

There are people in Czechoslovakia also to whom a debt is due as indeed there is to the British Council who in awarding me a Research Scholarship in the first place enabled me to work for a two-year period in the libraries and archives in Prague, Olomouc and Brno. Thereafter, my research was hugely facilitated by help from "Olomoucký Standa" who provided me, one way or another, with books and printed sources otherwise unavailable in the United Kingdom. I could hardly forget the contribution of "Ostravský Rolfajs" either. Long discussions with him of his expectations before 1948 and his experience of post-revolutionary Czech society in a short career in its aparát helped clarify some of the essential features of a "Czech Road" which were not so different from the early 1920s.

Though this may be the first full-length study of Šmeralism to appear in English, it is far from the last word on the matter, though it may well be from me. It was a salutary experience to learn on a recent visit to Ostrava that there are as many as 60 full-time researchers in Czechoslovakia working on the historical problems thrown up by Šmeral's life and works. The limitations of their research such as they are not infrequently derive from constraints of a non-scholarly nature. However, I have no such excuse and the shortcomings of this study are all my own work.

Prague
Olomouc
Linz
Brighton

B.W.

# Introduction

This study is concerned with one aspect of the history of socialism in the Czech Lands. It focuses mainly on the years 1917–1921 and deals with the radical socialist movement identified with the name of its leader, Bohumír Šmeral. This is not an arbitrary choice, for Šmeralism, the convenient shorthand for the movement, related to the Czech political environment in such a way that it posed a grave threat to the Establishment. My interest in the radical Left then lies in its importance as a phenomenon which sprang up in response to the social and economic conditions of the time. Indeed there were other political fractions and movements which posited radical alternatives, for example the anarchists of Northern Bohemia. But they were not remotely as important as the movement Šmeral led. Within the environment, the aims they offered bordered on the utopian, while Šmeral's objectives were on the other hand realistic and perceived as such. The fact that Šmeralism appealed to a large part of the population and developed into a powerful mass movement contrasts with the fate of anarchism which had withered by 1920 and prompted many anarchists to seek their salvation in the ranks of the radical socialists.

The importance of Šmeralism however lies not simply in the fact that it was the most powerful of the anti-Establishment movements. First and foremost, it represented a challenge to Social Democratic orthodoxy and as such provided the major focus of opposition in the early years of the Republic. This tends to be confirmed by the fact that the Social Democratic Party [hereafter SDP] and successive governments, not seldom acting in tandem, worried by the radical socialists and alarmed at the possibility of far-reaching change, made determined attempts to halt Šmeral's progress. Secondly, and in its implications for the future of socialism perhaps more important, Šmeral's reluctance to allow the radical socialist movement to embrace Leninism was a challenge to the other pole of socialist orthodoxy which from 1920 was peddled with increasing vigour by the Comintern. This raises vital questions concerning the viability of a "third way", of a road to socialism different from the established orthodoxies, which I will return to later in the introduction.

That the mainstream of the radical socialist Left led by Šmeral provided the major focus of opposition to Social Democratic orthodoxy in the early years of the Republic can hardly be doubted. That the failure of Social Democracy to solve the economic and social crisis led in the short term to a great increase in social radicalism and finally to the founding of a communist party is also an eminently reasonable view. Both statements however conceal a number of important questions. Can we legitimately suppose that the conflict between Šmeral and the orthodox SDs was purely an inner-party affair centred on the most appropriate tactics to be used in pursuit of common aims or was Šmeral's concept of socialism sufficiently different and bound to clash with that of the SDs? Did Šmeral have any coherent alternative system at all or was it simply a series of acts of policy unconnected with each other and knitted at random to situations as they arose? The effective challenge to the Orthodox SDs in the final analysis devolved to the advantage of the pro-Bolshevik wing of the radical socialist Left. Yet it must be asked: how much common ground did Šmeral share with Lenin and Bolshevism? This question can also be fruitfully posed vis-á-vis the group of former Red Guards who became known as the Czech Bolsheviks. Šmeral's movement generated wide popular support. But what was the nature of its appeal and which sections of society looked to him and his movement for their salvation?

The acceptance of the Comintern's Twenty-One Conditions by the radical socialist Left was soon followed by the founding of the Czechoslovak Communist Party [hereafter CPC]. Yet this institutional split which put Šmeral forever beyond the pale of Social Democracy was not a spontaneous rift based on petty causes, but the outcome of a long process of polarization. This was already visible in the late 1890s when Bernstein's ideas had taken a firm hold among certain Czech SDs whose champion, Modráček, contested the party's self-ascription as Marxist, revolutionary and proletarian. Following Bernstein, he argued that the socialist parties' methods for achieving their aims, principally class-struggle and the dictatorship of the proletariat, were rendered unnecessary in the light of the slow but steady increase in the number and scope of political reforms and a gradual advance in economic growth. He also observed that the strongly reformist practice of these parties conflicted with their Marxist ideology and urged them to recognize that they were indeed democratic parties of social reform.

# INTRODUCTION

Support for this view grew as changes in the social composition of the party made themselves felt. So-called "new workers", former craftsmen, bankrupt small-traders and peasants drawn to the towns, combined with the better-paid skilled workers and the embryo of a workers' bureaucracy in the party apparatus (mainly employees of the party, the unions, co-ops and workers' insurance companies) to introduce a different spirit into the SDP. The type of "worker-bureaucrat" (dělnický byrokrat) contrasted as strongly with the type of "professional revolutionary" in Russia as the conditions in which the workers' movement in Russia had developed differed from those in the Czech Lands. After 1897, electoral reform gave the SDP representation in the Imperial Council and prompted certain sections of the intelligentsia, mainly from the Progressive Party, to enter the movement. These gradually took over some important positions and with support from the rank and file, they set about attenuating the Marxist ideology of the party into a programme for the gradual growth of capitalism into socialism.

This became the occasion for a dispute in which the party press declared its neutrality, though its claim that its competence was limited to the solution of "more practical questions" was tacit encouragement to Modráček who, from the late 1890s to 1919, provided the focus of an opposition movement composed mainly of reformists and centrists. The latter represented the mass of the party functionaries who favoured the paths of gradualism and "practicism" and frankly opposed the left-wing's insistence on bringing the conflict into the ideological arena. Many of them had not been schooled in the philosophy of their party while others regarded an ideological struggle as irrelevant in the light of their day-to-day work in the local organizations. The rank and file in general sided with them as they concluded that any such conflict was gratuitous and would only lead to an unnecessary weakening of the party. It was the affair of "a few individuals", as the official SDP organ observed, while the power of the party consisted in having regard for "the real needs and conditions of the working people".[1]

Modráček's attack on the Marxist programme of the party was met with great vigour by the Left. This was roughly speaking an alliance of the old workers' leaders, among whom Josef Hybeš was prominent, and the young socialist intelligentsia, the first generation of university-educated party workers of whom Šmeral, Vacek and Houser were typical. The Left then sought to combine the proletarian traditions of the workers' movement with the intellectuals' grasp of Marxism, in which, according to the Soviet orthodoxy, the latter ultimately got the upper hand. This it has been alleged provided the stimulus for a section of the bourgeois intelligentsia to come out in favour of socialism after October 1918 with unhappy consequences for the labour movement in 1919–1920 and for the CPC in its early years. This is a question having an important bearing on the kind of party Šmeral was aiming at and why he differed from the Leninist notion. However there was little the left-wing could do to halt the progress of Modráček, who with Tomášek, Soukup and the new arrivals from the left-wing of the Progressive Party, made a great impact in the conditions of the time with their championing of national and democratic demands.

Šmeral did not oppose them for their support for democratic rights which he believed an essential part of the general democratic struggle on the road to proletarian revolution. He did however object to them on at least two other grounds. Firstly, their activity in the party was aimed at strengthening the independence of the Czech SD organizations and at deepening the national divisions in the common all-Austrian SDP, beginning with the MPs Club in the Reichsrat and also partly in the union organizations. This amounted to an extension and not a solution to the nationalities struggle though this lay at some undetermined point in the future after a revolution had brought socialism to the whole of Austria. As an internationalist, Šmeral could not see conditions developing in Austria facilitating the self-determination of nations. He believed that a sharpening of the nationalities struggle would only support the current of bourgeois nationalism with dire consequences for socialism. The various national bourgeois parties would first be drawn into mutual conflict and later form a united anti-socialist front. Against the unity of the bourgeois classes, he placed his faith in the international unity of the Austrian proletariat. He accepted that fundamental social change could be more easily facilitated in Austria where conditions were more promising than in an independent Czech state, whether monarchy or republic, where the political and social preponderance of the bourgeoisie would make itself felt to the detriment of the working class. Šmeral's internationalism presupposed the continued existence of Austria-Hungary albeit in a changed form. He was influenced in this respect by Palacký who had argued that the survival of Austria was indispensable if the Slavs were not to fall a prey to the designs of Tsarist Russia and Imperial Germany, a view which was widely accepted and persisted until the threat from Prussia receded early in 1918.

Šmeral's views, which he gave mature form in his address to the IX Party Congress in 1909,[2] remained more or less unchanged before 1914. He persisted in his opposition to the demand for a national state. Austria, as a geographical rather than a political entity, internationalism and socialist democracy remained the corner stones of his thought. He urged the party to work for national autonomy organised on language and cultural lines in which the democratization and decentralization of the state administration

# INTRODUCTION

would provide the basis for the replacement of the Dual Monarchy by a family of small Central European states with equal rights. However the way to such a federation led through fundamental structural changes in the political and constitutional make-up of Austria–Hungary which presupposed not only a consistent democratization of the existing representative organs but also of the institutions of state and administration. Their power would he believed ultimately reside in popular self-governing organs. The means to this end was a socialist revolution which would provide the opportunity for a kind of socialist united states of Europe, the final aim of international social democracy and the path to the solution of all social problems of which the nationality question was one.[3] After October 1918, Šmeral was confronted with a new historical situation, and as a result he altered some of his attitudes. Nevertheless the outline of his views presented here is to be regarded as the basis for the reconstruction of the views he held in the Czechoslovak Republic.

Neither Šmeral nor Modráček occupied the highest positions in the party before the war. These were held by centrist-reformists typically represented by Antonín Němec, a workers' leader of the old school who counted himself a success if he was able to maintain party unity. For him compromise was the key and he mistakenly thought that Šmeral and Soukup would resolve their differences given the opportunity to work closely with the leadership. His decision not inappropriately reflected his sympathy for proletarian aims and reformist practice. Soukup was indeed persuaded to give up his openly revisionist attitude while Šmeral found himself to all intents and purposes tied by the reformist practice of the party. Yet this arrangement in the long run deepened the degree of polarization and this ultimately worked itself out in the new historical conditions of the Czechoslovak Republic and led to the foundation of a communist party.

The emergence of socialist radicalism was not simply a response to the failure of orthodox Social Democracy to solve the economic and social crisis which afflicted the Republic in the immediate post-war years. It was to a significant degree the embodiment of Šmeralism and reflected the working out of the pre-war polarization in the SDP in the conditions of the new state. We have seen that Šmeral opposed the drive of the radical nationalists for a Czech state. But once the Republic had become a reality, did he continue in his opposition to the national state? Or were there other equally deep differences of principle and practical policy which divided Šmeral from these reformists who, in the wake of the national revolution, graduated to the governing class and became members of the Establishment? The principle of socialist orthodoxy on which their appeals to the loyalty of the working class were based rested on the political environment under which they had developed. In the Austrian half of the monarchy, this involved a developed capitalist system, with a sizeable working class, the existence of political parties and a parliament elected by a system of limited suffrage. Šmeral like the Establishment SDs had been weaned on this type of state. It is natural therefore to pose certain questions; namely, where did his concept of socialism differ from theirs? Did he share any of their political assumptions, for example, regarding political legitimacy or the role of parliament? Was the conflict between them simply about means or did their aims also clash? Or was the controversy to some extent contrived so as to create a situation which Šmeral could exploit to facilitate his own political rehabilitation?

It seems axiomatic that Šmeral was in competition with Social Democratic orthodoxy for the leadership of the socialist movement in the Czech Lands. The acknowledgement of Šmeral as co-founder of the Czechoslovak Communist Party would tend on the face of it to suggest that he shared or willingly embraced some or all of the values of Leninism. Nevertheless, his resolute rejection of SD orthodoxy pushed him in the direction of Leninism. However, can we uncritically accept that the existence of a Communist Party nominally if not then practically founded on Leninist principles necessarily entails the conclusion that Šmeral was a Leninist? Certain questions are worth formulating in the endeavour to delineate the essential features of Šmeral's thought in comparison with Lenin's. For example, did their views on the state and revolution coincide? What were their notions of the role of the party or of its internal organisation? And did the notion of the dictatorship of the proletariat have the same importance, or indeed any, for Šmeral as it did for Lenin? Just as Social Democratic orthodoxy was based in the Austrian state form, so was the Leninist principle of orthodoxy based in a type of state characterized by a lack of representative institutions, a tradition of Tsarist autocracy, little developed industry and its concomitant, a very small working-class, together with all the other features of an agrarian society. Fundamental differences therefore may reasonably be expected to emerge. If Šmeral's conception of socialism differs from the Leninist orthodoxy, then the founding of the CPC must be seen in an entirely different light, not as the beginning of institutionalized socialist radicalism in the Czech Lands, rather as the end of "a third way" which was in effective competition with the Comintern.

We must pose the question then whether the founding of the CPC was an indication of Šmeral's failure to hold the "middle radical" ground. Can it properly be argued that his conception of socialism was unrealistic insofar as it could not expect to survive the squeeze between the two major socialist

# INTRODUCTION xvii

orthodoxies? Šmeralism had a great impact in the Czech Lands, but was it mistaken in the belief that a "Czech road to socialism" could survive in the embrace of the Comintern? It is known that Šmeral was a reluctant partner in the formation of the CPC. Did he then resign himself to the view of the majority of the Marxist Left that a strong framework of international support was a prerequisite for a revolution? Or did he regard this as a preliminary working-out of a clash between his conception of socialism and Leninism which raised his hopes that, given the security of the Soviet Union, he would regain freedom to manoeuvre and develop his road to socialism in his own way?

The starting point of this study is 1917 and this is for two reasons. First, this was the year when the radical nationalists in the SDP achieved a significant victory. The wrangle over states-rights in 1889 which led to the birth of the National (later Czech) Socialist Party (hereafter NSP), Modráček's championing of Bernstein, the defence of national trade unions at the Congress of the Second International (1910) and the general and active acquiescence in the sweeping away of the Austrian International even before the outbreak of war were all to a greater or lesser degree symptoms of the presence in the party of a new spirit which rejected revolution and internationalism. Yet the representatives of this spirit were still in a minority and, until the origin of the Czech Union (Nov 1916) brought a fundamental shift, the leadership held firm to its support for Austria. The radical nationalists in the party quickly grew in importance under the impetus of the popular movement which developed in the Czech Lands and its demand for the suspension of sectional and class interest in the struggle for the national ideal induced the SDP to embark on a path which led to the abrogation of certain of its basic principles. This amounted to a revision of socialism and this was carried over into the new state where the prestige enjoyed by the radical nationalists, then a majority, as joint creators of the state gave their view the status of orthodoxy.

The second reason why 1917 has been chosen as the point of departure is because it was the year of the Russian October Revolution, an event no less fundamental in its impact on the SDP than the changes in the leadership of the party. At first, the radical nationalists welcomed it and more particularly the stir it caused in the Czech Lands which could be harnessed in the drive for a national revolution. They were chagrined to discover that after October 1918, it still remained an issue of vital interest. Try as they might to dismiss it as of little or no practical significance to the working masses in Czechoslovakia, it remained a source of inspiration to socialist radicals of all shades who were discontented with the new order and especially with the role of the SDP in government. Bolshevism however soon became more than an inspiration. It offered itself initially as a model of socialist revolution and as an alternative to the gradualism of Social Democracy. With the founding of the Comintern, it cast itself in the role of socialist orthodoxy, a view it purveyed with increasing prominence and intolerance from late 1919 and early 1920. The social disaffection of the last years of the war, which had abated in response to the proclamation of the national state, continued to grow despite its change of focus. The government's failure to come to grips with the social and economic crisis was often laid at the door of the Establishment SDs and the tide of support the nationalists in the pre-war party had won with their decision to divide SD organizations on a nationality basis was paralleled after 1918 by the rapid growth of the radical socialist wing.

I am not specifically concerned here with the character of the increased pre-war support for the party as this involves statements about the other socialist or quasi-socialist parties and it is not my purpose to cover the whole spectrum of socialism either pre- or post-war. However it will be instructive to look at aspects of the social composition of the radical socialists' following. To what extent were they genuinely proletarian? Was this the kind of situation of which Lenin often wrote in which the "petty-bourgeoisie" proletarianized by the war vacillated on the side of labour? Did the presence of large numbers of intellectuals in the ranks of the Marxist Left indicate the persuasive qualities of Šmeralism or a romantic infatuation with the idea of Bolshevism or indeed something quite different? We may also ask questions about the nature of popular attitudes to radicalism in general and to the CPC in particular. Why for example did Šmeralism enjoy an apparently greater numerical support when informally constituted as the Marxist Left than in the guise of the CPC? Was it felt to be a political organ alien to the traditions of radicalism in the Czech Lands, neither home-grown nor free of the bonds of orthodoxy? It is of course not always easy to determine whether those who sympathized with the radical socialists favoured Šmeral or the other individual leaders, some of whom stood closer to Lenin. Where evidence on this is lacking, I have relied on extrapolation to establish to what extent the mass of radical supporters followed the Czech Bolsheviks or Šmeral. It goes without saying that these extrapolated notions do not have equally strong explanatory power.

Šmeral's alternative to Leninism and Social Democracy I shall identify as "the Czech Road to Socialism" which not inappropriately reflects a contrast with the foreign roots of these movements. This view of socialism was epitomized in the figure of Šmeral who was central to the ideational dispute between the mainstream radical socialist Left and the SDs and also to the separate controversy which developed within the ranks of the Left itself, many of whom emerged as his opponents and supporters of the Comintern. However the first task is to determine whether the phenomenon of a Czech socialist movement answering to the name of "Šmeralism" can be discerned at all. With this in mind, I have devoted the first part of this study to an examination of his concepts, not only on the basis of his theoretical writings but also as they were reflected in the activities of the political organizations in which he played a leading role, the Marxist Left and the CPC. Where appropriate I have juxtaposed his political values with those of his opponents in an effort to draw out the essential differences. This is not always an easy task. While it is relatively simple to discredit the SDs view of him as a Bolshevik, it is considerably less so with regard to the Comintern's line. This described him as a centrist, but arguably this description was based on a set of values in competition with those of Šmeral and likely to be more interested in making a political and polemical point than in accurately classifying his stance. The German section of the Left in Liberec echoed and often amplified the opinions of the Comintern, such that even Lenin himself felt moved to intervene and moderate Kriebich's bitter attacks. Though Kreibich's polemical tracts are interesting, we may legitimately regard them as not always helpful for our purposes. The Orthodox SDs inclined to a different view and although their criticisms are couched in less dense language, they too bear a strongly polemical stamp. Šmeral had forever squared the pitch as far as they were concerned by his persistent refusal to change his pro-Austrian stance, which in the parlance of the day was known as "war-opportunism". Secondly and, in their eyes, equally unforgivable, he had refused to throw his weight behind the all-national coalition even in the dying days of the Monarchy. The climate of hostility thereby engendered made him the butt of public hatred influencing even some on the Left to treat him with suspicion. The attacks on him were not restricted to the non-socialist press. The SDP organs reserved their abuse for him too, adroitly distracting national and party attention away from other "war-opportunists" who retained favour in party and aspired to government, of whom Tusar was but one. This campaign too papered over serious differences in the party. The programmatic statements made at Party Congresses, meetings and so on reflect the latter aspect and these efforts to play down disagreements in the interests of party unity continued even as late as the summer of 1920.

Šmeral however is more revealing about his own attitudes. From 1899 when he became an editor of the party daily *Pravo lidu* until the year of disgrace, 1917, his output as a writer, journalist and propagandist was enormous.[4] The crisis of confidence and the threat of physical attack after the day of liberation caused him to suspend his activity for a time. After accepting the party's offer to go to Switzerland in 1919, he was encouraged to take up his pen once again which he used with considerable effect not only in the inner-party struggle but also within the broader setting of the propaganda-war over the nature of Soviet Russia.[5] Despite the difficulties presented by Šmeral's sense of diffuseness, I have relied heavily but not exclusively on his contributions, first to the newspapers and journals of the SDP, and later to the independent publications of the Marxist Left and, albeit less so, of the CPC. Another major source, quite apart from his published theoretical writings, are the agitation broadsheets on which he worked and many of these are preserved in state and party archives in Prague and Brno. Parliamentary records help to complete the picture, as far as this is possible.[6] However Šmeral's philosophy cannot be accurately re-constructed only from his statements but represents a relation between statements and his activity, theory and practice.

The ideational dispute is central to an understanding of the clashes between Šmeral and the two socialist orthodoxies. It was not simply a sharp difference of views. Šmeral made explicit statements about the nature of change in society and the agents of change which, as will be demonstrated, broadly governed his political strategy insofar as his grasp of the historical events unfolding before him was adequate. This aspect is important as it throws some light on the coherence of Šmeralism and ultimately its viability as an alternative. Leninism was a development of orthodox Marxism which grew out of the specific historical conditions in the Russian Empire. It retained the essential features of Marxist philosophy, for example the view of the state, the aims of socialism and the need for change by revolutionary means. It also had certain distinctive features, however, chief among which was a novel view of the role of the party in the revolution. Šmeral often expressed his commitment to Marxism and to the Russian Revolution, yet on several basic principles of socialism, he diverged more or less sharply from Leninism.

Šmeral's attitude to the role of the party is not always clear. He did not give it the systematic attention in his writings which, for example, Lenin did. Nevertheless, it is known that he rejected elitism as a principle and took a negative view of its manifestations whether in the Establishment SDs or in the Bolshevik party. He believed that in their different ways both relied too heavily on elites, although he allowed that in the case of the Bolsheviks historical conditions on balance tended to justify it. Yet in the Czech Lands, the existence of a party elite in the conditions of the national revolution and after led to a reduction in inner-party democracy, a narrowing of the base of representation and to the formation of a more or less immoveable

INTRODUCTION                                                                    xxi

oligarchy, all of which offended his democratic sensibilities. Šmeral's commitment to the interests of a major part of the social democratic constituency, that is, the industrial proletariat, won him few friends in the SDP who regarded this in effect to be a challenge to the national revolution. He was sensitive to the opinions of the rank and file and felt it his duty to address himself also to the demands of the socialist intelligentsia. His championing of their claims brought him into conflict not only with his own left-wing, whose interest lay in the formation of a revolutionary avant-garde, but also with Lenin. The Bolshevik leader was critical of his unwillingness to impose his own values on the rank and file in the vigorous and direct manner Lenin had made his own. In effect, Šmeral rejected the Leninist canon which suggested that the party was the sole determiner of the aims of the working class. He did not presume to speak authoritatively on all matters, preferring on the other hand to take due account of his constituents' wishes and endeavouring to steer them in that direction, yet without losing sight of the objectives he regarded as essential for the achievement of socialism. In this regard, he was influenced by his experience as a practising politican under the Empire although his view of the role of the Reichsrat was not always positive. Political legitimacy tended therefore to have a greater importance for him than for his militant associates, many of whom were "new radicals." Lenin's distrust of legitimacy in general and Šmeral's long experience of social democratic politics in the Imperial parliament in particular seemed to provide sufficient reason for the Soviet leader to lump him with the Orthodox SDs, a question of some interest and importance.

Differing concepts of the nature and role of the party lead naturally to a discussion of the means by which society should be changed. This, together with the aims of socialism, informed Šmeral's view of the party and vice versa. The Orthodox SDs' notion of social achievement arose out of the national revolution in a gradual way which provides grounds for questioning their commitment to socialism. This question can be usefully examined from the point of view of their social origins and their disposition in the party. It may also throw light on a problem which, according to Lenin, afflicted Šmeral's party, namely the alleged priority given to the liberal or liberal-socialist intelligentsia over the proletariat. The Orthodox SDs' enthusiasm for the Russian Revolution evaporated after October 1918 and where they had once whole-heartedly supported the self-determination of nations in their own benefit, as the guardians of the new state, they rejected the same principle when it was invoked by the national minorities. More relevant for the socialist movement was their overturning of a founding principle of their party, change by revolution. The violent overthrow of the state was good and necessary only if it was a foreign institution. On the other hand, in the conditions of the new state, violent revolution was an attack on the people themselves and violated legality and institutional continuity. The victory over the Austrians had been achieved, more or less by the emigration and the National Committee and this institution, dressed in parliamentary clothes, came to be the principal and approved method of inaugurating change. Universal suffrage, the second sacred principle of the Orthodox SDs, was expected in the course of time to leave the field entirely clear for the SDP to complete its work.

Šmeral's view of parliament was not consistent. Parliamentary manipulation in the Reichsrat and the suspected irregularities surrounding the origin of the National Committee contravened some of his most dearly held principles. First, it gave no place to the direct participation of the masses, apart from a sextennial vote. Second, it created a new kind of government elite built on the shoulders of the party elite. Third, he had strong doubts about its ability to represent. Finally, he was sceptical about parliament's ability to achieve rapid and radical, social and economic change, which for many of his supporters was the essence of the national revolution. Šmeral's attitude to the problem of change is puzzling because it appears on the available evidence that he disapproved of revolutionary violence but at the same time strongly favoured revolutionary change. Violence was for him a negation of a fundamental tenet of socialism, quite apart from the fact that his experience and personality did not cut him out for the role of a fire-eating revolutionary in the mould of, say, a Lenin or a Trotsky. While conscious of his own incapacity to break the SDP Executive's grip on the nominations of MPs to parliament, he tended to reject the gradualism of the parliament in Prague and its concomitant, compromise. He did not accept the Comintern's strategy vis-á-vis parliament, simply to use it as a sounding board for revolutionary views. This, with his refusal to split the party along the lines of the Bolshevik/Menshevik struggle, is at least a partial indication of his independent way and a sign that an open, mass party closer to the traditions of the SDP offered the greater potential for the ultimate victory of socialism than a narrow conspiratorial organisation made up of professional revolutionaries. As he well knew, conspiracy was anyway alien to Czech historical conditions. Despite all its dangers, some of which materialized, a broadly based party made revolutionary violence unnecessary. It provided a vehicle for the participation of the masses at local levels, followed the norms of legitimacy and inner-party democracy—even enlarging them bearing in mind some of the less-respectable SDP Congress practices—and to an extent fulfilled one of the fundamental aims of socialism, the raising of the

INTRODUCTION xxiii

consciousness of the working-class from which the other aims would flow and thereafter be achieved.

Yet Šmeral was not so clear-cut in his ideas. As we have seen, his attitude to parliament was ambiguous. Though he seems to have rejected it as much for its failure to properly represent as for its inherent tendency to be packed with self-seeking dullards and time-servers, he was very hazy regarding an institution which would more properly meet the conditions set by his political values. He was against cold-blooded violence but was known on several occasions to have uttered threats which he implied would be backed up with the force of the working class whose mobilization as a mass actually made this unnecessary. While a rough pattern emerges in his thought, the maze of his writings and his activity appear not seldom to be contradictory and at variance with each other, and this aspect forces some consideration of the question of the coherence of Šmeralism.

The founding of the CPC in 1921, it will be argued, was the final stage in the polarization of the SDP and was the decisive opening shot in the struggle to alter the character of Czech radical socialism. The pressure of the prevailing socialist orthodoxies proved too great for Šmeral to keep the middle radical ground. But this does not answer the question of whether Šmeral recognized the pointlessness of attempting to work outside the two socialist power blocs, a recognition which caused him to undergo a fundamental change of opinion; or did he simply resign himself to membership of the Comintern deceiving himself that the 21 Conditions as they then stood would not move matters beyond his control? It can now be claimed some sixty years on that Šmeral did not understand nor predict the consequences of membership and was consequently mistaken in his belief that despite basic differences he could maintain an operational latitude. What is by no means clear is whether this resulted from a belief that a politician of his experience and stature in the labour movement could conceivably rescue something from the ashes. Šmeralism in the event was defeated. But to what extent did he contribute to his own defeat? Was it simply an unmitigated disaster for Czech socialism or did it contain any positive aspects, elements of victory? And where did his defeat spring from? If, as evidence suggests, support for his movement derived from popular appreciation for the solutions he offered to the principal social problems, then Šmeralism related more closely to the Czech environment than any other political creed. Did it fail then because of his conscious decision to abstain from violence? Or because he failed to realize the depth and complexity of the still unresolved nationalities problem? Or even because he addressed his solutions to the intelligentsia and the already-converted proletarians, leaving the uncommitted, who could easily have tipped the scales, lost in the subtle theoretical distinctions between Šmeralism and Leninism? Šmeral then was squeezed and to demonstrate this I propose to show the constraints under which he was forced to act and which ultimately led him to join the international communist movement. All of the questions already raised will be placed in their appropriate setting which break down naturally along the lines of internal and external limitations. This corresponds roughly to constraints emanating from the national or domestic setting and the international setting respectively.

Part One is devoted to a discussion of the aims and tactics of Šmeralism and this is juxtaposed where appropriate with those of the two figures representing the corner-stones of the II International and the Comintern.

I proceed in the first chapter of Part Two to an examination of the impact of nationalism. It looks at this phenomenon as a factor in the de-radicalization of the masses and one which leads protest away from the real causes of unrest to pseudo-causes. It examines the extent to which nationalism was likely to weaken radicalism and how it affected Šmeral's movement. It also makes some evaluation of the SDP's answer to the problem which in the conditions of the time seemed more appropriate than Šmeral's.

Chapter Two is concerned with an analysis of the difficulties springing from the Czech political environment. It deals with the change in the political structure from the period of the Empire in the Czech Lands to an independent republic. This system built on parliamentary democracy and universal suffrage effectively consummated the national struggle. It had a very powerful appeal in the nation and produced a desire in the majority of Czechs to set about the problem of national reconstruction with great enthusiasm. It also allowed many to work out their national prejudices against people they regarded as their long-time oppressors the Germans. This situation tended to obscure the class struggle and produced a variety of pressures on Šmeral some of which he was unable to cope with. I proceed to show the historical tendencies which acted as neutralizing factors and which helped to dilute the affect the radical socialists had on the discontented population. The conditions of great social and political fluidity also tended to act as a neutralizing factor rather than the opposite insofar as they affected the nature of permanent party political support.

The third chapter is concerned with the radical challenge to the new state which involved not only Šmeral but the radical socialist movement as a whole. Here my purpose is to show that they were not united among themselves and although presenting an alarming spectre to the Establishment were permeated with many different kinds of radicals, some committed, others less so. It demonstrates their reactions to the new state and to each other and the solutions they proposed to the major problems. Sections of the radical socialists supported Šmeral. Yet a powerful and influential minority did not and sought to bring him under their control.

The economic and political demands of the radicals and their supporters form the basis of Chapter Four. These demands embodied the resentment of a large section of the population against an apparently inefficient and often deceitful government and a restrictive state. Though it spilled over on frequent occasions into violence, it will be shown that the Allied fears of an impending revolution were groundless. The nature of these demands contributed to some extent to Šmeral's confusion or hesitation and, given the political constellation, were not realizable. It is legitimate to ask whether his reaction to the opportunity implicit in the situation was adequate.

The fifth chapter concerns the social problem and the distinction between town and country forms its basis. There are good grounds for believing that Šmeral had great support in the urban industrial working class as the evidence I have presented in other chapters suggests. For this reason, apart from a summary of these points introducing the chapter, I restrict my remarks almost exclusively to the situation in the countryside. The chapter heading may therefore appear to be misleading. The countryside did not at all provide fertile ground for the reception of radical socialist ideas, although the evidence suggests that one section at least could well have provided a basis for the support which Šmeralism sadly lacked. Yet Šmeral only paid cursory attention to the land question in his theoretical writings if anything at all. At all events, he did not give the same weight to agrarian problems as to those of urban industry where the revolution had perforce to lie. To that extent, he was firmly in the traditions of the SDP who pre-war had scarcely been involved at all with the land question. Šmeral, unlike the Orthodox SDs, was marginal to the controversy over the Land Reform and his failure to get to grips with it not only restricted the scope of his movement almost entirely to the towns but in effect contributed to the construction of Agrarian power in the countryside which became the bulwark of the pre-war system. Šmeral did not and probably could not effect a link up between the peasantry and the proletariat, as the Leninists would have wanted. It is doubtful if social conditions on the land allowed this and these played a part in his ultimate failure.

A note should be added here on Slovakia. Its experience under Hungarian rule had given it a social and economic character reflected in a political development quite at variance with that of the Czech Lands. Though I make reference to Slovakia, particularly in Part Three in respect of events in

Hungary, it should be emphasized that my attention is centred almost entirely on the Czech Lands.

In conclusion of this introduction, we come to the significance of the failure of Šmeralism for the important question it raises about the problem of radical socialist parties in general. Šmeral is but one example of the failure of socialism over the last 100 years to meet the needs of the movements and societies which produced it. Why have political parties pressing for socialist policies found it impossible to achieve them? Is there something in the nature of capitalist society or its institutions which confines or subverts the policies of socialist parties attempting change without violence? If the capitalist system is unresponsive to radical change, are radical socialist parties faced with the choice of accepting the limitations placed on them by capitalist society as a whole, thereby sacrificing their aims or of a wholesale, sweeping-away of these institutions involving a tactical principle they reject? We must enquire if a radical socialist party can maintain its structure, organization and objectives and, if it cannot, and assuming it is uncompromising in pursuit of its aims, then is it forced into the arms of Soviet Communism? Can it be shown that such a party must always satisfy the demands placed upon it by the centre as the price of maintaining its objectives? And do these demands turn on notions of party organisation, centralism and ultimately obedience to the centre of the international communist movement? Open and broadly based democratic radical socialist parties of the Šmeral or Martov type have historically tended to come off worst in their struggles with Leninist elitism. Is it the case then that the achievement of radical socialist aims is always paid for by the enforced adoption of the general features of Soviet institutional and civil practice, arguably a partial denial of these aims? The decision to go it alone, with its implied rejection of the solutions proposed by a party of "the army" to the problems of representation and accountability is a vote for the maintenance of democratic rights and an acceptance of the moral values of that society. Does this then lead to the perpetual postponement of the realization of these aims until democratic norms have been abided by? Or is this playing into the hands of the dominant class, as Lenin might say, who would simply fall back on the organs of state to maintain their domination and its vehicle? If this is so, then the party is forced to abrogate a basic objective—rapid, radical change. If in pursuit of its aims, the party comes into inevitable conflict with the capitalist system, must it invariably abandon its commitment to moral restraint? Historically, it seems that the problem is intractable. Each system, it appears, is incapable of dealing with the demands made upon it. The demands, it would seem, have therefore to be scaled down

# INTRODUCTION

such that all radical socialist parties in Western Capitalist Society tend to become reformists and all radical communists in Soviet society, Stalinists. This study then seeks to show that Šmeralism, though incomplete, arguably forms the basis for a third way to socialism of unusual if not unique significance in that it presented the gravest political challenge in the conditions of the pre-war Czech liberal capitalist democracy and also subsequently in those of a bolshevized Czechoslovakia.

**Part One**

## Šmeralism

Šmeral's general views on political change, society and the aims of socialism were strongly influenced by the specific nature of the problems besetting the SDP under the Empire. His career up to 1914 throws considerable light on those central political values which informed his postwar activity as a radical socialist, although some of these he altered more or less in response to the new historical conditions which emerged from the national revolution. Like most Czech Social Democrats, his primary concern was the achievement of a just settlement of the nationalities question. Unlike many however, he did not expect the problem to disappear after 1918. Rather he argued from the outset of the Czech state that its structure would do little to eradicate the underlying causes of racial conflict. Subsequent developments appear to indicate that he was not far wide of the mark.

At all events, Šmeral's response to the problem of the nationalities in the Habsburg Empire provides an important line of inquiry into his views on the nature and role of the party, on political legitimacy, democracy and the participation of the masses. It also reflected his views on the aims of socialism and the means of change within society as a whole. In contrast to the Orthodox SDs who assumed that the Republic was the end of the matter, he did not accept that any system which gave one nationality mastery over a national minority could provide an adequate and lasting solution. In some respects however, as we shall see, Šmeralism, although theoretically sound, ignored aspects of the struggle which ultimately contributed to its defeat.

Before 1914, Šmeral stood closest to the Austro-Marxists for whom the model of Central European revolution following the Marxist canon of 1848 was binding. Although they accepted that the victory of a revolution in Germany was the essential point of departure for the victory of socialism in Europe generally, they looked askance at Marx's view that Austria was simply a boundary region of Germany. Most approved of the amendment

Kautsky had made. They no longer considered the small non-German nations as non-historical national remnants entirely dependent on the tutelage of the German Empires and as such the natural supporters of counter-revolution. The growth of the social democratic movement, particularly in the Czech part of the Austrian Empire, went far in eliminating their alleged inferiority although the Viennese Austro-Marxists, Renner and Bauer, still endeavoured to maintain a special and leading role for the Germans in the overall direction of the labour movement in the Empire. In this regard, their views clashed with those of Šmeral whose belief in the basic equality of nations ruled out any privileged position for the Germans. By the same token, he was an enemy of the system of dualism deriving from the December Laws of 1867 which had given rights to the Hungarians at the expense of other nationalities. Austrian and Hungarian Imperial domination of the subject peoples excluded the masses from electing a government and from participating in administration and hence was not only undemocratic but also politically illegitimate. The central political objective for Šmeral against a background of the crumbling of the dualist system and the onset of the social and economic crisis in the 1890s was not a socialist revolution. Rather was it a regulation and adjustment of the relations between the nationalities which would bring full civil and democratic rights to each nationality, avoid any repetition of the political conditions leading to an expansion of militarism and ultimately, war, and finally provide a firm and stable basis for economic development which in the fullness of time would assist the SDP to secure its aims.

Federalism, at the time largely an unknown quantity, provided Šmeral with the solutions to the burning question of the day. It helps shed some light on his political and ethical values and enables us to take his measure compared with one or other of the socialist traditions. Economic and cultural development had continued apace among the subject nationalities since 1867 and the impulse of industrialization, particularly marked in the Czech Lands in the last decades of the century, found an expression in a change in the political and constitutional order. The first step in this process had been achieved with a successful campaign for the introduction of universal manhood suffrage in which Šmeral himself had played a significant part.[1] The extension of the franchise however was double-edged. On the one hand, it was an important first stage in extending democratic rights not only to the peoples of the oppressed nations within the Empire but also to Austrian and Hungarian workers. On the other, it did little to solve the nationalities problem and, to the extent that the majority of the newly enfranchised irrespective of class origin tended to support not the SDP but the Progressive and State Rights movements, in effect intensified the divisions between the nationalities. After the Imperial Elections in 1907, the SDs' support had declined. This was mirrored for the most part in gains for the NSP, which made Šmeral aware of the increasing power of the radical nationalist message among the working class.² The signs had been visible earlier at the final conference of the All-Austrian Trade Unions (December 1904) and the last joint Congress of the Austrian SDP in October 1905. At the first elections held under the new system in 1907, the Czech SDP enjoyed a considerable degree of electoral success. This minor victory was attributed partly to the decision to divide SD organizations according to the nationality of the membership. Indeed Němec was not far wrong when he suggested that numbers in the party had increased six times over as a result.³ Much of its support can be put down to popular perception of one wing of the party as part of the radical nationalist wing of the State Rights and Progressive movement. The 1911 elections showed the SDP to have lost ground to them in that the votes the SDs polled fell from 390,000 (in 1907) to 357,000,⁴ an eventuality which frustrated Šmeral's expectation that an extension of democratic, voting rights would automatically tend to swell the ranks of socialism. The SDP did indeed grow in strength but, as we shall presently see, it attracted support from a constituency which Šmeral found unacceptable in an essentially proletarian party.

Šmeral presented his view of federalism in a more or less developed form at the IX Congress of the SDP in the debate on the nationalities question.⁵ His solution involved the constitutional transformation of the Empire into a democratic federation of free and equal nations. In outline, he proposed national autonomy on the basis of individual rights in national and cultural matters; the democratization and decentralization of the state administration with the election of a parliament and government having competence in all national and cultural affairs financed by taxes from the nationality electing it. Šmeral envisaged further that there would be popular representation at provincial, county and parish level all responsible to the national parliament and that each nationality would naturally use its own language in administrative and judicial matters. In all other areas of state administration, the dualism between self-governing and provincial administrations was to be abolished, the functions of the latter passing to autonomous bodies having general and equal voting rights and in nationally mixed areas, proportional voting rights. This second system of popular autonomy would be as far as possible decentralized. In respect of civil rights, each adult member of every nationality in the Empire would be guaranteed full democratic freedoms of assembly, association and the press. Moreover, Šmeral stressed the equality of each nationality in the Empire and hence rejected the Austro-Marxists view of a German *primus inter pares*. However, the significance of federalism lay not simply in its capacity to solve the nationalities question. It was also superior to State Rights in organizing the Empire economically. It was capable of giving each person within it a share, especially the industrial working class, for whom the bourgeois parties, the mainstays of the States rights movement, had made no provision thereby cutting them off from democratic participation in the process of production.

While the political transformations inherent in Šmeral's plan were aimed at achieving legislative unity and governing sovereignty for each nationality, he also argued for a fundamental change in the centralist organization of the Empire economically. A federalized state as a whole could offer economic and industrial development to all nations according to their capabilities but in a manner far in excess of the levels achieved by the centralist policies of the Habsburgs. Hence, against the idea of autonomy and independence in national, administrative and cultural life, he postulated the notion of a united and integrated economic policy within the borders of the Empire whose economic needs—to be adequately satisfied—demanded a large state organization. Quite apart from the better-balanced industrial and economic development federalism was expected to bring, it opened the way to an authentic international solidarity with workers of other nations. It was hence a genuinely all-national policy directed at achieving equality for the nation as a whole and for each individual member. In conditions of industrial growth, this would strengthen the class policy of the Czech proletariat, likewise those of the other nations, which ultimately was directed at the removal of capitalist domination. Later, on the eve of the war, Šmeral recognized that the historical forces ranged against his conception were too strong and he admitted that the organization of the Empire on a federal basis was possible only after the victory of socialism and not as the way to it.[6]

Federalism then satisfied the internationalist and democratic dictates of his socialist philosophy while State Rights did not. Broadly speaking, he opposed it on national, social and party grounds. Initially, given the ethnic structure of the Czech Lands, it implied a reversal of national domination which far from securing the future of the Czech nation would ultimately endanger it. The social and economic content of State Rights would do little to solve the material problems of the Czech people and nothing to improve the lot of the working class. Thirdly, it tended to bring disreputable people into the SDP who would in all likelihood affect the social composition and the class character of the party. His critique of the radical nationalists not only provided insights into the basic deficiencies in party structure but also of the role they could be expected to play in the direction of any future Czech state. Further, his analysis of the social and economic character of the Czech Lands proved to be equally applicable in the changed conditions of the Republic.

For Šmeral, the very fact that the State Rights programme was based on a very uncertain historical justification made it the duty of every Social Democrat to reject it. He implied that its protagonists were manipulating the Czech people by drawing a veil over the free choice the Czech state had made to unite with the Austrian and Hungarian territories and by referring exclusively to the national catastrophe resulting from the defeat at the White Mountain. He regarded this misuse of the truth as indefensible and as playing a role in the political conditions of the time analogous to the part the forged Manuscripts had played in attempting to establish Czech cultural bona fides.[7] There seemed to him to be little connection between a political system appealing to historical reasons and the working class operating in more or less industrialized economic and social conditions. Leaving aside the purely constitutional aspects, there were good democratic reasons for rejecting it. The claim for a Czech state based upon the historic Crown Lands required an abrogation of the principle of national justice for the Germans settled in the ethnically mixed territories. If State Rights was not to be interpreted selectively then the three Sudeten territories should equally have rights to organize their own state which in the prevailing conditions could be realistically realized and maintained as a sovereign parliamentary state within a federated Empire. If the State Rights movement did not include the Sudeten territories in its own claim then, according to its own canon, it was not a Czech program. Further, it made no mention of the historical claim for association with the Slovaks. The erection of a state on the historic frontiers of the Czech Lands in which Czechs would have a permanent majority over the Germans was for Šmeral no different from the situation in which the Czechs found themselves under the Imperial system. It was in effect to sanction an unjust and undemocratic system. Although Šmeral's view was swept away by national passion in which the desire for national freedom concealed the probability that once achieved, it would work itself out one way or another in national revenge, it accurately characterized the folly of founding a Czech state in these conditions, a point not lost on Masaryk who however did not bargain for the scale of the consequences.

Šmeral was unimpressed also with the means by which the State Rights movement hoped to achieve its aim. As its leaders Kramář, Fořt and Herold reluctantly admitted, nothing short of a "catastrophe" or, by another name, war would realize it. In the event, they were proved right and after the war they did not hesitate to use every opportunity to pillory Šmeral, not only for his failure to understand that the nationalist sentiments of the Czech workers would triumph over their class solidarity[8] but also for his underestimation of State Rights as a realizable program. This however is to miss the drift of Šmeral's position. A primary concern of his was peace. War simply invited wholesale destruction and tended to affect those at the lower end of society more directly and more deeply. Time after time the struggles of the great continental powers had been fought out in the Czech Lands with disastrous consequences for economic and social progress. The experience of the Poznan Poles was the most recent example which convinced Šmeral that an attempt to erect a Czech state could end up as an attempt on the life of the Czech nation. To a degree, he was in the tradition of Palacký. The founding of a Czech state itself provided no answer to the question of the German minority, who, imbued with an implacable hatred for their new masters, would look to Austria and the German Empire for support and ultimately their salvation. The nationality problems of the Empire would not therefore be solved but simply transferred to a smaller plane of operation in the first instance. Just as Austria had failed to find a lasting solution to the problem and had felt driven to the use of force and an expansion of militarism, Šmeral predicted that the Czech State, permanently under the threat of German intervention to protect the Volksdeutschen, not to mention its vulnerability as a landlocked state dependent on exporting industrial products, would be incapable of organizing itself so that the widest sections of the national community would achieve any fundamental social or economic benefits, as the State Rights' camp claimed.

Quite apart from its failure to take account either of the economic needs of the time or of the danger implied in their refusal to accept the need to integrate Czech national interests with the historical tendencies of Germany and Austria, Šmeral rejected State Rights for its social and economic content. In his view, it was a policy acting against equality for the proletariat in the nation and designed to foster bourgeois class interests. There was no doubt that it was capable of whipping up national passion and engaging the mass of the people. But the question remained whether it could satisfy its proletarian supporters won over by the promise of equality in a national state. Šmeral was in no doubt that it could not. But the emergence of a group of radical nationalists within the SDP in the first decade of the 1900s brought home to him the need to defend the class and internationalist principles of the party if, as seemed possible, the revival of the old rivalry between Austria and Prussian Germany brought a change in the international situation. Although it was still official SD policy in 1913, federalism could not be said to have stemmed the tide of nationalism within the party. It remained for

Šmeral to hold fast to his democratic socialist principles, despite his progressive isolation, in anticipation of more auspicious times.

Despite some early support for a State Rights solution within the framework of a federated Austria,[9] it was clear that the bitterness of the nationality relations gave Šmeral little reason to believe that his federalism would prove a success. He turned his attention to the state of the party whose democratic, socialist aims were being progressively damaged by the influence of the radical nationalists. His reaction to their efforts to alter the character of the party is an important basis for understanding his position when it came into conflict with Lenin's and the post-war orthodox SDs. He would not accept any change in its basically urban proletarian membership. He hardly considered the peasantry at this stage nor even the rural workers.[10]

In his student days, he had vigorously opposed the drive to win over university students to the SDP on the grounds that it would alter its proletarian character.[11] He believed changes in party membership embracing the lower-middle and middle-class would drastically affect the party's policy of proletarian internationalism. For this reason, he was instrumental in removing Modráček, his co-editor on *Studentský Sborník* for agitating for the organizational detachment of socialist youth from the Austrian SDP.[12] This was the first step in his campaign against the recent arrival in the SDP of former members of the left-wing of the Progressive movement, Soukup, Tomašek, A. P. Veselý and Skalák who, with Modráček, had embarked on their own policy of splitting off the labour movement as a whole from Austria and integrating it into the nation.

This tendency was strengthened by the effects of the anti-clerical campaign initiated by the SDP after the discovery of the fraud at the Svatováclavská záložna, a savings bank connected with the Catholic church, and the doubtful dealings of the archbishop of Olomouc, Kohn. The popularity of satirical pamphlets on these notorious affairs caused Šmeral to note with regret the deficiencies in proletarian consciousness even in party and union organizations.[13] Yet he was more concerned at that stage with the effects of the anti-clerical campaign which had helped blur the lines between the SDP and the Progressive movement, the latter having hitched itself to the campaign. The impression of a single camp united in the struggle against the Catholic Church and its political expression quickly grew and took a long time to be dissipated, particularly as it later became identified with the broader struggle against Austria. Anti-clericalism was widely regarded as "progressive" and consequently not only the bourgeois parties rushed to this standard of anti-Austrianism. It was a reaffirmation of the Hussite tradition and a stimulus to Czech separatism which found a ready echo in the SDP.

Anti-clerical, atheist organizations rapidly grew up from within the SDP which suggested that the initial gain in popularity had to be paid for in a loss in internal cohesion. One of these groups was "Volná myšlenka" (Free Thought) which published two influential magazines *Havliček* and *Kacířské epistoly* and sold them through the distribution channels of the party. They appeared to all intents and purposes to be organs of the SDP,[14] although they rarely retailed the tenets of socialism. In many cases, the SDP and the Freethinkers held joint political meetings, even on occasion with the bourgeois parties and the NSP. The Freethinkers courted any group which opposed Austrian Catholicism and divided the struggle against clericalism from the class and political struggle of the Czech labour movement. They rejected Šmeral's view that clericalism was the result of the conditions deriving from capitalism in the Empire and accordingly reduced the struggle against it to attacks on the clerical parties, a stance they shared with the bourgeois parties.[15] Groups like the Freethinkers attacked all Catholic SDs whether deputies in the Reichsrat or the few artless supporters of the party in the countryside. They also helped to foster an anti-clerical fashion within and outside the party which encouraged members of the intelligentsia in particular to float between one or other of the political manifestations of anti-clericalism.

As the radical nationalists in the SDP grew in strength fed partly by these anti-clerical organizations, the Freethinkers among others became defunct and were replaced by associations like the Union of Socialist Monists.[16] Stych, a former anarchist, and F. V. Krejčí, chairman of the union and later prominent in the CSP, both came to rest in the welcoming arms of the SDP. This willingness to accept all streams into the party to underpin its mass basis was a more or less faithful reflection of the values of the trade-union leaders who still dominated the leadership. These conditions had repercussions on the unity of the party and on its basic policy of opposition to class-reconciliation. In Šmeral's view, anti-clericalism had allowed certain people entry who had no rightful place in a workers' party. Young workers in particular were entranced by the persuasive mixture of nationalist and socialist aims and came to reject proletarian internationalism. Šmeral was also concerned by the development of a section of the petit-bourgeois classes, craftsmen and small-traders reduced economically and socially by the onset of large-scale production who were acutely sensitive to the suggestion that their plight was attributable to national discrimination.[17] Their links with the working class outside the framework of the SDP enabled them to influence opinion by stressing the social aspects of liberation. Their growing presence in the party also made Šmeral's plan for a federated Empire impossible, for in his view, the most powerful agent working in favour of the maintenance and reorganization of the multinational Empire, the working class, was in its political expression, seriously weakened by them and the academic intelligentsia.[18] His efforts to stir the leadership into some kind of counter-initiative met with little response. The social differentiation in the party also had its effect on party discipline, and members of the intelligentsia—Winter is but one example—felt free to write for the bourgeois parties' press and this represented another stage on the road to class-reconciliation and integrating social democracy "into the nation."[19]

Němec, the party leader had noticed as early as 1903 that the radical nationalists were attempting to divert the SD movement from its socialist aims.[20] He was referring to the group in which Modráček played a leading role. The differences and divisions which separated him from Šmeral in the pre-war years are instructive in that they are a groundwork to an examination of the significance of Šmeralism after 1918. Although Modráček resigned from the SDP in May 1919, many of the Orthodox SDs who remained in party and government more or less shared his political values. He was above all an admirer of Spencer and Darwin and their notions formed the basis of his own view of society.[21] Briefly, Modráček favoured a gradualist approach to the solution of social questions and his support for peaceful methods was vindicated to a degree by the successful campaign for universal manhood suffrage and the election of the so-called "People's Parliament" in 1905. Šmeral remained unimpressed with this institution as the means of change in Austria and referred to it as "the executive organ of the owning classes".[22] Modráček rejected the Marxist view of society and change and asserted that the differences between social classes were artificial, promoted by the unreasonable stress individuals in the SDP placed on ideological matters. He therefore felt no committment to Šmeral's principle of "a clear and unqualified opposition stance . . . the absolute principle of the party in a class state".[23] Accordingly, he attempted to reconcile class differences and the national question provided him with an ideal vehicle for bringing the party into a rapprochement with the bourgeois parties. His defence of cooperative socialism which derived from Proudhon[24] conflicted with Šmeral's and was in keeping with his aim to transform the SDP from a proletarian party into one with a socially broader range of support.

Before we move on to an examination of Šmeralism in the new conditions after 28th October 1918, it might be useful to summarize Šmeral's values deriving from his pre-war activity. The aims of socialism as far as he was concerned were not fundamentally different from those of the classical socialist thinkers. They involved the transformation of the capitalist order into a collectivist society in which all productive private property would belong to or otherwise be administered by the whole of society.[25] Private property had given rise to the origin of classes and the class state, and had to be abolished for it provided the means by which the working class, most noticeably, was exploited economically and dominated politically. This offended Šmeral's notion of democracy. His aim was a democratic, popular, socialist republic in which universal, secret, direct voting, to all political and economic institutions, on the basis of proportional representation, would give the people decisive control over laws, the apparatus of political and economic administration and the officials operating it. His view of universal suffrage was sobered however by the limitations imposed by the Empire and, while he expected much from the first parliament embracing a partly enfranchised working class, he did not assume this would provide the fundamental means of change. His experience as a practising politician in the Reichsrat tended to confirm this, although he never quite lost his belief in political legitimacy which was partially formed by this acquaintanceship. The aim of socialism was a revolutionary transformation of society. But there is a conspicuous absence in Šmeral's pre-war thought of revolution as the means of change.

On the other hand, this view was to be modified as he rejected the early socialists appeal to moral or religious reasons to provide the basic stimulus to change. He regarded selfishness as the basis of human behaviour,[26] whether capitalist or worker, and the struggle of interests thereby engendered could only resolve itself by power. Class struggle was in the first instance the means by which capitalist society necessarily matured to collectivism. To achieve this end, it was the duty of every politically conscious worker to become a party- and union-member so that these institutions could exert pressure in their respective fields of activity in accordance with their size and organization. In the conditions of 1907, Šmeral argued against revolutionary romanticism and the voice of the street and for the voting slip and legal methods. He made no mention of resorting to violence nor of the dictatorship of the proletariat. These beliefs governed his attitude to the State Rights movement which broke up the international organization of the proletariat and attempted to effect a reconciliation of classes on the basis of a promise of social equality once national liberation had been achieved. Far from achieving liberation, the working class would be subject to even greater constraints in a more tightly organized class state.

The founding of the Czech state appeared to indicate that the radical nationalists' solution to the nationalities problem was more appropriate in the conditions of the time than Šmeral's. However it was not the final stage in the working out of the contradiction between nationalism and socialism. The

## ŠMERALISM

nationalist intelligentsia had split the working class into national fragments and then mobilized it against the ruling class of the multinational Empire. Federalism had no answer to this. But their solution backfired on them for the national revolution created a new national Czech ruling class. This destroyed the assumption that the removal of the German ruling class necessarily entailed the abolition of all forms of class rule. It indicated that class oppression was not exclusively associated with national oppression. Class domination for the Czech proletariat continued in the new Republic while the Germans had to confront the new experience of national domination. In the long-term, federalism arguably provided a more adequate answer to these two problems although in pre-war conditions it appeared unrealistic.

For the Orthodox SDs, it was a vindication of their decision to accept Modráček's revision of party ideology in which the annulment of the principle and practise of class struggle occupied a prominent place. The reconciliation of social classes which was reflected in the political expressions of those classes organized in the National Committee (and later in successive coalition governments) was the basis of their view of the state. For them, the Czech state was an embodiment of the national revolution whose success had been substantially owed to the unity of all classes to whom political equality would unreservedly be given. They claimed political legitimacy for the state by reference to "the right of revolution" and to the right of the Czech people to democratic self-determination in their struggle against the Germans. The unity and amity of all social classes was carried via the coalition principle into government where it was expected to achieve the same success in political and social questions as the revolution had seemed to indicate it had had in pursuit of the national aim. There was little common ground between Šmeral and the Orthodox SDs regarding their attitudes to the state. A comparison of their views provides a useful point of departure for a discussion of the essential differences on this and related questions from which we can feasibly reconstruct some of Šmeralism's basic features.

Šmeral had already accepted the likely emergence of a Czech national state in March 1918,[27] and although unable to halt or transform progress towards its attainment, he was at least able to mobilize proletarian pressure so that its eventual form corresponded more closely to the wishes of the strongest social force in the nation. Accordingly, a type of state grew up on the ruins of the Habsburg Empire which was to a significant degree historically progressive compared with its previous form and, which in Šmeral's view, offered a more favourable framework for the proletariat to fight for its aims.

Šmeral, in contrast to some of his colleagues who had been in Russia, was to that extent, positive in his attitude to the state.[28] A republic with a parliamentary system of government and universal adult suffrage could not on the face of it fail to provide more opportunities for the working class to impress its will on the political process than the old despotic monarchy had offered. However, in contrast to the Orthodox SDs and closer to the Leninist canon, Šmeral saw the state as having two principal functions. Firstly, it sought in erecting the organs of state on a more or less purely Czech basis, to correct the claimed democratic imbalance caused by the pre-war social domination of the Germans. However the inauguration of a Czech state, as Šmeral noted, simply reversed the roles of subordination and domination against the Germans, deprived them of their rights temporarily, except for those whose economic holdings remained untouched, and to that extent primarily affected the working classes of the national minorities. Far from effecting a successful conclusion to the nationalites problem, it simply fuelled further resentment. Secondly, the state was a product of the National Committee, in which the representatives of the Czech nation, were of a predominantly bourgeois complexion. With the aid of the Orthodox SDs, whose efforts to moderate the class-exclusiveness of the proletariat and harmonize the interests of all classes had helped conceal the true interests of the proletariat, the bourgeois classes had created order, legalized it by "the people and the act of revolution" and prepared the defences[29] for the day national euphoria would wilt before the renewal of class conflict. Deprived of certain means of struggle, the proletariat was therefore driven into illegality. The state, subject to external pressures unable to find an immediate solution to the national minorities problem in the early years of the republic would tend to rely on force and, Šmeral asserted, the old Austrian militarist inclinations would reappear albeit in a changed form.

This would provide the last line of defence against a militant proletariat. The revolt leading to the founding of the state had been led by a proletarian movement inspired by social motives but which had fallen victim to Czech nationalism as the ready means to salvation. The state which grew out of their efforts did not respond adequately to their needs and despite the advent of new democratic representative institutions, the economic bases of society had with some minor exceptions remained unchanged. Control had indeed been wrested from unaccountable foreign aristocrats yet the state was a bourgeois republic organized in benefit of the capitalist classes. The limitations placed on deep, structural change were justified by the Orthodox SDs on the grounds of the effect on the overall renewal of production and the expected international repercussions of a campaign of socialization.

The Orthodox SDs did not regard the Czech republic as a bourgeois state but as the first step to socialism.³⁰ Hence they placed its preservation above all other considerations and this helps to explain why in difficult and sometimes critical moments when the power of the labour movement was seen as a serious threat to the state, they were willing to act in concert with the bourgeois parties and the President to see the republic through. Other considerations too suggested that they were not overly concerned with representing proletarian interests. Initially, an influential group led by Bechyně no longer accepted the special role of the proletariat in the party.³¹ On the contrary, the Orthodox SDs regarded themselves not as the political expression of any one class, but a party of the intelligentsia, craftsmen and tradesmen as well as of the proletariat. The working class then had to alter their aims to harmonize with those of the other social strata and were not justified in using class struggle as the means of change. Democratic representation would anyway ensure that their interests would be safeguarded. The stress the Orthodox SDs placed on universal suffrage as the sole means of changing society was an implicit recognition of the power of the extra-parliamentary struggle and of one or other forms of direct democracy. It was a matter of great significance then to reduce the participation of the masses to a reliance on the voting system. However the structure of the political system and the operation of the coalition constrained the popular movement. There was a degree of optimism that the relatively wide-ranging and progressive social reforms achieved in the early days of the republic without recourse to violence would be the prelude to a more fundamental social and economic transformation of society. Yet what little socialization or nationalization did take place, mainly land and forests, was undertaken less in the interests of shifting power in favour of the proletariat, than in benefit of national security. As regards industry, the Orthodox SDs followed Kautsky. They considered it inappropriate in conditions where the means of production had been ravaged by the war to press for the socialization of industry. On the other hand the reconstruction of industry on an unchanged property basis would bring a strengthening of the power of the proletariat. This would enable them to agitate more effectively through union and party channels without recourse to violence.

Šmeral differed from the Orthodox SDs on nearly every issue. Although closer to Lenin on certain of these, he also maintained views significantly different from those of the Bolshevik leader. We have noted that in 1918 Šmeral regarded the Czech state as offering more potential for achieving the aims of socialism than the Austrian Empire. However he disagreed with the Orthodox SDs assertion that the national state met the needs of the proletariat equally with those of other classes and provided the framework for the full implementing of democratic rights. The differences derived to some extent from their different views of the party which expressed divergent notions of democracy and class interest. The Orthodox SDs had abandoned the working class of the national minorities and cast them in the role of potential enemies of the state even helping to deprive them in the short run of democratic rights. Further, the manner in which they had hoisted themselves into government via the formation of the National Committee using the "key" from the 1911 elections was from the strictly democratic viewpoint dubious.[32] Their gratitude to the masses in the build-up to the national revolution contrasted strongly with their distrust for them after it. The Orthodox SDs once they had entered government postponed party congresses and willingly assisted the destruction of those expressions of direct democracy which challenged the accepted view of representative government. They had supported the abolition of local National Committees and likewise the maintenance of the old Austrian laws restricting freedoms of assembly and the press.[33] On the other hand, it is clear that within the coalition, the Orthodox SDs would not compromise on the issue of universal suffrage.[34] It is equally certain that they regarded this as the acceptable level of the democratic participation of the masses in both republic and party. Given the class and nationality relations in the state, it was unlikely that universal suffrage would give the SDP the most powerful position in the government and, as the Orthodox SDs claimed, thereby pave the way to socialism. The international reaction to fundamental economic and social change tended to contradict this and the Orthodox SDs gave a wide berth to any action which might alter the attitude of the Allied powers to the state.

There were other important issues quite apart from the problem of the vote. Šmeral was certain that he was dealing with a new form of party hierarchy which appeared to be insensitive to pressure from below and was rapidly transforming itself into an élite. The Orthodox SDs had broken the constitution of the party by not summoning a party congress to elect candidates to the National Assembly. They had simply co-opted those known to be favourable to their cause.[35] The fact that SD ministers were given authority by the National Committee also struck Šmeral as a breach of democratic probity. In effect, the Orthodox SDs were sharing in government legitimized by the bourgeois parties without reference to popular sovereignty, at least in the early stages. This provided the basis for a system which, elections notwithstanding, has some resemblance to a party and state oligarchy in which power and influence were shared among a relatively small group of individuals.

Šmeral then was deeply critical of the Orthodox SDs whose claims to be democratic rested on shaky foundations. On the one hand, they appealed for a peaceful, gradualist road to socialism through the ballot box. On the other, they were aware that this method was very unlikely if not impossible to achieve the aims of socialism in the conditions of the time. The mandates were the property of the Executive Committee, the great majority of whom were Orthodox SDs. This enabled them to keep tight control over those entering parliament. In those instances, when the Orthodox SDs held important posts in government, there was no thought of abandoning the coalition and returning to an uncompromising class policy which inspired Šmeral's actions in this period. They resigned their positions within it only in response to the threat of Šmeralism which by September 1920 was found to have attracted a majority in the party. Hence, Šmeral was bound to say that democracy as practised by the Orthodox SDs was selective and inadequate. His experience of parliament under the Empire and in the Republic gave him an ambiguous attitude to it and nudged him to the solution of the problem of power from another direction. Suffrage in these conditions was not sufficient and when the most powerful social force could be more or less overlooked then the most persuasive remaining argument was revolution. However the parameters he had given himself to work within in themselves became a source of constraint. These were the democratic and the radical socialist and his political philosophy could not allow him to abandon one in favour of the other. As a result, his short-term tactic was constrained. In a sense, he wanted it both ways. The democratic parameter strongly suggested that he should have given himself ten years instead of two to organize the mass participation of the workers into a revolutionary movement with clear and more or less permanent lines of support. Compelling reasons existed however, tied up with the post-war revolutionary wave, which convinced him that the short-term prospects were more favourable. Yet a major problem presented itself insofar as non-party mass participation could not be translated into an institutional framework as rapidly as Šmeral demanded. The radical parameter also presented a major difficulty for the working class did not always behave as Šmeral wanted. Given his democratic values, he was loath to force them. Short-term conditions did not allow him to overcome these two problems, although the long-term prospects for them were more encouraging.

One aim of the social democratic movement itself implied that Šmeral could not achieve a revolution in the time-span he had given himself. For Šmeral, the movement was as much about raising the political consciousness of the working class as about the transformation of the property bases into collective ownership. The "practical methods" of the party before the war had done little to liberate them from the prejudices and blind faiths which capitalist society had placed between them and full participation in the decisions controlling their lives. Relative success had to a degree sanctified party practice which tended to restrict agitation to purely economic issues. Šmeral was critical of this which influenced his view as to the kind of party organization most appropriate to the realization of educational and revolutionary aims. The party was "the most conscious vanguard of the proletariat"[36] gradually leading the thinking of the masses forward to the fundamental principle of the social revolution. It was not, nor was it designed to be, exclusively proletarian, although the working classes were numerically the most powerful element around which the strategy of the party had necessarily to be built.

Šmeral however believed there was a place for elements which were not in the strict sense proletarian. In contrast to the pre-1914 situation when a more or less bourgeois inflow had damaged the party, Šmeral was prepared to accept those whose class-interest was not proletarian, on the conditions that they were anti-nationalist and that bourgeois representation did not involve a bourgeois majority. This included principally a section of the intelligentsia who, like Šmeral himself, were alienated by the values of bourgeois society and attracted by proletarian ideology. As such they were the natural allies of the workers playing a vital role in education and propaganda on which Šmeral laid such stress. Equally important was their task of instilling and maintaining a revolutionary spirit and theory into the movement. Šmeral was confident of winning them over if their reservations concerning the threat the radical socialists posed to the existence of the state could be overcome. Their talents would be more readily recognized and rewarded in a socialist economy.[37]

One peculiarity of social development in the Czech Lands—the tendency of a considerable part of the non-urban working class to work in a factory besides farming a small piece of land with their families, an occupation which brought them into a more or less close relation with peasants, small-traders and craftsmen—also caught Šmeral's attention. Despite their social conservatism and their unwillingness to identify themselves with any class, he regarded them as a natural target through which the party could reach the peasantry. This social group occupied an important place in his plans. Before the war he had more or less excluded them. But from 1919 when the Orthodox SDs had all but given up on the peasants, he attempted to join them to the mass movement and allowed them a place in the party. In contrast to Lenin who regarded them as useful political allies and was willing to steal other parties' programmes to win them over, Šmeral was not interested in temporary expedients which would be overturned once they had had the desired effect. The peasantry was important by virtue of its size as a group which made it capable of breaking the power of the numerically smaller rich peasants and capitalist farmers who, organized in the Agrarian Party, were the real enemy.

To build a mass, democratic movement, Šmeral had to win the peasants and maintain their allegiance and to do this he had to respect their wishes and way of life which required the maintenance of their forms of agriculture.[38] With this in mind, he excluded the small and medium property owners from socialization. This and his assurance to preserve the savings of small and medium investors in banks and financial institutions suggests a firm intention to form a bond between these non-proletarian classes and the party.[39] In the struggle against the only enemy, great capital and its representatives, Šmeral saw the role of the party as uniting not only those members of the proletariat organized in the CSP, the Catholic and Agrarian parties, but also the semi-proletarians, small and medium proprietors in towns and villages, minor officials in state and local administrations and the intelligentsia whose active neutrality in the struggle was needed to help tip the scales.

Šmeral's view of the role of the party was sufficiently different from Lenin's so that ultimately they were bound to come into conflict. The considerable cultural traditions, the expansion of science and art particularly in the western parts of the country, a mature and well-organized educational system formed the basis for a natural connection between the labour movement and the intelligentsia. These were to be found to a degree in the cooperatives, social and financial institutions run by the party. As a result of these historical conditions, which were quite different from those in Russia, Šmeral was not averse to throwing his membership paragraph[40] open to include everybody who accepted the program of the party, class struggle and internationalism. The visible difference between this and the membership paragraph accepted at the first Congress of the Czechoslovak Communist Party in Nov. 1921 was small.[41] The wording was similar but the promise to accept the programme of the Communist International covered an entirely different view of the party which, however, was not immediately apparent. Lenin's narrow and exclusive view of the party, which was reflected in his frequent calls to Šmeral to found a communist party based on a relatively small group of professional revolutionaries, was to misunderstand the conditions of struggle in the Czech Lands. Firstly, there were few professional revolutionaries as such, unless we include Alois Muna whose experience in Russia in the revolution appeared to equip him for the organization of a violent struggle for power.[42] In reality however, his strategy did not match the violence of his oratory. Of the others, neither Vajtauer, the anarchist, nor the ex-lieutenant Kostyál, whose "Organization of Ex-soldiers" in Moravia planned an armed revolt,[43] would have won more than a temporary place in a Leninist party, as their subsequent fates indicate. As Šmeral knew, Czech traditions were against violence of this sort and as the Hungarian episode in Slovakia showed would only serve to reawaken nationalism in the working class.[44] Neither could the affects of the recent world war be ignored. These were displayed most prominently in a general unwillingness to be involved in an armed conflict where the security of the state was not an issue. A civil war in these circumstances was unlikely.

Apart from the membership paragraph, other aspects of party organization indicated a clear difference of opinion between Šmeral and Lenin, chief among which was the relation between party centres and local and provincial party organizations. Šmeral favoured a wider leadership formed from two organs, the Executive Committee elected by the party congress acting in tandem with a Managing Committee made up of representatives of the cooperative organizations, provincial trade union council, the Union Association, the SDP MPs Club and one SD senator.[45] This dualism was later abolished and transformed into a united, centralized leadership, responsible only to the party congress and the Comintern.[46] In Šmeral's movement, local organizations were given a degree of autonomy in their dealings with non-party organizations (co-ops., DTJ, women's and youth organizations)[47] and in deciding the tactic in organizational and agitation work. These secondary organizations in which sympathizers but not party members could have their say were not admitted into the meetings of the CP after it had been founded.[48] Further the Executive Committee, later the Central Committee, imposed the obligation on all institutions of the party to keep the centres fully briefed on all matters of party activity and membership, enforced complete obedience on the communists in parliament and gave the right of veto to all members of the CP Executive acting as delegates in all institutions of the party.[49]

The introduction of these rules of organization, which as Šmeral foresaw would ultimately give the Executive Committee access to and control over all communists down to the smallest group, ran counter to many of his essential values. The abolition of the committee investigating complaints against party officials, the initiatives to narrow down the party, the missives to elect only those people with organizational talent to the party organs[50] and the refusal to allow proportional representation for the national minorities[51] in elections to party organizations appeared to narrow the basis of democracy within the party and was a distinct move in the direction of the exclusion of the masses. The firming up of party discipline with the introduction of expulsion, which Šmeral only favoured in extreme cases, and the move to illegal work appeared to him to indicate that conspiracy was being introduced into the party as an organizational principle although there was no practical need for it. The stress on strict, centralized organization and on the talent to operate it was in certain respects a negation of a proletarian party proper. There was initially the likelihood that it would be turned into a bureaucratic organization run by a leader or a small number of individuals who, given the right conditions, would seek to engineer a putsch. They would have little regard for the wishes of the masses who were by definition politically unconscious and would anyway not be represented in the party and hence excluded from popular participation. In the Czech Lands, with a long history of proletarian struggle against capitalism, a mature and relatively educated working class, party organizations at every level inviting democratic participation and the widening of contact with society as a whole through the press, educational circles and the non-political party institutions, such as savings banks and health insurance offices, it was eccentric to close off the party from the masses and quite against Šmeral's tactic.

Šmeral made no bones about the fact that the different historical conditions in the Czech Lands made the application of a model of revolution developed and tested in an environment entirely unrelated to his own undesirable in terms of his own objectives. The principal problem afflicting the Czech State and one having important implications on the tactic and role of the party was its size which made it peculiarly vulnerable to the economic competition of the great capitalist states and likewise to the political ambitions of certain of its neighbours. This and the related problem of the nationalities composition of the state, as in old Austria, demanded a federalist solution which, given the general mood of the imminence of revolution, Šmeral saw in a united socialist states of Europe. Nationalist sentiment to which the origin of the state was due would not in the long run guarantee the existence of the state and, applied to the minorities, would tend to work in the opposite direction. Any revolutionary party therefore which was seen to be associated with an outside centre, and more particularly one which had sponsored a movement in a neighbouring country, which, though covered in revolutionary socialist slogans, was perceived simply as a disguised form of irredentism, could not fail to strain the class sentiments of its main constituency.[52]

Hence Šmeral felt constrained to keep Lenin at arm's length. His efforts to impel Šmeral to go about the immediate founding of an international communist party simply awakened fears for the safety of the state and lost him popular support. Nationalism had to be overcome gradually and could not simply be ignored by the expedient of the leaders coming to an agreement to found an international party, as indeed was the case after the disappointment of the December general strike. Even in 1921, the greater part of the Czech workers distrusted their German and Hungarian counterparts as they had been members of the ruling nations and for the fact that their SD parties had played an opportunist role towards their bourgeois classes in wartime. On the other hand, the German and Hungarian proletariat regarded the presence of the SDP in the coalition as a sure sign that the Czech proletariat placed state and national interests above those of class. In these circumstances, an internationalist organization of the proletariat in Czechoslovakia was politically unrealistic and indeed the founding of the CP was from this viewpoint premature judging by its short-term effects on party support. Far more perceptive was Šmeral's view, to encourage workers of all nationalities to first take part in common political action which, combined with the rejection by the Czech workers of the Orthodox SDs' coalition and social-patriotic policies, could feasibly form a genuine basis for internationalism.

Other considerations persuaded Šmeral to distance himself from Lenin which argue in favour of an independent tactic, not least his view of revolution. Unlike Lenin, whose revolution was based upon a relatively small group of professional revolutionaries prepared to use any means to seize power at the centre of government, Šmeral envisaged the unleashing of a revolution from below breaking out in the form of local insurrections in many different areas simultaneously and ultimately taking control of a disintegrating government apparatus at the centre. The position of the Czech Lands in relation to any world revolution ruled out any realistic seizure of power, quite apart from the reservations Šmeral held about the kind of party needed to achieve it. Further, the repositories of power which Lenin had had to overcome to make his revolution were of quite a different character to those in the Czech Lands. Moreover, he had been assisted by Russia's involvement in a disastrous world war. The war had brought the Czechs a national revolution but this had stopped short of a social revolution. The driving force in the struggle for power was the mobilizing of the masses at critical moments, as the Bolsheviks had early shown. Accordingly, Šmeral aimed at winning over the greatest number of people in a mass party which at the same time was an expression of their participation and more or less faithfully reflected their aspirations.

There was another important area dividing Šmeralism from the Russian method which was reminiscent of Martov and centred on an educational element[53] providing an important stimulus to the proletariat and maturing them to the conviction that they no longer wished to live in the old way. Instead of forming a determined and intransigent revolutionary communist heart with the body of the workers movement based on the centralist principle and quasi-military discipline, Šmeral, in the conditions following the national revolution, regarded the most appropriate method as one aimed at raising the revolutionary consciousness of the proletariat. The party's role then was to bring the object lessons of class reality to the proletariat and never to force them to the recognition of revolution nor to outrun their feelings and aspirations so that the party and the proletariat parted company. This was anyway unacceptable because Šmeral was intent on leading the proletariat in such a way that it would be capable of administering the state after the revolution had been achieved, a task in which the party would not play the leading role. The need for a mass party was the most fitting conclusion deriving from the traditions of the labour movement informed by and reflecting the proletarian orientation to which Šmeral believed the workers instinctively found a way. A revolutionary sect no matter how disciplined, although capable of initiating an armed revolution given outside help, would be isolated, provoke a flight of proletarian support to the Orthodox SDs and put back the cause of proletarian revolution for many years to come. The tactic hence was to remain within the SDP but maintain a policy of strict opposition to the Orthodox SDs whose support for the bourgeois parties would gradually bring increasing numbers of proletarian supporters over to the radical socialists enabling them to take control of party institutions and at the same time demonstrate to the proletariat of the national minorities that class interest bulked larger than bourgeois national interest. Given time, the initial disappointment with parliament as an institution providing immediate solutions to the economic and social problems of the time would fuse with the popular mood aroused by the Orthodox SDs contravention of the rules of political legitimacy. This would generate an irresistible mass movement which would not ignore parliament as a useful platform but would bring relentless pressure to bear in the form of municipal committees and workers councils. The local socialist councils disbanded in late 1918 indicated that this was not simply conjectural. Yet, as we have noted, Šmeral did not leave himself time, while his decision to win over local party organizations and involve himself only marginally with workers' councils suggests a serious problem in mobilizing and channelling support from non-SDP members.

The Orthodox SDs and the bourgeois parties both accused Šmeral of being a communist. Lenin regarded him as a centralist and a social democrat. In reality, they were looking at different aspects of Šmeralism. The Orthodox SDs drew attention to his aims, principally the socialization of production, and concluded that this marked his allegiance to the country where a communist revolution had been successfully achieved by a small highly disciplined party using the methods of violence and terrorism. Lenin's strictures on the other hand centred on those features of Šmeralism which seemed to him to be strongly reminiscent of Menshevism. In particular, his stress on the elective principle, his refusal to force the masses by violence, his willingness to accept self-criticism and tolerate opponents and his commitment to collective leadership all ran counter to the Bolshevik view of the party and the revolution. While the Orthodox SDs tried to cloak his movement in Leninism by emphasizing his revolutionary socialist aims and all that that implied for the security of the state, Lenin saw it acting in competition with him for the middle radical ground, not in terms of radical socialist aims but as a method of revolution more appropriate to developed industrial nations which conceivably could be erected into a model in competition with his own.

Šmeral saw no difference between communism and genuine social democracy.[54] Communism was simply the stage of development social democracy entered when a revolutionary situation emerged demanding a sharpening of discipline and a strengthening of the leadership. This however was substantially different from the Bolshevik view which envisaged "hard centralism" from the outset, shifting its emphasis away from a popular mass and democratic basis to the narrow, the bureaucratic and the centralist. At one stage, Šmeral was optimistic that the will of the proletarian masses would carry the day against the wishes of the Comintern on the issue of the party's name. However on this and the policy of proletarian dictatorship, there were great differences.

Šmeral did not have the faith in parliament which Lenin attributed to him and to that extent is not to be classified with Martov. On the other hand, universal suffrage was an important gauge of opinion within the state and a mirror of the elective principle in the party. In September 1920, he broke the coalition and formally took the Marxist Left into parliament as an opposition party bent on undermining the political expressions of the great landed magnates, financial and industrial circles in which part of the proletariat was organized. It was in Šmeral's estimation within the capacity of the proletariat, as the trend of events appeared to show, to gain a socialist majority in parliament, an eventuality which depended on maintaining the unity of the largest section and gradually bringing together the worker parties of the other nationalities. He doubted if the bourgeoisie would accept this majority however and he had no reason to think they would not find a way to undermine this as the Orthodox SDs had done when they had learned that a majority of the party favoured the radical Left. They had achieved what amounted to a dictatorship of the minority. This abrogation of the democratic principle had necessarily to be answered with the dictatorship of the proletariat in the interests of the majority who, by one or another artifice, had been excluded from democratic participation. Šmeral was aware that such results could be achieved in parliament, but it was the mass movement of the proletariat educated by the practices of the Orthodox SDs which would inaugurate a strong government and destroy the violent resistance of the minority. Workers council would play a role in this endeavour similar to the function of the National Committees in the days of the national revolution and, as in late 1918, they would cut across the boundaries of party and class.

Šmeralism was abandoned in 1920, although given a decade it might have succeeded. In conclusion of this chapter, some brief consideration should be given to its coherence and realism in relation to political conditions and, more particularly, some of the reasons for its failure. It should be stressed however that these points will be discussed more fully in those later chapters covering the specific areas into which his thought and activity naturally fall. The long-term prospects of Šmeralism were not at all bad. There was powerful support for his economic programme throughout the First Republic, though the internal wrangles of the Communist Party was one of the factors causing it to ebb and flow. His emphasis on mass, participating democracy and criticism of elitism and hierarchy corresponded to the more or less iconoclastic and egalitarian traditions of Czech working people.

Yet the short-term conditions did not allow him the flexibility to manoeuvre which in practise produced a clash between his radical socialist and democratic values. He failed to appreciate fully the restraining character of the coalition and he underestimated the Orthodox SDs. He did not anticipate that they would get help from the structure of the political environment and directly from parties and individuals within it. The attempt to remove the SDs without resorting to violence was met not only by the SDs but by most of the other parties, and this he did not bargain for. He was more or less aware of the affect of the national state on his supporters but he was unable to do anything about the external factors which interposed. He had no answer to the volatility of the mass movement which increased as a result of this and the Czech workers' tendency to identify the national minorities with irredentism. These conditions, hence, forced him to operate within narrow boundaries and deprived him of tactical room. This was particularly visible in respect of his federalism. Arguably this could have provided a solution to the problems of the national minorities. Yet circumstances were not appropriate in the short term to the maturing of the proletariats of the different ethnic groups to common political action, the prerequisite for a mass, democratic socialist revolution on which a federalist system could be built. The Orthodox SDs' solution ultimately led to further nationality problems, but the support they syphoned off from Šmeral placed significant constraints on him in the short term. The response of the Czech Bolsheviks in conjunction with the Comintern to force the minorities into a united international communist party, little more than a mechanical application of internationalism, was an attempt to force the pace of the revolution. The decline in popular support for the newly founded Czech CP suggested that it misfired, but more important for Šmeral, the Comintern, after allowing him an independent path in the summer of 1920, had second thoughts. The failure of the December General Strike was assumed to be the failure of Šmeralism and its leading figure hence was placed in a quandary. His reluctance to be identified with Bolshevism was not purely tactical. It was determined by socialist principle as much as political realism. His entrance into the CP was not a recognition of the superiority of Bolshevism, more a sign that in the aftermath of the strike an independent communist party was unrealistic. Yet this was not the death of Šmeralism for it was to raise its head on more than one occasion in the subsequent history of the CP.

# Part Two

*Chapter 1*

**Nationalism in the Czech Lands**

The impact of nationalism on Šmeral's movement was considerable. It led protest away from the real causes of discontent to the pseudo-causes, in effect defusing proletarian socialist radicalism. It played a significant role in preventing the cooperation of Czech workers with those of the national minorities, in particular the Germans. It was also a factor in restraining Czech workers especially in mining- and light-industry from swelling the ranks of the radical socialists, though they espoused social and economic aims closer to Šmeral's than those of the two Czech socialist parties. In an ethnically homogeneous state, they might well have supported him. As it was, in conditions of threat to the state most visible in the case of Hungary,[1] their nationalist sentiment proved stronger than their class solidarity. They typify to some extent the puzzling relationship between nationalism and socialism discernible in even the most revolutionary centres of proletarian socialism at this time. In the specific conditions of the struggle for liberation, the two elements in the relationship seem to have formed a significant degree of unity. However, the new stage of historical development reflected in the foundation of the Czech state brought the contradictions between them to the surface. Working-class support for nationalism was conditional on the achievement of socialism. Yet the transformation of the SDP from a proletarian internationalist to a nationalist party made this difficult if not to say impossible. National sentiment was ultimately bound to clash with class sentiment, and the inability of the Czech working class to resolve this contradiction was one of the primary causes of Šmeral's failure.

Czech proletarian nationalism emerged more or less as a response to the SDP's unwillingness and inability to come to grips with the nationalities question. The first stage in this process was completed in 1897 when Klofáč broke away and founded a new Czech socialist party. This provided the impulse for the entry of a new spirit into the SDP itself which gradually brought changes in its leadership and direction. In the social and economic conditions before 1914, the stance the Austrian SDP displayed to the nationalities problem was, like that of the Czech SDP, likely to alienate a considerable section of the industrial workers' support. This was most marked, as we shall presently see, among workers in light industry and in the small industrial towns in the ethnically mixed regions. The policy of the SDP faithfully reflected orthodox Marxist doctrine. This was based on the assumption that members of the working class had no nationality insofar as their existence was primarily defined by their relation to the productive means. This forced them to the logical but erroneous conclusion that the proletariat would invariably give priority to class allegiance over national sentiment. Accordingly, the SDP emphasized class struggle, international proletarian solidarity and likewise international organization. However, other considerations interposed both practical and theoretical which ran counter to these notions. These were derived from the particular conditions governing the nationality relations in the industrially more advanced regions of the Empire. The situation in the Czech Lands was more or less a denial of those social democratic principles which stressed the individual's right to an education and to use his native language in his work. [While class struggle was acceptable to the Czech proletariat concentrated in large industrial conurbations, where national divisions coincided more or less with the pattern of ownership of productive private property, it was rejected as inappropriate in the economic and national conditions of certain areas mainly in the north of Bohemia.]

Though the SD leaders themselves were theoretically of an internationalist persuasion, the structure and direction of the party was an approximate reflection of the German-Austrian domination, which was the rule in many other areas of the economic and political life of the Empire. In practice, it seemed reasonable for socialists belonging to the most developed region in Austria-Hungary to exercise the decisive influence in the party's affairs. As they rightly argued, the success of the socialist movement as a whole depended on international, political and union organizations stretching throughout the Empire with co-ordinated policies and administration. Yet certain Czech SDs complained that this amounted to Austrian domination by other means and as such contravened the democratic and socialist values of the party.[2] In this case, proletarian internationalism clashed with the growing national consciousness of the Czech workers, and indeed with the nationalist sentiments of their German counterparts, though that concerns us less here. The Austrian SDs understood and occasionally sympathized with the Czechs' aspirations to national equality. Their response to the increasing pressure was simply to counsel patience. Nothing could be achieved until after the revolution when a socialist federation of autonomous nationalities would be brought into existence. In their own interest and those of the revolution, they chided the Czech SDs for their insistence on immediate national autonomy which they regarded as a de facto weakening of the international socialist movement.

The reality of the day-to-day economic struggle tended to undermine the Austrian SDs' view of the primacy of international proletarian solidarity. The notion of the common struggle of German and Czech workers against the real enemy, the capitalists, was more or less sound theoretically. Yet the conditions were such that they were unable to accept internationalism. The struggle for their daily bread interposed and instead of uniting them made them enemies. The affects of large-scale Czech immigration into newly industrialized and predominantly ethnic German regions were most marked in the competition for employment.[3]

Czech workers often had the advantage over their German counterparts as they were prepared to accept lower rates of pay. The German employers tended to remain true to their class interest and rejected any claims on their sense of national solidarity which appeared in the form of appeals to take on German in preference to Czech workers. The collision of national consciousness was compounded to a significant degree by a form of class antagonism which had its source in the fact that many of the Germans the Czechs were superceding were proletarianized masters or *Gesellen*. The Czechs on the other hand were usually either unskilled workers, first-generation labourers fresh from the countryside or even small peasant landholders working in industry.[4] The areas where this aspect of the clash of nationalities was most acutely felt lay mainly in North West and North East Bohemia.[5] The conditions of economic and social life and the more or less close contact with the mixed-nationality areas provided a significant contrast with those of the workers operating in the large concentrations of heavy industry and mining in the almost purely ethnic Czech hinterland.

This was reflected in an important difference in consciousness, which, in the conditions of the new state, produced a divergence in political allegiance that Šmeral was unable to bridge. The large numbers of workers employed in the industries of Prague, Plzeň and Kladno, for example, were less directly affected by the clash of national consciousness, except inasmuch as their class struggle was directed against their predominantly German employers. Heavy industry naturally attracted large concentrations of workers. It provided conditions in which proletarian consciousness crystallized and expressed itself in the foundation and development of an extensive network of union and party organizations. It was hardened especially in the struggles of the early 1890s when the emergence of the mass strike gave them a new awareness of their power. This was true also to an extent in the industrial areas of northwest Bohemia, though the concentrations of workers were much smaller. Yet the structure of industry as a whole in northern Bohemia inhibited the growth of political and particularly union organization among Czech workers. This region was the home of "small-shop" industries employing up to five workers which in 1902 formed 36% of all workers in Bohemia.[5]

This situation favoured the employers who successfully prevented efforts to improve pay and conditions and likewise to unionize the shop by calling on the waiting and more mobile pool of cheaper Czech labour. Czech workers acquired a reputation as strike-breakers and scabs and effectively alleviated the German workers of the means to conduct successful strikes. Yet not only the jobs of the German workers were at risk, so too was their way of life. This was frequently bound up with the cultivation of a piece of land which affected their economic mobility.

The Austrian SDP was confronted with a dilemma. The SDs could not champion the claims of the German working class over those of their Czech counterparts, as this was a clear abrogation of the principle of international proletarian solidarity. On the other hand, their recommendation to wait until wages paid to Czechs equalled the going rate for Germans, thereby giving them an equal chance in the labour market, was considered inadequate. The prerequisite for that was a powerful trade union movement, which was lacking, but to introduce and develop union organizations, especially in the light of the employers' resistance, implied the work of at least a generation. The SDs' proposal could not satisfy the German workers' demand for an instant solution. Indeed it aggravated national antagonism because the Austrian SDs appeared to be siding with the Czechs. Accordingly they turned away from them and worked out their resentment directly on the Czechs whenever they could in factories and workshops. The Czech workers too came to the conclusion that proletarian solidarity in these conditions tended to equal German domination. The German employers inflicted on them lower pay and poorer working conditions than German workers would accept, which strengthened their conviction that they were exploited as proletarians by the capitalists.

More immediate, however, was their daily experience of persecution and harassment as *Untermenschen* by German workers. This caused them to resist the spread of union organizations which were ultimately of German provenance. National antagonisms then allied with their conditions of life and work in light- and home-industry and handicrafts constrained the development of a strictly proletarian consciousness. Rather, national consciousness overpowered their awareness of their relation to the means of production and the political struggle against capitalism became secondary to the nationalist struggle against the Germans. However in certain conditions, they were combined for the nationalism of the Czech workers often expressed itself in attacks on German capitalism. Yet in the first instance, they looked for a political organization which rejected internationalism and sought to achieve democratic aims, in the expectation that ethnic division would provide the answer to the nationalities problem.

The practical effects of internationalism were not everywhere the same; for example, in Reichenberg (from 1918) the union association was composed of Czech and German workers.[6] In Ostrava, too, strikes were organized jointly.[7] But for the Czech workers in light industry especially in northeast Bohemia, internationalism was primarily associated with foreign domination. This view persisted well into the era of the Republic despite the gradual shift in ownership of industrial holdings in favour of the Czechs which began in 1918.[8] In the medium term, Czech workers might have supported Šmeral's struggle for socialism. As it was, they were more or less diverted by among other things the renewal of the nationalities struggle after the Czechs had become the ruling nationality.

The Czech workers, just like the Germans, turned away from the internationalist Austrian SDP and looked for a party which would genuinely fight to protect their interests. Such a party emerged in 1897 when Klofáč, reacting to the failure of the SDP, broke away and founded the Czech National Socialist Party (hereafter CNSP). Its principles were significantly different from those of the SDP. Klofáč rejected proletarian internationalism for what it had done to Czech workers in the mixed nationality regions. Further, he gave the industrial proletariat no special position as the agent of change. Rather, he broadened the category of worker to include not only those labouring in the mines and industry, but also those in handicrafts and home-industry, the self-employed craftsmen, peasants, clerks and small shop-owners and businessmen. His aim was to form a broad front of Czechs from different social classes to fight for the removal of foreign influence in the Czech Lands. This was felt most strongly in commerce, industry and agriculture. Though Klofáč himself did not subscribe to the demand for the socialization of the means of production, he successfully passed himself off as anti-capitalist insofar as his stated policy was to divest the Germans of their economic holdings. They were situated in Czech territory and in his view rightly belonged in Czech hands. Czech workers of all kinds stood to gain security and a greater share of the national wealth, though on the basis of private property, an aspect of the debate which however did not become clear until later.[9] The broadening of the definition of worker naturally led Klofáč to abandon class struggle and substitute instead the harmony of all classes as equal parts of the nation in the struggle against the Germans.

Within a short time, the NCSP began to put down roots among working people initially by sponsoring relief and educational associations. This effectively brought them into the forefront of the social struggle against German capitalism and a political struggle against the Austrian state, insofar as these secular and native Czech institutions amounted to a rejection of Austrian clerical and political ideology. By 1902, they had grown into the nationalist trade union organization, the OČD,[10] and in 1908 they had 16, 141 members.[11] Though small compared with the Czech SD Unions, this figure represents a significant rate of growth and the OČD continued to expand such that in the following six years it increased five times over to 70,000.[12] Their growing popularity was also reflected in votes cast for them at elections. At the Reichsrat elections in 1907, they gained 71,773 votes to the combined Czech SDs' vote of 278,113,[13] which they raised by more than 40% to 101,214 in 1911.[14]

Their success was most noticeable in the northern national borderlands, though it was not associated exclusively with one class or social group. They achieved probably their greatest single success in the early 1900s, with the winning over of the Czech railway workers who resigned en masse from the old international socialist union and joined both the CNSP and its union. They also won the adherence of workers with quite different aims and viewpoints. Some like the handicrafts workers in the northeast under the Krkonoš mountains had anarchist leanings and were attracted to it as it gave them an opportunity to express their anti-Marxist and anti-state sentiments. Others like the miners in Duchcov and Most had a more specific social programme which, broadly speaking, consisted in bringing the mines into the ownership of the Czech nation. The textile workers who were suffering from the low pay and poor conditions associated with the competition between mechanized and handicraft industries had the more modest aims of achieving some improvement in their circumstances. The party was not united except in its opposition to the Austrian state and its instability was reflected in the wide range of views held by the leaders on social and economic questions. These of course did not fully appear until after the national aim had been achieved.

Other factors contributed to the rise of the Czech National Socialists. In 1902, 56% of all workers in Bohemia were employed in concerns with fifty employees or less.[15] The Czech SDP tended to overlook them, not because many of them were in the forefront of the clash of workers of different nationalities, but, as Social Democratic theory demanded, because their primary aim was to unionize and politicize workers in large industrial conurbations. Party and union resources anyway could not stretch to every area and with an insufficient number of full-time workers they had to be content to work in regions where they could reach the maximum number of workers, which meant large industrial towns. By and large, these were in the ethnic Czech hinterland. Between 1902 and 1912 there was a substantial increase of workers in large factories from 1.57 million to 2.2m.[16] This appeared to the SDP to offer a golden chance to transform the scale and organization of the labour movement from its basis of relatively small-scale and scattered proletarian struggles, often isolated from each other, into a numerically overwhelming and organized mass movement. Yet even in the large industrial towns, the SDs did not have things all their own way. The people who drifted to the towns to find work were from a more or less rural environment. Some were impoverished artisans, others small peasants who had given up the struggle against a pitiless land system and taken to the towns to remedy the problem of income while keeping their allotments.[17] Both explained their predicament by referring one way or another to foreign domination and, though some gravitated to working in heavy industry, they were not to be won for the SDP. Rather, particular sections of heavy industry supported the National Socialists, for example, the metal-workers and chemical workers in Prague and Plzeň.

The Czech SDs could do little about the conditions contributing to the emergence of nationalism in the labour movement. Though the writing was on the wall already in 1896 when the suggestion for a trade union centre independent of Vienna was narrowly defeated at the II Czech SDP Congress,[18] the workers still had not lost all their enthusiasm for social democracy, at least judging by the SDs' success at the elections the following year. They polled more than a quarter of a million votes, representing some 30% of the votes to the Fifth Curia, and most were cast by their traditional supporters in the large industrial areas.[19] This success was one of the factors which induced the Czech SDs to reaffirm their commitment to internationalism which they expressed in their anti- State Rights declaration in the Reichsrat. The policy of the Czech SDs was seen as a betrayal, not only of the nationalities program itself, but also of socialism. They were unable, too, to escape the contradiction in the character of the declaration itself, which was not the work of all SD delegates in the Reichsrat, only of the Czechs. This suggested that it was simply a kind of national matter which sat uneasily beside internationalist principle. Secondly, though it was a specific attack on the nationalist aspirations of the Czech bourgeois parties, there was a conspicuous absence of protest against the national oppression of the Czech nation by Austrian imperialism. It deprecated historical rights and as such was directed against the widening of the reactionary principle of monarchy, yet there was no protest against the repressive Austrian monarchy. Their basic aim, the struggle for a socialist republic, was not mentioned either. In effect, they acquiesced in the dominant position of the Germans in the Austrian SDP and supported the Emperor and the Dual Monarchy. In these conditions, they could do little to prevent the bourgeois parties increasing their influence in the Czech labour movement. Proletarian support for nationalism in the event led to the subordination of the final interests of the working class to those of the nation which, as it was led by the bourgeois classes, entailed a subordination to their social, economic and political values. Before it came to this however, the reaction of the Czech SDs to the secession of Klofáč set in train a process which ultimately worked itself out in a deep split in the SDP itself.

Shortly after the anti-State Rights declaration of the Czech SDs, Badeni introduced his language decrees by which he intended to give the Czech language equality with German in the Imperial bureaucracy. This affected the Czech SDs in a number of ways. They had no quarrel with the content of the decrees as they had long been agitating for equal rights in language use. However, they objected to them on the grounds that these matters were properly the business of parliament, though they well knew that even if the Habsburg system had allowed this, the German national majority would never have voted them through the Reichsrat. They placed themselves in an impossible position. Their commitment to democratic principle led them to oppose government by decree ignoring the likelihood in this case that this would have opened the way to a greater degree of democratic participation for the Czechs in society. In so doing they played into the hands of the German nationalists, the sworn enemies of all Czechs, whose sudden and unaccustomed role as champions of democracy and parliamentary government in the Reichsrat contrasted with their sponsorship of pogroms in the national borderlands. The Czech SDs identification with them on this issue amounted to something like political suicide. It was at the same time a major factor in the discrediting of the SDs and likewise in helping to boost the fortunes of the bourgeois nationalist parties. In these conditions, it was likely that the Austrian SDP would begin formally to recognize the aspirations to national equality in its constituent national parts, which in the final analysis required a softening of its line on international proletarian solidarity. It did so as much in response to the growing movement of nationalist SDs as to undercut the appeal of parties like Klofáč's to a large section of its proletarian constituency. In deference to national aspirations, it transformed itself into a federation of national and autonomous parties, which was outlined in theoretical terms by the Brno Nationalities Programme. In reality, the realization of its aims was as distant as the coming of socialism itself. The Czech SDs felt no more equal nor autonomous than before. The power of decision remained firmly in the hands of the Germans.[20]

Although this did not become a conspicuous trend until after 1907, the workers and sections of the petty-bourgeoisie and intelligentsia saw little reason to offer their support to a party still dominated by the national enemy, particularly when the NCSP had a programme combining State Rights and a pledge to fight for economic and social demands not markedly dissimilar from those of social democracy. The signs of the drift away from the SDP emerged as early as 1901 when the votes cast for them fell overall and most noticeably in the Czech Lands. The workers' enthusiasm subsided as the Fifth Curia became a battleground for competing nationalist groups.[21] The campaign for universal suffrage from 1905-7 enabled the Czech SDs to rescue some of their damaged reputation. Their struggle was understood as a national as much as a democratic battle against the Austrian system. This helped to conceal the changes taking place under the surface of party life and also the nationalist disintegration in the labour movement as a whole. The prominent role of the SDP in the movement for voting rights was reflected in their victory in the 1907 elections, but this did little to ameliorate the national antagonisms within its ranks[22] and, at least as measured in election results, it went thereafter into a gradual, if temporary, decline.

The attitude of the leading Czech SDs to the Austrian SDP changed most noticeably after 1907 when the federation of national social democratic parties had been in existence for ten years and still showed all the signs of German domination and few of the national equality which it had been set up to achieve. The Czechs came to believe it was merely an expression of the German attempt to maintain a united labour movement, not as an expression of internationalism, but more as a certain kind of great power nationalism which was a reflection of the general relations between Austria and the subject nations. Adler's reproach that they were "minderwertig in Internationalismus"[23] cut little ice as in these conditions international proletarian solidarity amounted to national domination. They had some justification for their views, most notably on the issue of education, which helped to integrate the SDs into the wider national conflict against Austria, and on the question of party finance, which was intimately connected with the unions. The first was probably more inflammatory in that it touched the Czech nation as a whole, while the second was restricted more or less to SD sympathizers. Both however were interpreted as examples of national discrimination.

The right to an education in the native language was a fundamental tenet of social democracy. This explains the bitter recriminations which followed the Austrian SDs' outright rejection of Czech claims for a new university in Brno, which was based on the false grounds that Germans were in a majority in the city. This and their voting against a proposal in the Reichsrat to subsidize and nationalize the school of the Czech minority in Vienna[24] suggested that they were no different from the German bourgeoisie as far as protecting their power was concerned. They too seemed intent on slowing the growth of national education through which the minorities hoped to achieve some sort of parity. This created great resistance among Czech SDs in Vienna, but, more significant for the future was the effect on those in Northern Bohemia. Hitherto they had maintained solidarity with their German comrades voting at elections for German SD candidates.[25] Their reaction marked the beginning of the end of this practice. The second bone of contention was the finances of the party which affected not only the administration of the party organizations but also its ability to reach the masses through agitation and propaganda. Here again the Czech SDs felt themselves to be hemmed in by restrictions which came one way or another from their German counterparts. They had experienced this as early as 1897 when, after the setting up of the SD federation, the Germans had refused them, contrary to established practice and international solidarity, financial help in the launching of their independent party newspaper *Pravo lidu*. They were refused money, too, in 1901 to help fund the new organ of the Czech SDs in Vienna, *Dělňické listy,* which, placed beside Adler's support of Polish and Hungarian SDs in similar ventures,[26] was interpreted as national discrimination, though this was recognized as more or less marginal to the central problem of party finance. The main financial prop of the party was the unions which had developed from the symbiosis of party and union organizations. Although both sets of institutions grew stronger, the Czech SDs did not reap the benefit directly, as Vienna still controlled the economic sources of the party, federation notwithstanding. Nowhere else in Cis-Leithan Austria did a national constituent SD party, at least the equal of the Germans in its influence on the mass, hand over its affiliated union-members' dues to the Viennese centre without having some say in the uses to which the money was put. This made a nonsense of the whole idea of equality within a federation and the advantages to the Austrians were such that it was unrealistic to expect changes of any significance.

The conflict over trade unions at the Copenhagen Congress of the International (1910) was therefore as much about the destination of Czech trade unionists' financial contributions as about national division, though these issues were closely connected. The Czechs' decision to build their own trade unions and attend the Congress as a social democratic party in their own right was denounced by Adler as the destruction of international proletarian unity. Yet the nationalism of the Czechs lay only in their demand for equal rights which the Germans were unable and often unwilling to give. Although the International cast them in the role of destroyers of internationalism, they were no more nationalist than the Germans in whose favour internationalism worked. As a party, the Austrian SDP was no larger than the Czechs. Yet the structure of the leadership, which was little more than a group of federated leading organs having the external appearance of international representation, enabled it to speak at the International in the name of the whole Austrian SDP. This tended to push aside the internal needs of the party and while the Germans controlled the leadership there were few grounds for believing that change would follow.

In the Czech Lands, proletarian opinion was more for the autonomist SDs and against the decision of the International. Despite the inroads of the National Socialists on their support, the SDs did not lose their authority over the masses. On the contrary, the International was seen as an instrument of the great nations which hardly understood the needs of small, dependent nations. On balance, the Czech SDs remained the real representative of the Czech working class, which does not however necessarily suggest a greater inherent inclination of Czech workers to nationalism. It is after all a moot point whether a genuine representative of internationalism existed at all in Austria. In the conditions of the time, internationalism represented national domination and the proletarian reaction to it could only work itself out in a nationalist way. To that extent, it found its natural allies in those movements which were also fighting to bring German domination to an end, though their social and political values were of quite a different order from the traditional aims of the SDP. The merging of the Czech SDs with these groups and their subsequent division were of great significance in bringing about a squeeze on radical socialism.

By 1911, the Czech SDP had taken significant steps towards becoming a nationalist party, though this was not completed until late in the war. These changes however were not always discernible in policy statements. Němec, the leader, strongly supported a strengthening of the independence of Czech SD organs and likewise an extension of the principle of national division into the hitherto all-Austrian organs such as the SDs Club in the Reichsrat. On the other hand, he agreed in principle with Šmeral's solution to the nationalities question[28] and supported his demand for a revision of the Brno Programme (1899) and a genuine attempt at international solidarity from all sides. This became official policy at the IX Congress.

A number of aspects suggested that time was not on his side, as Němec suspected. In practice, the split into Autonomists and Centralists was a repudiation of this doctrine while on the other hand, it brought a considerable increase in the size of the Czech party. A minority view voiced by Meissner rejected Šmeral's solution as identical with that of the Austro-Marxists and he firmly set his face against it. Yet the rank and file as a body were not all anti-internationalist. Some like František Náhlík, the Pisek SD leader, did not agree with the Autonomists and on the contrary supported the international unity of the unions. But, as he warned Adler[29], in the case of a split, he felt obliged to abandon the Centralist secessionists and hail to the Autonomist majority. It would of course be imprudent to suggest that this was the rule, but it does at least indicate that apparent displays of nationalism need not be per se anti-internationalist. Šmeral reiterated his scheme for a federation at the XI Congress, albeit in a slightly changed form, and though he had moved from his position of a reform of the Empire to a socialist revolutionary solution, he was unable to counter the forces operating within the party. The war brought a fundamental change in the character of the SDP in that it sharply intensified nationalist feeling. In contrast to the Czech politicians at home and abroad, who more or less quickly abandoned the idea of the maintenance of Austria-Hungary and looked forward to a radical and violent turn of events to settle the Czech question, Šmeral retained his belief in the necessity of a federation of nations on its territories until the bitter end. He foresaw that the nationalists in the SDP and the working class would be drawn into the broader struggle for national liberation and seduced into supporting national interests in the belief that this would further socialist interests. Proletarian nationalism then, though not homogeneous, was conditional on the achievement of socialism. The outcome of their support for nationalism was the national revolution which ultimately furthered the interests of their class enemies, the bourgeoisie. The working-class as a whole reacted more or less negatively to this and, to that extent, nationalism came into conflict with socialism. Yet the character of their reactions varied according to which socialist party they supported.

In contrast to the Austrian SDP, the Czech SDs (Autonomists and Centralists) gained in strength over the period 1907 to 1911. Their share of the vote rose by more than 100,000 from 278,430[30] to 366,244.[31] Though this was hardly reflected in their representation in the Reichsrat, a mere 2 delegates,[32] it showed at least that the Autonomists policy of national division in union and party organizations had borne fruit. Increased support for them was most visible in Bohemia, though the internationalists after the Autonomist/Centralist split in 1911 were not entirely abandoned as Náhlík had portended and maintained a truncated power base largely in the two areas of heavy industry, Brněnsko and Ostravsko, where Czechs and Germans and, in the latter case, Poles worked side by side. Nevertheless, the rise of nationalism in the SDP as a whole could not be denied. Nationalist sentiment too was growing, arguably at a faster rate, in the CNSP. Votes for them grew by just under 50% in four years[33] and the involvement of their unions in the struggles of the textile workers in North East Bohemia in 1911 and their efforts to fight the mass lock-outs in the Central North Bohemian metal-working industry was significant in the expansion of their union base.[34] They also profited from the reluctance of SD union functionaries to use the strike weapon which is not to say that they won many recruits from the OSČ, rather that in those areas where unions were weakly or not at all established, the ČOD won a reputation for defending the interests of the small worker. This was underpinned by the common attitude that the SD unions were only interested in the industrial proletariat in the large towns.

The war played a decisive role in burying the socialist precepts of internationalism and class struggle which ultimately brought about the final transformation of the SDP into a nationalist party. It also created the conditions for the SDP and CNSP to converge, signs of which had been visible since 1911 in the secret overtures of Meissner.[35] But for events abroad, this might well have led, if only for a time, to a fusion of the two parties. The outbreak of war engendered a curious form of patriotism which brought a brief reconciliation between Czech and German. This soon faded however in the light of the Central Powers' early military successes which left the Czechs wondering whether, as seemed likely for a period, the Germans would repay them by intensifying national domination in a more rigidly organized post-war Empire. Although the Czech workers as a whole had had little faith in the Second International, its failure to prevent the war tended to deepen their sense of disillusion with international socialism as a force. The German SDs vote for war credits, sustained by Adler, seemed to reveal the true nature of internationalism and deepened Czech opinion against them even further. Šmeral's plan to support those forces leading to democratization inside

Austria and peace and neutrality externally was swept away by the hard reality of the Austrian international administration. In conditions of savage dictatorship, the Czech SDs "correct attitude to the war"[36] was bound to affect their popularity. Perhaps more significant was the narrowing of the base of the party and unions, not that the number of organizations as such declined radically, but rather that they were more or less emptied of members. In the first year of the war, about half the workers organized in SD unions went to the front. Many of them were classified as dangerous or unreliable as were certain younger party activists. Conscription and the internal dictatorship made a class-socialist policy unrealistic[37] and this induced a political passivity which further alienated many SD supporters. Not only were the party and union bureaucracies left more or less untouched, likewise the people working within them, but so too were their press organs. In contrast to the censorship on the organs of the CNSP which banned *Český dělník* (1914) and *České Slovo* (1915) completely, the Austrian regime was content to allow the problems caused by heavy financial losses and the paper shortage, which began to bite in 1917, to act as an effective substitute for censorship.[38]

By contrast, the CNSP was made the subject of the most punitive measures. Its newspapers as we have noted were closed down. Klofáč and others, already marked men for their pre-war anti-militarist, anti-clerical and anti-Austrian activities were thrown into prison. One of them, Josef Kotek, was tried by a military tribunal and shot.[39] This provoked a wave of sympathy and, in the light of the later reversal of the verdict, became a cause célèbre whose echoes carried over into the new state. The National Socialist unions condemned the protestations of OSČ that war conditions did not allow union activity. Though it was doubtful if they could have done anything at all, the SD unions did not resist the militarization of the key industries nor the removal of workers' rights gained pre-war in respect of working-conditions and hours and, likewise, pay.[40] Apart from their general incapacity, there were examples of SD union behaviour which did not look dissimilar from collaboration, notably the translation of labour in the wake of the closure of significant numbers of light industrial factories in Northern Bohemia in 1914 into armaments factories. While on the one hand it was possibly the only realistic way of solving the problem of unemployment, it was seen by others almost as an act of betrayal and caused much ill-feeling. Such developments with conscription caused a notable decline on its membership from 105,000 (1913) to 24,000 (1916).[41] The efforts of the ČOD to protect its workers' interests were short-lived and an extensive organizational basis ceased to exist, except in sections of the metal and rail-transport industries.

Šmeral's policy of "hibernation" he later described as a strategem to maintain the organizational basis of the party intact.[42] It did indeed deflect the attention of Austrian militarism but at the price of a loss of respect among the working class. The mood of the people diverged sharply from the sentiments of the party proclamations expressing loyalty to the Habsburgs. In conditions of war, there seemed to be little choice nor harm in suspending party differences in the interests of the preservation of the working class on whom the war itself placed a heavier burden than other social groups. A form of national unity came to be expressed through the Czech Union in which the bourgeois parties, who like Šmeral still held firm to their pro-Austria position, seemed to pose no great social threat. He became not only an active member but for a time also de factor leader of the Union fighting mostly in vain to assuage the worst excesses of both the militarization of the factories and likewise the internal military administration. The socially conservative politicians represented no danger for as Pan-Slavists they had been put in prison. Yet his efforts to work for the lifting of the suspension of civil rights did not satisfy the SDP leaders who came to an accommodation with the bourgeois parties on the basis of their new position on the Czech question and had found a solution in the form of national self-determination.[43] They were reacting to the slogans of the spontaneous popular movement among which the slogan of State Rights had taken on an irresistible appeal. Support for Austria helped neither the social conditions of the people nor promised to bring national equality. An Austrian victory would merely turn the screw of national domination, hence they placed their hopes in the victory of the Allies and they looked to the emigrés in Paris for action. It was only a matter of time before the SDP officially revoked their anti-State Rights declaration of 1897 and, in the national question, they came out openly with the bourgeois parties, though in the manner in which this political arrangement worked itself out, this had serious implications for the socialist dimension of the party's programme. These however were not revealed until the new state came into being. The social movement connected an improvement in living and working conditions with the demand for an independent national state,[44] but as its impact intensified, the former gradually gave way to specifically socialist demands.[45] Nevertheless, the first workers' demonstrations gave priority to the demand for a national state.

This reflected the influence of the SD radical nationalists, Meissner and Habrmann who, as leaders of the Metal-workers Union, were in the forefront of the struggle. Their prestige among the uncommitted on the SD Executive where they too had seats rose strikingly as a result. A second aspect of the situation indicated that nationalism among the workers was on the march. The industrial workers had long before lost faith in their SD union officials who, for one reason or another, had not caught up with the new stance of the party apropos Austria.[46] They removed some of them, notably in Prague and Plzeň, more specifically for their failure to defend their rights. They were replaced by officials of rump ČOD unions or proletarian sympathizers of the National Socialists. This was a significant departure which for a time helped to overcome the suspicions that the more committed SD sympathizers had had in respect of the socialist aspirations of the CNSP leaders. It was only a short step to the united approach of all Czech workers, irrespective of political or even union affiliation, with the likely exception of the Christian Socialists in Moravia. Support for the new direction within the SDP and its partners in the CNSP entailed a de facto acceptance of an informal coalition with the bourgeoisie.[47]

The agreement of all sides to rule out a one-party solution in the government of any future Czech state suggested that bourgeois dominance of the national movement did not imply bourgeois domination of the socialist movement. It was not foreseen that the national revolution would legitimize the concentration of political forces and enshrine it in the coalition system with unhappy consequences for the aims of socialism. Nevertheless, the fears that the bourgeoisie would determine proletarian social policy were dispelled to a degree by this accord. This was reinforced first, by their pledge not to interfere in purely workers' matters and secondly, by the slogans they adopted which, especially after the Russian October Revolution, took on a very radical character.[48] Yet the national character of these proposed expropriations was hidden in proletarian assumptions that the productive means would necessarily be the subject of change in a radical socialist sense. The presence of an anarchist contingent in the CNSP, some of whom, like Vrbenský, were noted radicals in social matters, was also considered a good omen insofar as they provided some stiffening within their party, whose constituency reflected only imperfectly proletarian socialist aspirations and whose leaders had had too long a history of close association with the bourgeois Young Czechs. Yet, opinion at the grassroots of the SDP was placated by the National Socialists' acceptance of the principles of social revolution and class struggle.[49]

Šmeral could not accept the radical nationalists' solution. Neither was he able to resist the tide of popular opinion in the party which on the national question converged with that expressed in the Czech Lands as a whole. Cooperation with the bourgeoisie only led to disaster and, as he correctly predicted, the national revolution would only further their interests. Appeals to national unity were a smoke-screen to conceal the reality of class domination and de-fuse proletarian socialist radicalism. Neither could he accept the position of parity in the labour movement accorded to the National Socialists which was not only a minority, but scarcely proletarian, the political reflection of the "petty-bourgeois . . . hotbeds of national hatred."[50]

His resignation as party-leader was a recognition of a situation which had been in existence for some time. It signalled the formal termination of proletarian internationalism, a repudiation of "the German doctrine" and a de facto abrogation of class struggle, though this was not admitted. Thereafter the radical nationalists occupied the leading positions in the SDP and attempted to formulate a specifically Czech type of socialism. In this scheme, the industrial proletariat occupied a no more significant place than any other class of worker, manual or mental. The ideal of the new social democratic philosophy, ironically enough, reflected Kautsky's influence in that it centred on a parliamentary democratic state guaranteeing a gradual evolutionary path to the solution of all social problems. In practice, it favoured a fundamental economic reorganization of society only insofar as it touched foreign-owned productive assets which, though they were to be nationalized by the state, were widely expected to be divided among and run by self-regulating cooperatives.[51] In principle, this programme was not basically different from the programme of the National Socialists. The emphasis on the similarity of certain parts of both SDP and CNSP programmes gave some reason for believing that they might go as far as fusion and found an entirely new Czech party without the undesirable associations or unacceptable traditions of the hitherto German-dominated party.

The particularly acute character of the nationalities' conflict in the Czech Lands brought home to all socialists the significance of nationalism for the working-class. It could not be reduced to a specifically Czech problem, although the close attention paid by the Second Comintern Congress to this phenomenon in its Czech milieu occasionally gave the impression that it was. Yet nationalism was recognized as a major problem by all radical socialists affecting socialist movements of other oppressed nations quite as much as that of the Czechs. This was reflected in the controversies and in the differing solutions to the problem, not only in the international socialist movement with the polemics of Lenin against the Polish SDs, but also in the disputes within the Bolshevik party itself, as indeed in the Czech social democratic movement.

Bolshevik orthodoxy[52] regarded nationalism in relation to Europe at this time as positive insofar as it was capable of furthering the cause of socialism in combination with proletarian revolution. It was a significant influence on proletarian consciousness and had to be recognized as a factor affecting class struggle and as a barrier to class solidarity, particularly in small, nationally oppressed nations. There was hence a necessity to prevent the proletariat being sucked into the national movement as an undifferentiated social force, rather to maintain an approach independent of the bourgeoisie and directed to its expropriation by means of a social revolution. If on the other hand, the leadership of the labour movement were taken over one way or another by the bourgeois parties, then the nationalist struggle of the workers would be guided away from class struggle and, though it might result in the achievement of radical democratic demands, such as universal suffrage and a Republic, it would not lead to an attack on bourgeois political and economic interests and hence would be of little use in furthering the social revolution. This had been the case in the Czech Lands where, in addition, nationalism tended to contradict internationalism insofar as it amounted to a restriction of the rights of the minorities. In these conditions, proletarian internationalism required the Czech labour movement and its leaders to fight for the self-determination of the ethnic minorities although, as Lenin recognized, a reversal of national domination could be expected to increase national hatred for a time making this task more difficult.

The Orthodox SDs argued that internationalism would ultimately come out of nationalism in that, through the parliamentary system, socialists would gradually achieve the abolition of classes and class-interests. In practice, they gave their support to the maintenance of the frontiers of the Historic Provinces which implied that they were not prepared to extend the principle of national self-determination to the minorities, though they had claimed it for themselves. They were against the demarcation of minorities in separate states and likewise against Šmeral's plan for national equality within the Republic. In this instance they rejected the principle of self-determination as they regarded it as inapplicable to a society moving towards socialism. Their nationalism then placed limitations on the rights of other nationalities and on their own proletariat in that it had little or no social content and, from Šmeral's view, was regressive as it strengthened the class state.

Šmeral opposed the SDs' nationalism on the grounds that it did little for the proletariat and was not a solution to the nationalities problem. Neither did he accept the crude internationalism of Muna, which was based on a too simplistic notion of false consciousness. In practice, it did not bring workers of different nationalities together in joint proletarian action against the bourgeois state, which was the real key to international proletarian solidarity. Both the SD and Bolshevik poles of orthodoxy failed in the Czech Lands. Though the former's nationalism was too strong in conditions of the reversal of national domination and overpowered Šmeral's federalism, it did not solve the problem of socialism. Their nationalism indeed was successful in diverting people's attention away from it. Bolshevik orthodoxy leaned too far the other way and its stress on proletarian revolutionary internationalism was seen as essentially anti-nationalist in character and not adequate to meet the needs of nationalistically inclined workers in small countries. Šmeral was at a disadvantage in respect of both orthodoxies. In contrast to his own position, those of the Orthodox SDs and the Bolsheviks were reduced, the former to a simple, nationalist pro-Czech republican stance, the latter to internationalism, which amounted ultimately to support for the Soviet Union. In the process Šmeral's federalism was more or less extinguished.

Although it lived on in one way or another in both parties, the "new" form of Czech socialism was seriously effected by the Russian October Revolution. Initially, it was seen through the prism of national ideals and this was reflected in the adoption of the slogans of peace and self-determination of nations in the strike-wave in early 1918.[53] Yet these self-same strikers were not motivated exclusively by nationalist sentiment for they were equally inspired by the economic demands of the Bolsheviks. This presented a serious obstacle to national unity in that it encouraged class conflict and sought albeit indirectly an end to the SDP's policy of class reconciliation. In most cases, the strike movement, as for instance in Ostrava, was directed against individuals in whom the roles of national and class enemies neatly coincided, in this case the steel magnates and mine-owners in Vitkovice.[54] While the Czech bourgeois parties were pleased that the Revolution had hampered Germany's war aims, they were fearful of the consequences of a renewal of a specifically proletarian dimension in the national revolutionary movement, a central lesson of the Russian events, which the parties representing the socialist movement had been trying to undo. Petitions from a whole series of towns in Bohemia and Moravia spoke of "a socialist nation" or "a people's state"[55] and these found consistent expression in the SD programme of 1st May 1918 framed largely by Šmeral. Beside the calls for peace and national self-determination stood those for the socialization of the mines and large industries and the expropriation of land.[56] The SD Executive reacted to this surge of proletarian socialist sentiment by dropping all talk about the new Czech socialism. They back-pedalled on Modráček's plans and likewise indefinitely shelved the idea of amalgamating with the National Socialists.

The nationalism of the Czech workers constituted the basis for a squeeze on Šmeral which displayed itself in different forms of constraint and did not allow him to operate within the strategy he had set himself. The first and arguably most powerful constraint related to the working out of the contradiction between nationalism and socialism. This appeared in one guise or another when the radical socialist movement threatened to take control of a majority of the labour movement, but most conspicuously in connection with the new state's problem with Hungary.⁵⁷ The second related to the practical affects on the political environment of the transformation of the SDP into a nationalist party. Thirdly, the impact of a type of national socialism peddled by the nationalist SDs in certain areas of the proletarian constituency and likewise by the CNSP in sections of the working class normally disdained by radical socialists affected Šmeralism insofar as it was unable to meet their challenge and win over all categories of worker into a mass democratic, but predominantly proletarian, revolutionary party. Fourthly, Šmeral was not able to adequately adjust his internationalism to the conditions he found among the working class. While he agreed in principle with Muna's internationalism, he rejected his scheme for introducing it in a nominally international communist party as more or less artificial. In practice, this worked itself out in the short-term, which is all the time Šmeral had at his disposal, in a squeeze from the Orthodox SDs who drew attention to the connections with Russia and revived memories, though this was hardly necessary, of the hard lessons vis-á-vis national domination learned from the experience of Austrian internationalism. Documentary evidence confirms the failure of the 1920 General Strike to be due largely to the incidence of proletarian nationalism.⁵⁸ Šmeral was not given the time for conditions in the working class to mature to a genuine internationalism and he had little option but to fall back on the only existing form of internationalist orthodoxy in the shape of Bolshevism.

Proletarian nationalism emerged in its most distinct form as the specific response to the problems encountered by the Czech workers in the northern national borderlands. It spread to other larger areas of industrial concentration in the hinterland though, for one reason or another, its impact was less marked than in Northern Bohemia until the conditions of war brought it out most forcefully in differing expressions of resistance. These often assumed radical socialist as much as nationalist forms. Nationalism in these circumstances was a part of proletarian class struggle and the national state regarded as the instrument by which socialism would be achieved. However in the way this relationship worked itself out lay a barrier⁵⁹ and not an instrument to socialism. A national state could well provide a platform for the achievement of their political aims, but, depending on the circumstances in which it was erected, this did not of itself coincide with nor provide a platform for the achievement of their economic aims. Events showed that liberation from national domination cleared the decks for an unambiguous class conflict. Or, to put it another way, the struggle of the oppressed nations for national liberation was little different from the nationalism of the ruling classes against the rights of the class oppressed after the jump had been made. In conditions of the early part of the war, the overall affect of the spontaneous and unorganized proletarian actions in defence of workers rights was slight. There was little alternative but to cast around for support among the SD nationalists. In the light of subsequent changes in the party, they had little option but to accept the nationalist struggle from abroad which was dictated more or less through the bourgeois parties at home. The consequences of this cooperation were of course not clear until later. Nevertheless, it is doubtful whether they would have supported them if they had not believed their interests would have been furthered thereby.

Though the political interests of the working class and the bourgeois parties met in the aim for a national state, their economic aims did not. A Czech state opened up all kinds of opportunities for the bourgeoisie in agriculture and especially industry[60] to extend their class domination. The proletariat more or less regarded the national revolution as part of an unfinished social revolution. Its subsequent sense of betrayal sprang from the realization that proletarian support for nationalism had worked itself out in such a way that the labour movement had traded the domination of a foreign predominantly aristocratic capitalist class in a semi-feudal monarchy for one of a native bourgeois class in a democratic republic.

Although nationalism and socialism did not have such a close correspondence in the working class in the new state as it had had in the last year of the war, it stubbornly refused to break down unambiguously. It persisted in shifting forms even in the most militantly socialist sections of the labour movement. The achievement of liberation produced a change in conditions which altered proletarian attitudes to the Orthodox SDs, yet the retention of nationalist values in one way or another made Šmeral's task of mobilizing a reliable, mass party problematical. The Czech miners' expropriation of the castle and estates of Duke Clam-Martinitz[61] is but one example of proletarian action prompted as much by radical socialist as nationalist sentiment, as it was in the similar action involving Prince Lobkowicz in Roudnice nad Labem.[62] Yet there were few, if any, expropriations of Czech-owned properties. Even the miners in Kladno, whose militancy had earned it the nickname "the Czech Kronstadt", had not worked out their views on nationalism and socialism. For example, they denounced the state as "a bourgeois republic" and "a capitalist state." Yet they saw no contradiction in donating 7000 Crowns to Rašin's "Fund for the Republic" and at the same time sending greetings to Lenin expressing their solidarity with Bolshevik aims.[63]

In practice, the wish to preserve the republic tended to defuse radicalism. The incidence of civil riot on occasions suggested that radical socialists were threatening the state, though many of the more extreme kind had little or nothing to do with the organized socialist movement. Nevertheless, they produced an unambiguously nationalist reaction in some of the leading figures in the revolutionary movement. Brodecký, Muna's henchman, for instance, abandoned his revolutionary path in the aftermath of the "Black Friday" hunger riots in Prague and the provinces (May 1919). He saw the choice as the state or the revolution and opted for the former, taking more than a few other radicals with him.[64] Stivín too, whose committment to the revolution had been rewarded with honorary membership of the Soviet Hungarian government renounced Šmeral[65] when the troubles in Slovakia for a time threw into doubt the continued existence of the Republic.[66] He was probably correct in his assertion that "there are two people our workers love: Masaryk, our President, and Lenin, the President of the Soviet Russian Republic."[67] But it was impossible to give them both support simultaneously in the situations which emerged in the autumn and winter of 1920 when an attempt to forge a movement to change the economic and political foundations of the republic was regarded as an attack on the state. The workers then were split within themselves not only as a class but also as individuals. In most cases, their nationalist inclinations triumphed over their class instincts, which was more often expressed in varieties of political passivity than in physical defence of the state. This triumph was borne out most clearly in an official report of the General Strike. It confirmed the suspicion that "its failure (is due to) the Czech worker being first a Czech and afterwards, a socialist."[68]

The Czech Legion also exemplified to a degree the puzzling and uneasy relationship between nationalism and socialism. In the Russian theatre of war, it was an explicitly nationalist movement concerned to help win a national state by defeating the Central Powers. Though SD sympathizers were in a majority, their aims as reflected at the 1st Congress of the Legion were no more than national and democratic[69] and were more or less the same as the radical nationalist SDs. Internationalism and proletarian socialist revolution had no place in their plans. However, the active principle on which their organization was based owed something to the conditions in which it developed and to the adoption of radical democratic political forms closely but not exclusively associated with the Bolsheviks' Soldiers and Workers Councils. An army of volunteers organized on the basis of a direct and participating democracy and common decision-making could not fail to clash with the values of Štefánik. The active national sentiment of sections of the Legion was significantly reduced, first by the proclamation of the Republic and secondly, by Štefánik's destruction of its voluntaristic and popular basis. The revolt he provoked was less about radical socialism, though some supported this aim, and more about the principles of "revolutionary popular justice." Nevertheless, the failure of their struggle to maintain the democratic organization of the army had repercussions in the Czech Lands. Explicitly socialist demands surfaced where before they had been more implicit or, more accurately, an accepted part of the organization of the community operating under pressure of conditions which made collective work more or less a necessity. The divisions within the Legion in Russia brought to a head by the arrest of its elected leaders[70] in 1919 were not in principle dissimilar to those in the Czech SDP in the Czech Lands after the liberation. National self-determination had been achieved, yet the issue of social and economic self-determination remained. Arguably, the proportions between radical proletarian socialists and nationalist workers content to accept the system as the bourgeois parties had constructed it, were not fundamentally dissimilar to those between the legionnaires who joined the Red Army or the Czech CP in Russia and those whose nationalist sentiment overcame their indignation at the destruction of the essential character of the Legion and induced them to stay. Of the 60,000 or so legionnaires in Russia[71] some 2,736 had joined their fellows in the Red Army bringing the total to about 5,000 in 1919.[72] Others found their way into the Czech CP which had 2,685 members in February 1919.[73] Veselý[74] is probably not too far wide of the mark with his estimate that 10,000 to 12,000 Czechs and Slovaks were at some time or another in either the CP or the Red Army before they returned to the Czech Lands.

In general, proletarian nationalism played its part in the Legion insofar as the great majority stayed loyal to the principles of the Orthodox SDs. Some sections, like the XX transport, returned imbued with the values of the III International and radical socialist aims.[75] Others broke out into open revolt, as at Železná ruda,[76] with the avowed purpose of installing Masaryk as dictator, the embodiment of the nation and its father and the only person they believed to be genuinely interested in fulfilling their demands.[77] The Kladno radicals too were actively involved and their calls for the government to be given over to Masaryk and for the introduction of socialization[78] not inappropriately reflected the nationalist and socialist aspirations of the labour movement. This seems to suggest that Šmeral was right in keeping Muna at arm's length for so long, although in the final analysis this did nothing to solve the basic problem which afflicted and ultimately condemned his movement to failure.

The growth of nationalism in the SDP effectively removed Šmeral from the leadership. This led to its transformation as we have seen into a nationalist party which had significant affects on the constitutional environment under which Šmeral waged his struggle. As he foresaw, the radical nationalists did not proceed independently in defence of proletarian interests. Instead of throwing off the political leadership of the Czech bourgeois parties, they more or less accepted their role as an auxiliary and not as an initiator of change. As a result the bourgeois parties were enabled to dominate the National Committee, frame the institutions of government and adopt and manipulate the "key system" which provided the basis for the first governments. This led naturally to the erection of the coalition system.[79]

Within the National Committee, the Agrarians and National Democrats were given special rights in respect of the economic organization of the state. The Orthodox SDs occupied an important even fulcrum position insofar as they acted as the mediator between the proletariat and the state. Their presence had to be maintained to pacify their constituents and to give the appearance that the national state was indeed the indispensible means to the achievement of socialism. Bearing in mind the provision of social reforms, this policy was not unsuccessful. Though this took some support away from Šmeral, the more important area of constraint lay in the relations of the Orthodox SDs to the bourgeois parties and ultimately the state. Šmeral was forced to address himself to the problems created by the political environment. Like a good democratic socialist, he tried to win the party by good democratic methods only to discover that it overlapped with the organs of state which ultimately rushed to its defence. In these specific conditions the party could not be won.[80] Šmeral's absence from the Executive made it difficult to warn the rank and file of the consequences of cooperation with the bourgeois parties and organize a struggle against them independent of the nationalist SDs. This was the significance of the strike of 14th October 1918, but its effect in this regard was limited by the preponderance of nationalist

SDs and National Socialists in the Socialist Council. The immediate reaction of the National Committee was to set up their own local organs with the help of the SD nationalists. This effectively squashed the growth of local Socialist Councils,[81] which might have given Šmeral the extra-party means to mobilize radically inclined workers he was later shown to lack.

An essential part of Šmeralism involved winning over workers, including those of a strictly non-proletarian character, whose sympathies were with other parties.[82] Though he made extensive gains within the SDP, as he represented the old socialist orthodoxy against the new policy of cooperation with the bourgeoisie, he made few inroads into the support of the National Socialists. This placed limitations on the scope of his mass movement which forced him after the General Strike to adopt a different line. Šmeral hence had to attempt a solution to the problem of nationalism within the other main party representing the working class, as well as within the ranks of the SDP. In practice, he was unable to achieve it and this can be partly explained by the similarities of their programmes which placed him in competition with the CNSP for more or less the same worker constituency. His failure in this regard is also connected with the traditional animosities springing from differing notions of party composition which had divided the SDP and the National Socialists in the pre-war period and remained present in the conditions of the new state. A significant factor too was the popular reaction to Šmeral's political past.

A powerful stream existed in the CNSP whose aims were not substantially different from Šmeral's seen strictly from the economic viewpoint. This was made up of the miners in North West Bohemia and of the anarchists who were influential in the small industrial towns in more or less the same regions. The fact that they were strongly anti-Marxist did not prevent them from espousing more or less radical socialist aims. It was said of them that their hearts beat for the revolution though their reason was for the state. They still associated Šmeral with the "German philosophy" and internationalism which they rejected as placing unacceptable limits on individual freedom. These factors and a significant degree of personal antagonism between one of their leaders, S. K. Neumann and Šmeral made integration unlikely in the early years of the Republic. Both the miners and the anarchists displayed in varying degrees revolutionary socialist and nationalist values. The protest strikes of the North Bohemian German miners against the state were answered by the Czech miners' regularly working two shifts without a break to make up the decline in output. But it was the anarchists who oscillated more dramatically between revolution and the desire to help the Republic, though Neumann himself was against its institutions and indeed gave up his mandate in parliament.[83] Though they contained their radicalism within the CNSP for the first vital years, it was Neumann who lost patience and demanded the immediate founding of a Communist Party against Šmeral's will. Nevertheless, he and Vrbenský were in the forefront of their party's drive for socialization. Its prestige, already high from the war, was significantly enhanced by the progressive face it presented to the working class on matters such as health and accident insurance and unemployment benefit, quite apart from the role it played in the initiation of measures designed to remove foreign and clerical influence from society. Vrbenský made a great impact with his efforts to give priority to the feeding of the poorest in conditions of near famine. Their efforts to protect the interests of the Czech workers were reflected in the constant growth of their unions and also in the votes cast at elections, though a considerable section of these were more or less members of the petty-bourgeois classes proletarianized by the war. Nevertheless, the ČOD concentrated about 20% of organized labour in its ranks[84], mostly in Bohemia. In 1920, this represented 350,000 workers, mostly in the small-scale industries. The SD unions made some inroads into their support in larger towns, not infrequently by means of intimidation, but in general no real attempts were made to win the great numbers of non-union labour in the light industries. This can be explained by reference to the legacy of the pre-war SD belief that these workers were not to be compared with industrial proletarians as the agent of change, a view held unambiguously by Muna and the Czech Bolsheviks. In practice, the nationalities struggle in the national borderlands which continued unabated in various forms is a more likely explanation. The fact that its proletarian and semi-proletarian sections still stood in the forefront of the Germans' reaction to the state helps to explain why the CNSP remained basically untouched by the process of differentiation in the SDP.

Šmeral's tactic then to create a revolution by means of the mobilization of a mass, democratic and basically, but not exclusively, proletarian movement was seriously affected by the impact of nationalism. He could do nothing about conditions in Northern Bohemia and hence nothing to weaken its affect. He could not win over the Germans either, though he tried in a desultory way on 14th october 1918, which simply hardened nationalist workers' attitudes towards him. Neither was he able to follow an internationalist line which did not come to be identified with that of Muna's and the Bolsheviks. Internationalism in those conditions, as Austria had shown, was associated with national domination and only in the special conditions of parts of Slovakia had it shown some promise as a solution.[86] Šmeral's strategy required more time to combat the difficulties created by nationalism. In the final analysis, he was more or less forced to capitulate to Muna's reaction to it. Šmeral's mass revolutionary party was in the short-term seen to be unrealistic and after the General Strike had shown just how deeply it had permeated the proletariat, he had little option but to accept the consequences of the squeeze between nationalism and Bolshevik internationalism.

*Chapter 2*

**The Challenge from the Political Environment**

A number of features of the Czech political system erected after the liberation created problems for Šmeral and hindered the ability of radical socialism to exert pressure within it. As a result, the movement was isolated from the political institutions of the state and, given his values on the means of change, ultimately gave a justification to those favouring violent revolution. Some of these characteristics derived from changes in the political structure itself. Others were related to the office and person of the President who occupied a central position within it. Apart from the direct constraints deriving from political institutions and presidential management, there were other indirect constraints of a more or less ideological nature which affected Šmeral's support. These were provided most tangibly by the drive for national reconstruction. The Czechs' enthusiastic support for this continued the nationality struggle by other means, with the crucial difference that the Czechs were the ruling nationality. In the process, there was a strong tendency for the struggle of classes to be obscured. Conditions of great social and political fluidity persisted throughout the early period of the Republic and these were reflected in more or less sudden and short-lived shifts in support for the political parties. This was related in part to the introduction of universal adult suffrage. As a consequence, there was little of the voting stability which is the rule in states with a tradition of parliamentary democracy where not infrequently voting behavior has a club or clannish character. The Czech proletariat like the other classes in the community did not respond purely and simply to their class interest. They were subject to violent changes in viewpoint in respect of questions only marginally connected if at all with their desire for economic and social change. The problem of Hungary was but one example.[1]

They were nevertheless diverted into other channels. The urge to organize was another tendency which marked the age. This was seen not only in the growth of the political parties, the founding of new ones and the increase in cultural and special interest clubs peculiar to the historical development of the Czech Lands. It was also mirrored in the growth of alternative organizations, some founded as a reaction against educational or ecclesiastical authority, some against the new political establishment. This pointed to a significant degree of fragmentation in society with shifting allegiances which affected Šmeral's plan to win power with a mass movement united on the basis of a common disaffection. Taken together, the interplay of forces produced by the political system and the historical conditions contributed to Šmeral's failure.

The declaration of 28th October 1918 initiated a process bringing fundamental changes to the character of the state as a whole.[2] It also set out the basic features of the political system which Šmeral was to find so troublesome. The most conspicuous change was the transformation of the Czech Lands and, after the borders had been determined, part of Silesia with Slovakia from provinces of one or other halves of the Empire into a republic. This was organized on the basis of a parliamentary democracy and universal adult suffrage. Ironically enough, Šmeral had a hand in the state-form finally settled on though,[3] as it turned out, it did his cause little good. The differences between the old and new political systems were considerable. Under the Austrian system, the Czech Lands had been provinces of Cis-Leithania in which the monarchy had been the most powerful political institution. Since 1867, the Emperor had technically been subordinate to the constitution. In practice, ministers were responsible to him though custom required them to obtain approval in parliament for their proposals often on pain of resignation or dismissal. After 1900, there was a tendency for the emperor to prefer "Beamten-ministeria" who had no formal party affiliation. This reflected his belief that important positions in government demanded specialists. It also made it more likely for their work to be taken out of the area of political controversy likewise easing the passage of legislation through parliament. As we shall see, this system was not jettisoned with the inauguration of the new state. Until 1907 when universal equal manhood suffrage was introduced for national elections, most Czechs did not have the vote and hence had little voice in the Reichsrat. Yet even after the electoral reform, the number of Czech deputies did not correspond with the numerical superiority of the Czechs in Bohemia.[4] A similar situation existed in Moravia. Both provinces had separate systems of local and municipal administration, likewise Provincial Diets, which remained unaffected by the reform. The Germans were enabled with the help of both systems to maintain their supremacy.

In general, the Czech people expected two things from the collapse of the Habsburg Empire and they expected to achieve them from the fundamental changes in the political system. The Republic itself was a sign of the passing of the age of kings and emperors and created the expectation that the new system would radically reform the voting rules. The acquisition of full civil and democratic rights provided the means of turning the tables on their former masters, the Germans. It also exercised a powerful appeal among groups, particularly at the lower end of society, who saw it as the key to the attainment of their social and economic aims. Institutional change did indeed assist the Czechs to work out their national prejudice but it did not allow, contrary to expectations, the socialist movement to have free rein. Šmeral became a victim not only of the renewed nationality struggles[5] but also of the pressures exerted by the political institutions which formed the legislative and executive basis of the Republic. The Provisional Government's main concern was stability. In practice, this meant reconciling the Germans to their new role in the state and pacifying the socialist movement. The necessity to impress on the Entente that extremes of political behaviour had little chance of realization produced the system of coalition government which, given the nationality and social composition of the Czech Lands anyway, was more or less inevitable. Before elections could be held, the Prague National Committee developed naturally into the first and interim government. This in itself had a significant impact on Šmeral, though not until later, as at that time a radical socialist opposition existed in only a rudimentary form. The "key system" however, by which the parties were represented in the government (via the National Committee), gave the bourgeois parties a double-success. Firstly, they gained a majority in the period when the institutions of state were being re-worked or otherwise set up. Secondly, the SDP was not given representation according to the results of the 1911 as had been agreed. This example of democratic sharp-practice had an influence on Šmeral's view of parliament and change. It is doubtful if this made much difference in the early months as the SDP were, anyway, nationalists. But it may have later put more supporters of the Marxist Left into parliament when Šmeral's drive to win a majority within the party was in full flow. The "key-system" strengthened the hand of the anti-socialists and the anti-proletarian bias was emphasized to a degree by the co-opting of certain artists, writers and public figures.[6]

The Provisional Constitution which brought the National Assembly into existence used the "party-key" as the basis for the balance between the parties' mandates. Yet the radical socialists were not only affected by the structure of the system which even in its early stages left them stranded outside it. They were also seriously affected by two acts of government policy. Initially, all the old Imperial laws were maintained intact[7] which in the conditions of the time placed restrictions on political agitation but for all stated purposes was aimed at German nationalists. This measure also imposed limitations on the activity of the type of Czech socialist who had staged the great strike of the 14th October which had challenged the authority of the National Committee. In the circumstances of the liberation, these were rarely invoked before 1919. Secondly, alarmed by the independent role of local national committees which in parts of Moravia had suspended and disarmed the police and deposed Mayors,[8] the government first reduced them to an advisory role to local authorities[9] then abolished them altogether.[10] The destruction of these local centres of authority, some of which were opposed to the government's plans,[11] removed the last vestiges of a dual power and enabled the coalition to set itself up as the unchallenged centre of political jurisdiction.

It was the primary task of the coalition to defend the Czech character of the Czech Lands which represented a settling of historical wrongs and democratic accounts. The system corresponded closely to the ideology and practice of the national revolution, but in changed conditions, two more or less antagonistic tendencies emerged which affected the parties and their relations in the coalition. The more powerful was the centripetal force which was displayed in the parties' acceptance in the last resort of restraint in the interests of the national state. The second aspect which on occasion obscured the first and tended to operate in the opposite direction was the antagonism of the political parties to each other.

There was a powerful current in favour of political differentiation which was not restricted to the parties' relations within the coalition but ran deeply through individual parties. In general, parties were not homogeneous in the sense of representing a single class or group interest. Arguably, only the National Democrats, whose members were drawn almost exclusively from the professions and the business institutions in Prague, constituted a possible exception. Most major parties however represented more than one class or social group and struggles broke out, for example, within the Agrarian Party, which were resolved, while in others, like the SDP and the People's Party, they went as far as a split. In both cases however, though there was considerable movement among the rank and file of those parties intent on change, the structure of the parties was such that the leadership was immensely difficult to shift including the case when, as evidence suggested, a majority stood against them. These leaderships represented their parties in the coalition where they attempted to exploit the fruits of victory to the full.

# THE CHALLENGE FROM POLITICAL ENVIRONMENT 61

Yet while they all haggled over individual policies, which often gave the public an impression of instability, there was little evidence that this put the state under threat. Indeed the violent disputes over the Land Reform were not simply about which party would achieve the most power and influence out of it. Behind them all was the debate on how the construction and execution of the reform could best strengthen the state. Significantly enough, it was the National Democrats, the party with the numerically smallest power base, who decided to withdraw from the coalition. The only other example was the SDs themselves who did not resign on their own initiative but as part of a carefully thought-out plan between the coalition and the President. The coalition then was a source of considerable stability built on the more or less unanimous urge to national reconstruction and a balance between the energetic assertion of a policy with the willingness to accept compromise. This resulted in practice in the coalition moving round a political centre which excluded extremes of political behaviour. Evidently, the price exacted for a share in power in the shape of the limitations imposed on the parties was not too high for there was no shortage of candidates. The system then placed a check on the misuse of power for no single party could rule alone, given the nationality and social composition of the state, which itself made a coalition more or less inevitable, and seen from the viewpoint of the individual party, it was under the control of the opposition.

Two other aspects are relevant here relating to the parties, which placed significant obstacles in the way of those like Šmeral who sought to challenge the coalition in parliament. Firstly, the parliamentary mandates came to be regarded as the property of the party, more precisely its leaders, whose authority did not derive from the parliamentary party and who often were not parliamentarians.[12] It ensured the mastery of the party over the individual, reduced the challenge from the local organizations and gave the leaders the right to withdraw mandates or veto inappropriate choices of candidate. This was closely linked to the second aspect, the system of "fixed voting lists" at elections. Originally, the National Democrats had proposed a voting system under which the voters would make up their own lists. They were acting on the assumption that the old "Austrian opportunists", notably Šmeral, were still hated by SDP sympathizers and they expected them to react by voting in "war-heroes" or specialists from other parties. The SDP resolutely opposed this.

The reality of the economic struggle between classes and not views in wartime determined voting behaviour among the working class, as the Orthodox SDs correctly predicted. Given the choice between a loyal, competent and usually obedient servant of the party, more or less the characteristics of the SDs co-opted to sit in the first parliament, and the passionate orators of the Marxist Left, whose promises of instant solutions combined with the anti-establishment and anti-authority attitude reflecting the mood of the time, the working class would, in all likelihood, have chosen the latter. Fixed voting lists then prevented a wholesale shift away from the Orthodox SD career politicians and specialists to the radical "men of the people." The wave of militancy was not then carried into the heart of provincial and local administration, nor into parliament, which allowed the Orthodox SDs to maintain cooperation in the coalition and effectively pre-empted attacks on the stability of the government. Free voting lists in all probability would have transformed the SDP overnight and by placing Šmeral in the leading position of the largest parliamentary party would have spelled the end of the coalition. A mass party led by radical socialists in parliament intent on rapid and radical change and committed to an opposition stance as befitted their role in a class state would, with all the advantages of incumbency and legitimacy, have been in a far better position to mobilize the uncommitted masses and intensify class struggle. As it was the Orthodox SDs' control of the mandates and the voting system made it difficult for Šmeral to dislodge them from their positions.

The strength of this system as a buttress against radical socialism was revealed in 1920. Prior to the general election, all the signs appeared to indicate that Šmeral had the support of a clear majority of the rank and file in the local organizations[13] and likewise among SD sympathizers as Peroutka attests.[14] Yet Tusar was still able to maintain overall Executive control over the nomination of candidates for the general election. The SDP gained 74 mandates at the election.[15] Of these, 24 hailed to the Marxist Left,[16] which suggests that in certain areas the tide of popular support for the radicals was so strong that the Executive preferred to accept them rather than provoke repercussions. The Orthodox SDs were helped in the majority of areas however by two other factors. Firstly in conditions of disputed authority, the old code of party discipline asserted itself and most followed the recommendations of the Executive. This was facilitated by the second factor, namely that a majority of the local officers of the party had remained unchanged since the war-years and these were more or less obedient to the wishes of the Establishment SDs. This related to another effect of fixed voting lists. It was widely publicized, as much by the Agrarians as the Orthodox SDs, that influence on the nomination of candidates for parliament could be exercised only from within the party.[17] People hence were encouraged to join a party and the ranks of the SDP as indeed other parties, swelled as a result.

## THE CHALLENGE FROM POLITICAL ENVIRONMENT 63

Yet these "recruits of socialism" who formed a significant section of the new members discovered that the structure of the party did not channel their dissent into effective action but on the contrary tended to contain it. The coalition system and certain institutional features and practical habits of the SDP together contrived to form powerful obstacles to the radical socialists. These were not removed by the introduction of universal suffrage nor by the holding of elections. Although the latter did something to correct the injustice deriving from the "key system" which gave the SDP 20 mandates fewer than the voting showed it deserved,[18] it could do nothing about the Executive's stranglehold on the distribution of the mandates. Universal suffrage under these conditions could do little to give free rein to the radical socialists, rather it was a part of the political arrangements of the state which tended to neutralize them. Nevertheless, the new electoral order specified in the Government Programme (Jan. 1919)[19] affected Šmeral in two distinct ways. One was practical, the other ideological. In the conditions of the time, he could not build a bridgehead into the party in the numbers which reflected the superiority of the radical socialists. Universal suffrage then was from two points of view more or less useless as the means of taking power. Initially, the rules governing mandates allowed no easy access and secondly, the social and national composition of the Czech Lands would scarcely ever give any one party a majority in normal circumstances. On the other hand, he had to face the fact that the Republic was a democratic state in which every adult had the right to vote. Almost everybody in the Establishment from the Orthodox SDs to the President was wont to remind him of that and of the fact that the ballot box opened the way to change. Any other means was a repudiation of democracy and to be shunned.

The political system then put him over a barrel. It placed him in the position of attempting to win over the party in the democratic manner when in practice it was not susceptible to it. And it blamed him for exerting pressure outside parliament when it was effectively closed to him. The ideological struggle too went against him, as the central aim of social democracy for achieving change was universal suffrage[20] and one for which the people had struggled for decades. It mattered little that in the political circumstances of the time, it was capable of changing little, at least as far as Šmeral was concerned. Nevertheless, the introduction of universal suffrage created a mood of optimism among the SD sympathizers, who assumed that the party would achieve an outright hegemony in parliament and thereafter complete the national revolution by a democratic, parliamentary socialist revolution. The Hodonín radical, Koutný, spoke for many with his assertion that it was the ultimate weapon enabling radical socialists to become "real Bolsheviks."[21]

The principal effects of universal suffrage however were quite different. In practice, it was first and foremost an instrument for the consolidation of the state, insofar as Czech majorities previously not enfranchised gained control of those areas in which German ethnic minorities held sway. The local elections did, as mentioned earlier, settle the dispute about the number of parliamentary mandates per party.[22] They also achieved the removal of foreign or Austrophile officials in local administrations and this was taken by the radical socialists as a step freeing their political activity from the constraints of the old Imperial laws[23] which, however, proved to be an over-optimistic assessment.

The local elections produced significant changes in that hundreds of town and village administrations came entirely under the control of the SDP. The socialist parties swept home with 48.74% of the vote.[24] The results demonstrated unambiguously the extent of support for them, reflected the emergence of women as a novel and potent political force whose sympathies were most often with the radicals[25] and helped ease the Provisional Government out the door. Changes took place in the coalition government, although there was no constitutional obligation, but these appeared to be more or less unconnected with the pattern of voting. Although the socialist parties had won, their failure to achieve a merger[26] and the bitter opposition the attempts had provoked in the local SD organizations made it more or less impossible for them to form a government. The influence of the radical Left anyway made the SDP vulnerable and effectively precluded it from entering government as the major party, which was a response to and a reflection of the Allies' views. On paper the socialists had what amounted to an election victory, but conditions were such that they would not and could not make use of it except to force Masaryk, whose vital role in the political system will be discussed presently, to install an SD as prime minister though it was against his wishes. The essential nature of the coalition however did not change. The Provisional Government had contained six parties[27] and this set the pattern for the period of the Republic during which not less than five parties were involved in forming governments. The fact that practically anybody was permitted to found a party tended to conceal the reality that political life was dominated by a relatively stable heart made up of only a few parties. The proliferation of new parties positing national and social alternatives was a great advance in democratic terms compared with the old Austrian system. Yet the coalition government was considerably less accountable than for example a government based on one party. It could not be forced to resign by the people as a whole and the structure of the parties too insulated their ministers from the possibility of recall. Changes in the coalition were not made on the basis of the results of elections but by the President, who paid some regard to the popularity of the parties as expressed in the voting before nominating ministers. The distribution of power in the state appeared not to be significantly correlated with the pattern of voting. Initially, the outright control of town and parish councils won at the local elections which promised a decisive shift in power was almost immediately eroded. As the price for supporting the new electoral order, the Agrarians secured the introduction of special financial commissions to control local government finance. In the main, the Agrarians controlled these commissions, which balanced the SDs political control of town and rural district councils, and by this means, the coalition was in a sense carried into local administration. In practice however, the Agrarians' unelected financial administrators had the whip hand, because few of the SD councillors had experience of either public administration or finance and relied heavily on the commissions. These were made up of village entrepreneurs and local professionals, more or less the natural supporters of the Agrarian party.[28] In central government too, the fundamental differences in power did not derive from the difference in the number of votes cast for each party. From the inception of the Provisional Government, there was a hint of arbitrariness which was usually expressed in practices favouring the parties of the right. The party key as we have seen favoured the bourgeois parties distorting, in the extreme case, the NDP's parliamentary strength by about 90%. Numerically, ministries were divided according to this criterion. The three governments from 1918 to May 1920 had a preponderance of socialist ministers and of these governments, two had a socialist prime minister. This gave them the appearance of socialist governments which did not at all correspond with their power as measured in the ministries they held. In the Provisional Government, the SDP held three, yet none of these was of a kind to have such powerful affects on society as they at first sight suggested. Indeed one of these, the Justice Ministry, was effectively subordinated to Švehla. Differences in power between the parties depended on who held the key ministries. In the conditions of the time, they were the ministries of the Interior and Agriculture which (with Public Works) were in the grip of the Agrarians,[29] and remained so until the Second War. The local election results prompted a change in government which nominally recognized the leading position of the SDP in the state, with the reluctant choice of Tusar. For Masaryk, he was the third choice behind Švehla, whose party managed only 15.3% of the votes,[30] and Tomášek.[31] Yet the bulk of the power was held by the Agrarians. The political system favoured them further by allowing the foundation and operation of the Domovina, which at its inception was strictly an illegal organization. This helped to build up an area of rural dependence and pre-empted the development of the socialist movement in the countryside.[32]

Though the principal repository of power under the new democracy was the coalition, it could scarcely have operated so effectively without the help of Masaryk. His influence on the political system was felt in a number of ways. The office of President gave him constitutional powers which he used to smooth the path of the coalition. Secondly, great personal prestige gave him considerable ideological power which helped pacify sections of the working class and likewise carried weight with members of individual parties both within and outside the coalition. His connections and success from the war gave him special rights over foreign policy and defence, while in internal politics he encouraged the party which he thought could do most to strengthen the national integrity of the state, the Agrarians. Finally, he laid the basis of a power centre which was more or less immune to influences from outside and went some way to fulfilling his wish for administration by experts. In their different ways, these all presented a challenge to Šmeral.

As President, Masaryk was to a degree the bearer of the political functions which under the Austrian system had been held by the Crown. He was the symbol of the nation and the stabilizer of the ideology of the state of which he was the creator. He accepted the role of the highest political authority and frequently mediated in the conflicts which broke out in the coalition. His moral authority and prestige as the architect of national liberation induced the parties to accept his arbitration as he had always appeared to be "above party" and inspired principally by his wish to preserve the state. The politicians readily made him head of state and C-in-C of the armed forces, as these positions carried little power. However, his powers though limited at the outset to the naming of individuals to the higher echelons of the army and the state administration[33] quickly grew despite the reluctance and opposition of the coalition. Masaryk won crucial rights to chair cabinet meetings and to name and discharge ministers including the prime minister. New laws also allowed him to address parliament directly and to refer bills back to committee. In practice, this amounted virtually to a veto, which is suggested in the constitutional amendments from 1919,[34] though it was never clearly defined and later documents make no reference to it. He also endeavoured to extend his rights into the domain of individual ministries. From the outset, his intention was to be involved in elaborating the programmes of individual departments and even to fix them in the inaugural decrees. The coalition rejected this as an incursion on the rights of the prime-minister, as they did his attempt to gain the right of parliamentary initiative.

The parties were clearly intent on maintaining their prerogatives in parliament undiminished. Despite significant differences in the outlook and attitudes of the parties in government, none of them represented the problem to the state which the SDP posed. It carried too much weight politically to be ignored and its popularity in the country as a whole suggested that there would be serious repercussions if it was. Masaryk's strategy for dealing with the socialist movement then was to affiliate that part of it represented by the Orthodox SDs to the cause of national reconstruction. The onus then was on the radical socialists to win over the institutions of the party. The Orthodox SDs as joint creators of the state would in all likelihood have protested vociferously had they been left out of a share in power. Though they would scarcely have gone over to the radicals, the popular reaction might well have strengthened Šmeral and gained the radicals leading and decisive positions in the party. But Masaryk rightly believed that the best method of containing the radical threat was to keep the official representatives of the social democratic movement in the coalition. Here at least, it had a semblance of sharing in power which, if it had not, may well have invited a confrontation between the organs of state and the popular movement. For this reason, Masaryk rejected the solution of Kramář whose reliance on force[35] would have undermined the claim to run a democratic state, played into the hands of the radical socialists and generated further open, and perhaps armed, conflict. There was no doubt of the Orthodox SD's commitment to the state and the risk of having them in the coalition caused by their vulnerability to their left-wing could anyway be minimized. The SDP, as we have seen, had its own mechanisms for preventing the ingress of radicals into positions of influence in party or parliament. This was complemented by the powers of the President in forming governments. His liking for specialists, a notion which in the public imagination connoted a degree of erudition with the quality of being above party, like himself, enabled him to gain acceptance more easily for his individual preferences for sensitive ministries, for example Interior and Finance, to which a more or less specialist character was attributed.

In terms of the power derived from ministerial office, the Agrarian party was the main beneficiary of the ministries in his gift. Švehla, a farmer by profession, became virtually an automatic choice for the first-named ministry and after the challenge of the socialists in the difficult early years of the Republic had passed, he and his colleagues went from strength to strength. From 1922, the Agrarians had a Prime Minister in every government. Indeed by the end of the decade, they had consolidated their power to such an extent that it was said to be "difficult to see where the state begins and the Agrarian party ends."[36] This is no doubt exaggerated. But it is arguably not a coincidence that after the Republic had ridden out its stormy early period during which the Orthodox SDs had three back-seat ministries, they were quietly eased out of office until in 1926 they played no part at all in the coalition. The Agrarians on the other retained and even increased their power. It can be argued that this was justified by the results of elections. Yet in 1920, the SDP won 74 to the Agrarians 28 seats while in 1925, the Agrarians scored 45 to the SDs' 29.[37] We can legitimately conclude then that a kind of bias existed in the system, a point I shall return to in connection with Šmeralism. In general the political configuration of successive coalitions was dependent less on public opinion expressed at the ballot box than on the will of the president who used every means at his disposal to neutralize those he regarded as bent on the destruction of the state.

Masaryk's pre-war relations with the SDP had been good and they were not sullied after the war by the preferential treatment he gave the Agrarians. He maintained his influence among them even after he had passed over their claims deriving from an election victory to provide the new government with its prime minister, though these were later accepted. In general, he preferred to keep his distance as befitted his position, but he still retained a direct line to the heart of the party through Bechyně. Together they organized the resignation of the SDP from the coalition in September 1920[38] which brought the crisis with the radical socialists to a head. Similarly, they were involved in working out the best strategy to win back the People's House from Šmeral. In their struggle, the Orthodox SDs were considerably aided by the President who mobilized the other parties and subsequently the organs of state in their defence. Bechyně's presence in the government, which Masaryk had nominated to return the nation to order in the aftermath of the struggle, was also indicative of this close relationship to the Orthodox SDs.

The industrial workers providing the backbone of the radical socialists were prone to violent changes of opinion. Oscillating between socialism when all the signs from government appeared to indicate that their calls for social justice had been forgotten, and nationalism when national danger threatened,[39] their political restlessness reflected the fluidity of the situation. Masaryk took it upon himself to throw his personal prestige into the struggle which in the conditions of the time turned on the debate regarding the means of change. The wave of riots in Prague, Brno and Kladno had been protests largely about the lack of food and extortionate prices and, to combat the radicals who were working to transform them into more cohesive action with political aims, he intervened. He helped to conciliate the large concentrations of workers in Plzeň, anyway a traditional nationalist stronghold, and in

Hradec Králové. His activities at the time when the crisis in the SDP was at its height in autumn 1920 were probably more important. He addressed not only militant industrial workers, as in Březové Hory,[40] but also members of the Czech Legion who had served in Russia[41] who were preaching Bolshevism to the home army.[42] In his speeches, he often made a point of appealing to older workers through whom, bearing in mind their experiences of life unenfranchised before 1914 and likewise of gradual economic progress, he attempted to bring over the younger, more radical socialists, who formed a considerable part of the Marxist Left, to his view of parliamentary democracy. He referred to the bloodless revolution which had brought them independence and recommended this as the Czech model for social change. Marx, he argued, had thrown over revolution in favour of evolutionary change. Lenin too he dismissed as a non-Marxist "more of a revolutionary anarchist . . . (or) . . . a syndicalist."[43]

This was not the sum total of his efforts to sway proletarian opinion away from revolution. He helped stoke up an old myth from the war by sponsoring a publication purporting to show the extent of German involvement in the Bolshevik revolution.[44] With official approval, it was disseminated in schools, church organizations, in cultural and special interest associations though he knew this to be a forgery. Most of the radical socialists' natural supporters were nationalists and the anti-German appeal of this publication caused many to reject Bolshevism for its apparent support of German irredentism, though they did not entirely give up their radical social aims. The President continued his campaign in the official organ of the CSP, České slovo. Beneš too took part, after his official adoption by the party in 1920, while Masaryk was accorded the right to accept or reject articles.[45] The magazine Čas also became the showcase for his views on why Czech conditions excluded the Leninist path.[46] The gravity of the situation was underlined by a series of publications based on his lectures and covering the themes of proletarian dictatorship and Bolshevism.[47] The operation of aspects of the land reform and the promise of a public enquiry into the nationalization of the coalmines gave substance to his assertion that the national revolution was indeed the point of departure for a socialist revolution, subject to planning and the agreement of international interests. His listeners were flattered by references to their cultural and educational superiority which, he asserted, made Russian methods of social change inappropriate. He constantly reminded them of the opportunities the new political system offered, suggesting, with a degree of dishonesty, that ". . . a revolutionary movement is a nonsense when you (workers) have the possibility to gain a majority in government."[48] Universal suffrage and the proliferation of parties did suggest that the new political freedom was not simply formal and as a result few among his listeners questioned the view that the vote was capable of bringing about change by altering party relations in parliaments. Important figures among the radical socialists, like Brodecký and Stivín, came round to his way of thinking after other experiences had persuaded them that revolution was undesirable.[49] They worked hard to unite the rank and file radicals on a common platform with the Orthodox SDs, ignoring the fact that the SDP could never in those conditions achieve an absolute majority.

The ideological campaign cost Šmeral dearly. He could not shake off Masaryk's identification of his tactics with those of Bolshevism. The president's evaluation seemed to be borne out by the putschist tactics of Muna in the December 1920 confrontation. Although this had little to do with Šmeralism, he was unable to keep the middle ground between the Orthodox SDs and Muna and ultimately felt more disposed to fall in with the latter whose aims, in contrast to those of the SDs, he felt able to agree with.

Šmeral had to find solutions to the problems posed by the political order which, as it affected him, was built on two institutional systems whose primary function was to filter out the kind of opposition he represented. The first and for his purposes most immediate was the party and its leaders, the Orthodox SDs. Their ability to distribute and withdraw parliamentary mandates at will enabled them to enforce obedience. Their party secretaries decided on candidates to elections and fixed agendas for branch meetings and congress. The operation and management of the party amounted to rule by a party elite who more or less ignored the clamour for change of the rank and file. Theoretically, they could be removed by decision of congress and Šmeral, in accordance with his values, worked assiduously within the democratic rules of the party to achieve this. In practice however the Orthodox SDs could not be removed from below and they were not prepared to recognize that the people and not the Executive was the highest authority in the party. As Peroutka, never a friend of the Left, later asserted: ". . . all power comes from the parties and whatever institution stands against them loses . . . something which is nowhere to be found in the constitution enables them, if it comes to it, to be more than a match for anybody."[50] The struggle Šmeral undertook against the Orthodox SDs was not simply a contest for power. It represented a conflict of two fundamentally different views of the party. In the conditions of the time, the Orthodox SDs insulated themselves from the rank and file and formed more or less an oligarchy, or at least an inflexible elite which was little affected by popular pressure. For Šmeral, it was a struggle of elitism against democracy, of representation against participation, likewise of the proletarian base of the party against professional middle-class careerism. The notion of political legitimacy had to be called into question in circumstances where the Orthodox SDs appealed to the radicals to accept universal suffrage as the means of change, but devised delaying tactics which strongly suggested a refusal to allow themselves to be tested within the party, when evidence showed them to be in a minority.[51]

Just as the Orthodox SDs were not responsive to the majority votes cast against them in the local organizations, neither was there a direct connection between voting behaviour and the configuration of the governing elites in the coalitions. On balance, the judgement of the President and not the number of votes cast for a party played a greater role in the distribution of power to the parties. It was clear to Šmeral that this restricted or undermined the power of the ballot box to achieve change. The extension of the coalition principle into local government after the SDs' victory at municipal elections was added proof that universal suffrage in the political conditions as they were was not sufficient. Changes did indeed take place in the coalition, yet there was little change in its nature. It was accountable more to the President than the electorate and to that extent shared something with the SDP whose parliamentary delegates were responsible to the Executive and not the party members. Democracy for Šmeral implied, to an important degree, the ability to choose freely and for that choice to be reflected in the political configuration of the state. This was difficult in the case of the party and also, though for different reasons, for parliament where he knew no one party could expect a majority. More or less the lynchpin in the entire system was the President whose personal prestige enabled him to legitimize governmental changes not provided for in the constitution and to ignore calls for elections when conditions might have justified it.

This set of circumstances could not fail to affect Šmeral's view of the means of change. The tactics of the Orthodox SDs in September 1920 could easily be reproduced in the strategy of the coalition. His own principle of "no compromise with the bourgeoisie" effectively shut him out of the coalition in which anyway he could have achieved very little. He did not reject the legitimacy of parliament as such, except insofar as the role of the parties and the President in it prevented a more accurate reflection of the wishes of the people. He did not exclude parliament but doubted if it was capable in those conditions of deciding about the socialization of the great capitalists, for example.[52] As it was unreasonable to posit change through the ballot box given the obstructions placed in his way by party and parliament, he settled on another kind of institution which however would not initiate the revolution. He was confident that the support for his aims he enjoyed from the Centrists, especially in Pardubice and even from sections of the Right in Ostrava, combined with that of legionnaires and some Czech Socialists, would see the party through its troubles and maintain its identity as a radical social democratic party. This would lead the mass movement to the revolution. However he envisaged the formation of workers' committees to organize the movement specifically to meet the challenge of the bourgeoisie after the programme of the socialization of large-scale industry had been forced through. They would also have the task of assisting and even taking over in the case of the state bureaucracy being overloaded or breaking down.[53]

The political system presented Šmeral with problems which in the timescale he gave himself were more or less intractable. He had achieved one half of the policy forming the means of change, namely the mass movement. But he failed to come to grips with the problem of the Orthodox SDs who refused to leave him in charge of the party, whose institutions were indispensible in harnessing the power of the masses and whose name was vital in persuading the unions in particular that his movement did not represent the new communism, but rather was a revival of the lost principles of social democracy. Šmeral underestimated the Orthodox SDs insofar as he assumed that they would bow to the will of the majority. Neither did he foresee that the other parties and the president would support them. In the conditions of the time, there was probably no way to guard against this as the general strike called in protest against the part the SDs played in the People's House showed. It indicated that Šmeral likely overestimated the power of the mass movement to alter the situation, or at least he misjudged the mood of the people inasmuch as he was unable to mobilize as many as he anticipated.

To a degree, this is a comment on the nature of the movement he led. His view of the party was such that he was not fundamentally opposed to the loose, relatively undisciplined elements which formed its basis. Yet the issues which precipitated the general strike were not such as to unite and stiffen the movement. Šmeral himself was unsure about the wisdom of his call when he knew that Muna and the Kladno communists were spoiling for a confrontation with the state. As he correctly foresaw, their commitment to armed revolt would only solidify opposition behind the government parties. On the one hand, he welcomed the outbreak of hundreds of revolts at local level and the forms of proletarian organization outside the party and the self-initiatives this would produce. On the other, he was not able to control them, which resulted in the movement having a splinter and factional character with a wide variety of aims and means. Perhaps if he had bided his time and reacted to the tactics of the Orthodox SDs in a more considered manner, he could have prevented the explosion which was effectively the end of Šmeralism. He might have been able to maintain the pressure of the mass movement on the SDP, even increased it given the economic conditions in 1922, forcing the other parties and the President to abandon them and at the same time given himself a breathing space to pursue the effective development of workers' committees. As it was, the general strike convinced the Czech communists that his means of change were not appropriate and the only way forward was armed revolt. This required a different kind of party. Yet the foundation of the Communist Party was the end of a genuinely mass and democratic radical socialist party. It gave the Orthodox SDs undisputed mastery of the party and its past and, with these advantages, it retained the allegiance of a large section of the working class and the unions whose aims were more in accord with those of Šmeral. It also made the job of the government and the state much easier.

*Chapter 3*

## The Challenge of the Radical Socialists

The first whiff of opposition to the social and political character of the emerging Czech state was initiated by Šmeral even before the Austrian Empire had collapsed. It was more or less a response to three connected problems. The first is related to Šmeral's integrity. In the light of the Allied victory and the firm control the emigration and the Prague National Committee exerted over the drive for national liberation, his political concept was often mischievously interpreted as a betrayal of the nation. In addition, he had to contend with allegations of careerism emanating from career politicians of all complexions and with the bitter personal attacks of individuals, some of whom shared many of his political and economic aims but not his internationalist values.[1] Šmeral's reputation in these circumstances took a hammering which did not leave the SD workers unaffected. He was forced onto the defensive and was not in a position to face the National Committee whose predominantly bourgeois character gave the socialists little hope for the incorporation of their social and economic demands into the fabric of the new state. To this second difficulty was added a third, namely how were the diverse sources of social opposition to find a voice when the cry on every Czech's lips was for a national state.

Even the group who later came to form the radical socialists were in disarray. They were caught unawares and unable to take up a position on the general question of the Czech state, self-determination of nations nor on the peace demands. This derived at least partly from the fact that the war had more or less accustomed them to leaving these problems to the Czech Union and National Committee.[2] Šmeral no doubt regretted having taken no part in the formation of the National Committee.[3] Although this was quite consistent with his stand of "no compromise with the bourgeoisie," it made it more difficult to counter the influence of the radical nationalist SDs. These factors and the abrupt change in party attitudes towards Soviet Russia[4]

75

convinced him of the necessity to show that not all of the party was willing to accept a subordinate role to their class enemies. He determined to show also that an act of signal defiance to the Austrian state could also serve as a salutary warning to the National Committee that proletarian power was a force to be reckoned with and was not to be forgotten when the time came to make the social and political arrangements for the new state. Šmeral's federalist hopes were clearly a dead letter in the face of the Allies' solution to the problem. But, while the representatives of the bourgeois parties at home and abroad could claim mastery over the international setting in which the Czech question would ultimately be settled, Šmeral was concerned to impress upon them that he still commanded wide support among the proletarian masses of the Czech and to a degree, the Bohemian Germans despite the campaigns to discredit him. This balance of forces was evident during those critical junctures which marked the early years of the Republic.

The Socialist Council, through which Šmeral made the opportunity to display his antagonism to the social dimension of the national revolution, had other aspirations. The connections between part of the SDP and German–Austrian social democracy, which had made no attempt to distance itself from the Austro–Hungarian system, continued to have a negative effect on its popularity and greatly assisted the shift of proletarian support from the Czech SDP to the CSP. Despite Šmeral's rooted objections to sections of the CSP, he considered it prudent to be seen participating in a body embodying the cooperation of all socialists in a united Czech national front. This helped to counter the influence of the National Committee where socialists were in a minority. In the given conditions, it was vain to argue that Czech social democracy, even the radical socialist fraction, could avoid being drawn into dependence on the bourgeois conception of the national struggle. It remained therefore to concentrate socialist forces of all kinds. Šmeral even worked for the acceptance of the Centralists, who were anathema to the CSP, in the hope that something might still be saved. If he had refused to participate, there would have been a danger that the social democratic workers still faithful to him would have abandoned him altogether. Further, there would have been no way to modify or otherwise hinder the seemingly inevitable progress of the CSP and SDP towards fusion,[5] which might well have affected the rise of the radical socialist Left. Šmeral at least drew comfort from the programme of the Socialist Coucil which gave precedence to the proletariat gaining power in the new state.[6]

The formation of the Socialist Council, was designed to end the mutual isolation of the socialist parties. It was also significant in another way as it fulfilled to some extent the call of the working class for united proletarian

# THE CHALLENGE OF RADICAL SOCIALISTS 77

action in the struggle for a socially just state. It presented to the people the general notion of socialist councils as a possible basis for the future struggle for the aims of the proletariat. These had neither the ideological strength nor the radical programme of the Soviets. Yet they created an admittedly remote possibility of uniting the proletariat across party lines. A new mood reflected in Stivin's reconciliation with the Zimmerwald centralists[7] encouraged Šmeral to believe that there was a strong possibility of the Socialist Council developing further, which in terms of sheer size might have given the proletariat the preponderant influence in the new state. Indeed it was involved in two actions whch suggested that the bourgeois parties were not entirely free to handle matters in their own way. Without prior discussion, it was announced that a National Assembly would meet in Prague and that its deputies would be drawn from both chambers of the Reichsrat, provincial government and representatives of the towns. Only the threat of the mass action of the workers prevented this[8] and it seemed that the predictions Šmeral had made on his lecture tour of Moravia, a reaction to Staněk's refusal of the Austrian proposals, were not far wide of the mark.

The second act of opposition centred on the administration of the strike of 14th October 1918 which, far from being an attack on the embryo of the Czech state was, among other things, a signal reminder to certain powerful figures in the Prague National Committee that the people would have no truck with their monarchist tendencies. The protest against the export of food was, at Šmeral's instigation, adroitly used to give voice to the popular feeling for a republic based on universal suffrage.[9] The strike emphasized both the anticapitalist and socialist sentiments of the workers forming the major section of the strikers and Šmeral's commitment to internationalism. It was intended to be the beginning of a series of concerted actions by the Socialist Council and not, as it turned out, the end. But Šmeral also addressed himself to the German workers of Northern Bohemia, emphasizing the class aims of the strike common to Czech and German worker alike and that the law of self-determination would apply equally to the German people as to the Czechs.[10] His enemies in the SDP and the NC were scandalized and alleged that he had acted in concert with either the leadership of the Austrian SDs in Vienna or with the German SDs in the mixed nationality border areas. Later in 1924 the official organ of the national revolution corrected this impression but could not undo the damage done to his reputation.[11]

Nevertheless, the National Committee was treated to an arresting display of proletarian power which demonstrated unambiguously the desire for a republican form of state. If the complete removal of class privileges was not everywhere stressed, it anyway emphasized proletarian expectations of social equity. Immediately before the strike, the Socialist Council had invited the Brno Centralists to take part in the action and also to join the Council itself. This was significant for a number of reasons. Their insistence on a republican form of state strengthened Šmeral's claim that this reflected the views of most workers on the future organization of the Czech territories. They even published a republican constitution which was seized by the Austrian authories.[12] In addition, Šmeral derived a considerable boost from their stress on the social and economic demands of the proletariat, which he had hitherto been attempting to propagate almost single-handed. Of more direct relevance for the impending struggle against the Orthodox SDs was their support for the entry of the Czech communists from Russia into the party. This helped to undermine the plans circulating in the Socialist Council to effect a complete merger of the SDP with the Czech Socialist Party. The Centralists then entered the Socialist Council albeit with reservations. This provided the signal for their provincial organizations to enter the local Socialist Councils which had begun to form around 14th October 1918. Their attraction to the Czech communists, like Šmeral's, flowed from their perception of them as uncompromising fighters for the cause of the social and political emancipation of the proletariat. They were less interested, if at all, in their advocacy of a new type of party organization. On the other hand, they feared the consequences of the founding of a single Czech socialist party built around the Socialist Council which would have made their task all the harder

In the meantime, they maintained their independence within it, simultaneously forming links with Šmeral's group and sections of the CSP around the anarchist, Landová-Stychová, who unlike most of her party, had not abandoned the principle of class struggle. These strands would develop and ultimately bring to life "a united party of Czech, class-conscious and international Social Democrats,"[13] which, had they known the true character of Bolshevism, might equally have led to the foundation of two independent Czech communist parties.

There was no-one in the labour movement capable of opposing Masaryk's conception of the struggle for the state apart from Šmeral and the Centralists. Nevertheless, the general strike represented a grave threat. Originally directed against the monarchy, whose local administrations were expected to use the army to quell disorder, Czech national leaders feared that it could be transformed into a mass and violent action against the authorities, in which the Prague National Committee and its local representatives too might be pushed aside. With the help of the Orthodox SDs and unions, the strike at least in the major urban conurbations was removed of much of its menace.

The circular Šmeral had inspired was only in a few places interpreted as an instruction to initiate a revolt.

As a result, the strike went off more or less peacefully. Yet the symbolic proclamation of the Czechoslovak Republic was not the only cause for concern. Nearly everywhere local socialist councils were formed composed of representatives of all socialist parties. They exceeded in number the provincial National Committees. Only after the strike was over did the order go out to expand them into every area to regulate the activities of the socialist councils.[14] Šmeral's promise of self-determination for the Germans also had some effect and German workers took part in the strike in the Brno, Ostrava and North Bohemian regions. This tended to show that the divisions between Czech and German were in certain areas and on specific issues not insuperable. The sheer size of the protest nationwide and the orderly and disciplined course it had taken had a significance which was not lost on Šmeral. Despite the parallels drawn by the Austrian authorities to the outbreak of a Bolshevik-type of revolt, he was confirmed in his view that in conditions of peace, such a mass strike demonstrating the revolutionary mood and determination of the wide masses organized by local party organizations could achieve fundamental political change. Despite the claims of the bourgeois parties, it had nothing to do with a Bolshevik conspiracy as such. It had more to do at one level, with the revolutionary potential inherent in a united working class and at another, with the absolute priority to be given to the participation of the masses.

The Socialist Council distanced themselves from Šmeral as a result of his initiative. But he had achieved a considerable amount. He had helped make impossible the aims of the small though influential group of monarchists in the National Committee. Further, and paradoxically, given the abject apology of the Socialist Council, he had with the aid of the masses ensured that the socialists would have a significant role to play in the operation of the state. It remained to exploit the problems implicit in the Orthodox SDs' efforts to transfer the all-national coalition, which had been successful in securing its war aims, to peace-time conditions.

Šmeral's part in the strike indicated on the one hand that the last remnants of socialism opposing Masaryk's conception of the struggle had been overcome and that the Czech revolt had finally become a genuinely all-national affair. On the other, it was clear that he had no intention of organizing a violent national revolution, preferring to wait for the end of the war which brought a new state-form and enhanced the possibilities for political struggle. Indeed, he had helped win the first argument against the representatives of the national struggle at home who were less progressive socially than Masaryk's group abroad. To gain control however of the national movement, Šmeral had first to destroy relations between Masaryk and the Allied Powers or alternatively to persuade a majority of the nation to reject his conception of the Czechoslovak state. The first was an illusion and the second was barely feasible given the existence of the state itself and the personal popularity of Masaryk. Even radical socialists, with the exception of Muna and certain of the Czech Bolsheviks, were unwilling to lay the blame for the defects of the economic and social system at his door.[15] The struggle hence had to begin in the SDP itself, whose representatives in governing circles occupied an important even fulcrum position in the fortunes of the state, spreading out to those radical sympathizers not organized in party or union. However as we shall see, a vital international dimension imposed operational limits on Šmeral[16] which, put very roughly, could not have allowed him to take power, even if he had had the entire mass movement behind him. This ultimately left him with little choice but to turn to Bolshevik Russia.

The inauguration of the Czech state brought a decisive change in the balance of political forces internally. Although the boundaries of the state were not fixed until the summer of 1919, there was no longer any need for people impoverished or otherwise reduced economically and socially by the war to restrain their radical aspirations, a feature of the situation when the origin of the state hung in the balance. The CSP formed from Vrbenský's North Czech federalists, several of the groups in the Czech Democracy movement and the National Socialists, had in association with the Realists ensured control over the masses by passing themselves off as political forces with a major committment to basic social change.[17] The influence of the intelligentsia among the people, an important factor defusing the threat of the radical movement, declined after the war and the radical programmatic statements of the majority of the parties were seen in their true light.[18] There was no longer a national need to respond to public pressure and move to the left. The Orthodox SDs, the traditional guardians of the anti-capitalist demands of the working-class were safely tucked up in the government. Only Šmeral remained and, as Kramář believed him to be against Bolshevism,[19] which was true but for reasons other than he thought, attempts were made to absorb him into public life. Švehla however was against leaving him to the short memories of the public and, also from personal motives, attempted to have him permanently emasculated politically. His parliamentary experience and intimate knowledge of the workings of his party made him the natural focus around which a radical opposition could form within the SDP. He had survived the post-war hate campaign and had not lost the regard of the working class for his singleminded and strenuous efforts to defend their interests in war-time. It was natural therefore in the aggravated conditions of post-war Czechoslovakia, as people became habituated to the existence of the state, to overlook his position in war-time and look to him for leadership in pursuit of their social and economic aims.

The instinctive reservations held by, among others, Šmeral and his group about the manner of the formation of the Prague National Committee grew in conditions of peace when it became apparent that the coalition and the National Assembly did not correspond to the real relations of party power in the Czech Lands.[20] Divested of the need to keep silent and encouraged by assumptions of freedom and democracy, for many the essence of the new state, they sought at first to clarify the principles on which it was founded and to examine the place of the Orthodox SDs within it. The first signs of resistance to the SDP arose not from Bolshevik agitators, as Kramář claimed,[21] but from the workers in the Škoda factories in Plzeň. At first, their demands which were a repetition of the programme of the SDP from 1st May 1918, expressed their wishes for the political and economic organization of the new state.[22] They were supported by similar petitions from Olomouc,[23] Poldiná huti[24] and Brno,[25] to name only a few, but it was conspicuous that these groups did not form an opposition movement as such, but were more concerned with impressing on the Orthodox SDs the urgent need for swift action to remedy their economic plight.

A series of important social reforms was enacted which, in a few cases, was a constitutional recognition of a situation brought about by popular pressure and even occasionally by the threat of violence, which the government could not anyway change.[26] Opposition indeed was at this stage amorphous which can be partly attributed to the uneasy state of the frontier regions and also to the fact that even the radical socialists were divided over the case of Šmeral and most were reluctant to be identified with him. Until he felt secure enough to return to public life in the Spring of 1919, resistance to the Orthodox SDs was expressed in a more or less haphazard manner. The hunger demonstrations in November 1918 were the most visible signs of dissatisfaction with the coalition, but these were for the most part ineffective as they were largely without leadership or concerted plan. They did however provoke a reaction which suggested that the Orthodox SDs were not opposed to the use of violence where it was in the interests of state.[27] It seemed that they were attempting to transfer the principle of class cooperation from conditions of war against a national enemy to those of a socially-aggravated peace. In the very process of bringing order and stability to the state, the political hegemony of the Germans was broken, yet their social and economic power was to a large extent untouched. Hence the active participation of the Orthodox SDs in the construction of the state was in these conditions paradoxically a de facto rejection of proletarian claims to social liberation and as such was bound to provoke the strongest opposition.

In the early period of the Republic, the Orthodox SDs in the related areas of government and party were regarded as having initiated or being an active partner in policies which were more or less directed against the interests of the working people. They had opposed Meissner's plan to abolish the old Austrian war restrictions on assembly and the press,[28] supported the abolition of the local National Committees and accepted without demur the Ministerial Council's abrogation of the principle of responsibility to the National Assembly. The principle of class struggle was jettisoned in expectation of the speedy introduction of universal suffrage even though the SDs had consistently voted to postpone general and local elections even when it was more or less certain that no one party could achieve an absolute majority. In respect of social questions, they favoured solutions devised by committees of experts,[29] an echo of old Austria, which stood oddly beside their decision not to appoint SDP representatives to the committee entrusted with the formulation of the first government programme. These factors and their implicit support of violence to maintain the new order significantly reduced their popularity. The challenge from the street fell as a rule on unemployed workers and women protesting against profiteering.[30] More significant was the ground-swell of opposition within the SDP itself which had ready-made organizations whose ability to reflect discontent was however limited by the influence of the SD executive. The Orthodox SDs also had a case to answer within the party itself. Quite apart from the question of class cooperation or class struggle, they had exceeded their mandate in that they had revised the party programme of 1912 without the express agreement of Congress, the highest organ of party democracy. It had of course not been possible to call one in war-time, yet this was invoked continually as a pretext for postponing the party Congress as was the case in late 1918. The co-option too of SDP representatives to the Provisional Assembly, which was achieved more or less in secret, awakened fears that the party was under the control of a small circle of people uninterested in popular, mass participation in government and whose tactics and aims were determined largely by the bourgeois parties.[31]

Pressure for change in the first instance came from below. Roughly speaking it was broken into two parts which had a greater or lesser degree of contact. The first, the mass of workers and unemployed marching in demonstrations held opinions no more revolutionary than those consistent with achieving a rapid and equitable solution to the supply problem and an end to unemployment. Many were sympathizers of the CSP and Catholic Parties. The second section on the other hand operated within the area and local SD party organizations and was almost wholly made up of younger individuals who, having returned from military service, were concerned to right the situation in which professional and paid functionaries of either the SDP, its business establishments or the union organizations dominated the entire apparatus of the party with little or no reference to the membership. Their highest priority was to correct the discrepancy in inner-party democracy and remedy "the absolute weakness and the complete breakdown in party and organizational discipline."[32] A separate conference was called at which some 300 party secretaries pressed their claims for a full Party Congress. They confidently expected to turn out the Orthodox SDs, introduce a greater measure of democracy within the party, for which an Action Committee of 18, half of them factory workers, had been elected,[33] and return along a reconstructed parliamentary road to the old principles of social democracy. Although Arno Hais, and Koníček, founder members of the Czechoslovak Revolutionary Council of Soldiers and Workers, and likewise of the Czech Communist Party in Russia,[34] were present at the conference, there was no call for a violent revolutionary solution.

The Congress of the SDP was more or less inconclusive seen from the viewpoint of the Party's radical left-wing. The Executive failed to produce the promised new programme, made no attempt to deal with the issues of inner-party democracy raised in the resolution of the November 1918 conference and indeed compounded their error insofar as they allowed a large minority of delegates to participate and vote who were not qualified.[35] Pik and Habrmann, the two bastions of radical nationalism, in Plzeň became the target for their own party organizations who, after two years isolation, had discovered that other views existed in the party. The generally bellicose mood suggested that this ran to many other sections. In an attempt to head off any outright party strife the Orthodox SDs welcomed the Brno Centralists into the party calculating that the resulting strengthening of radicalism would be balanced by the fusion with the CSP, a motion also accepted at the Congress to the indifference of the radical delegates.[36] In effect, they were seeking to maintain the Socialist Council by another name and, believing they could impose more or less the same kind of unity the movement had enjoyed in the last year of the war, they accepted individuals and fractions in the party with whom they were likely to conflict. In so doing, they missed a golden opportunity of removing Šmeral, if only temporarily. He returned to the Executive Committee on which the radical socialists held five seats while the others, the majority, were divided into discreet centre and nationalist blocs.[37]

This group within the party in general recognized the state, were willing to test the parliamentary system and work within the SDP to achieve their aims, at least for as long as it took them to discover its inadequacies as an instrument of radical change. Against stood Muna and the emigration in Russia which was of an entirely different character from that of Masaryk's. His tactic, insofar as he had consciously conceived one at all, differed markedly from Šmeral's. In this regard, his experience in Russia played a crucial role. Before the war, he had been habituated to the practice of political struggle found in the Union of Tailors in Prostějov where he had been a secretary. He had also stood for the Reichsrat as an SD MP. His more or less brief acquaintance with the style of politics under the Empire was obliterated when he witnessed the events in Kiev surrounding the Bolsheviks' seizure of power in the Ukraine. He had also come into conflict with Masaryk for the leadership of the Czech movement in Russia. His plan[38] for a union of independent democratic republics on the territories of Austria-Hungary was substantially different from Masaryk's. His failure to win over many sympathizers in the Czech Legion, quite apart from the complete split in the Czech SD movement in Russia, resulted in his movement acquiring a splinter and factional character as a counter-organization to the National Committee.

While the SD sympathizers in the Legion were committed to war, which was against the wishes of the Russian Bolshevik leaders, and prepared to work for national reconstruction when the state became a reality, Muna took the opposite view. Both the Petersburg and Kiev groups of radical socialist SDs rejected the legitimacy of Masaryk as leader and with the help of the Bolsheviks formed a Czech section within the Red Army[39] and a Czechoslovak Communist Party in Russia (May 1918).[40] These developments formed a significant part of Lenin's plans for Central Europe. Initially, he hoped that the propaganda campaign waged by Muna would prevent the translation of the Legion to France and by some miracle bring the legionnaires over en masse to the Red Army. Failing that, any addition to his forces no matter how small, was welcome in the struggle against the Whites. The opportunity to organize groups of crusading communists from the war-prisoners of the Habsburg nationalities ultimately destined for their own countries when hostilities had ceased was also a vital part of the plan for a general outbreak of European revolution on which, it was believed, the success of the Soviet Revolution depended. The outbreak of hostilities between sections of the Legion and the Bolsheviks made the first part of the plan more or less a dead letter and increased the prejudice Muna felt for the Czech state. There remained the organization of those Czechs committed to proletarian revolution and the most effective use of those who had hailed to the Red Army but whose numbers and reasons were such that they could make little difference in the civil war. These, like Anton Kubat,[41] although often of doubtful Bolshevik conviction, were allowed home to make propaganda for the Russian Revolution. This was planned at the convening of the "Austrian International" in Moscow immediately after the succession states had come into existence.

It is not entirely clear to what extent Muna followed or understood Lenin's advice. What is certain is that he adopted a position on most of the vital problems of the Czechoslovak state and the solutions to them quite at variance with those of Šmeral. Despite Lenin's insistence on tactical realism, Muna came to the Czech Lands as the chairman of the Czechoslovak Communist Party and the representative of the Bolshevik party. Circumspection had little or no place in his political strategy nor in his personality. He was irreconcilably opposed to the state and was bent on its destruction. Both he and Šmeral regarded it as essentially a class-state, but Šmeral, far from inviting a head-on confrontation with its organs, chose to work within it as a form of political and social organization expanding the opportunities for class struggle, which the Habsburg Empire had more vigorously denied the working class.

Šmeral's method was to exploit the growing discontent among the working people, which extended to sections of the intelligentsia, resulting from the post-war economic crisis and harnessing the ground-swell of opposition from below. He could thereby secure the removal of the Orthodox SDs in local party organizations, and ultimately in parliament, in the democratically prescribed manner. His stress lay on entirely legal methods emanating from the mobilizing and participation of the masses. This of course changed when the political system became aware of the power behind the challenge of the radical socialists and acted to close off their access to leading positions.

Lenin's advice notwithstanding, Muna frightened off local and regional party secretaries with his wild talk of violent revolution and they refused him entry to their party organizations. Illegality hence became not a form solely borrowed from Leninism, but a practical necessity in the light of his failure to effectively penetrate more than one section of the social democratic movement. He thereafter turned to the radical socialists in Kladno to provide the avant-garde of the revolution and the emphasis on their activities as a role-model for the rest of the radical movement contained within it the seed of centralism. Despite his enormous and successful agitation, there were serious weaknesses in the manner in which he set about creating a revolution in the Czech Lands which suggests that his understanding of the problem and of the historical setting was not as firm as Šmeral's.

Initially, he grossly underestimated the nationalist sentiments of the working class, assuming that their commitment to radical socialist objectives excluded per se any loyalty to the state and Masaryk.⁴² Although hungry for information about the new forms of social, political and economic organization in Russia, on which Muna was held up as an authority, the ordinary working people were often cool towards him for his scorn for Masaryk's revolution.⁴³ He made other tactical blunders too, principally his insistence on a Russian style of revolution and his assertion that had Kaiser Wilhelm won the war, little or no difference would have been noticed in the social conditions of the people. Much of the advantage gained from his experience of Russia and from his personal magnetism was offset as a result. Secondly, his attitude to the state governed his view of its political and parliamentary institutions. This was almost wholly negative. The SDP hence could not provide the path to the social revolution he desired and his inability to use it for his own ends reinforced the view he had learnt in Russia that violence, only to the exclusion of individual terrorism, was more appropriate.⁴⁴

This was strongly influenced by two further aspects of the political environment. Muna's arrest in early 1919 led to an unsuccessful attempt to make him the subject of military justice. This created for a time a tendency towards violent self-defence. Improper and unfounded allegations of his participation, or at least complicity, in the attentat on Kramář and rumours emanating from Russia of his incitement of the Czech Legion to rebellion, mutiny and desertion⁴⁵ threw into doubt the whole concept of due process of law, quite apart from the question of fundamental freedoms on which the republic had avowedly been based. Held without a warrant, he was released by armed workers in Prostějov who were prepared to fight for his freedom. For Muna, the incident was instructive in two ways. It demonstrated that the direct action of the workers was a realistic possibility given specific issues. Secondly, both the Orthodox SDs and the bourgeois parties were capable of turning a blind eye to contraventions of the legal code when these were directed against their opponents. In his eyes, they thereby forfeited judicial legitimacy. He was later confirmed in his suspicions when a legal warrant for treason was issued based upon one drawn up in Kiev before the Republic had come into existence, to which the Agrarians had in its publication in the party organ added that he might be taken dead or alive. Hence, he felt no qualms in offering the threat of violence to achieve his aims, although in practical terms the means to dispose of such power was beyond him. Even after the government ruled that there was no case to answer, he was wont to invoke the principle Masaryk had proclaimed in Russia: an eye for an eye.

Despite being secure from the legal viewpoint, he remained in some personal danger until his arrival in Kladno and in the light of the unlawful activities of certain legionnaire vigilante groups and the frequent destruction of SD meetings by the Agrarians, whose penchant for violence caused them to be called the "green Bolsheviks,"[45] gave substance to claims that the government's enforcement of the law was selective, moving even his enemies in the SD MPs Club to an official protest.[47]

Muna's case was of significance in other ways. It divided opinion within the nation and also polarized the SDP itself. It further provided the impetus for the radical Left in Prague to organize itself not only in defence of legitimate proletarian agitation but also as the defender of legal certainty and moral values.[48] This was quite at variance with Muna's views. The workers' defence of his right to address them and their own rights of assembly threw open many of the local Moravian SD organizations to him. This presented a direct challenge to the authority of the Orthodox SDs whose strict instructions to bar him from every facility of the party were consistently ignored. It demonstrated too that their hold on the lower echelons of the party was not strong which contrasted with their position in its leading organs. Neither was it lost on them that in a matter of a few weeks, the Prostějov organizations had on this issue turned against the local SD hero, Bechyně. Muna tried hard to maintain the appearance of illegality, hiding and organizing secret meetings often against the wishes of the secretaries of the local party organizations in Moravia who were helpless in the cross-fire of the Orthodox SDs, who favoured his deportation,[49] and the pressure from the rank and file, who protected him and facilitated his agitation. His experience of the Russian revolution and the focus he provided gave people the opportunity, in the absence of a strong centre of authority which had collapsed with the Monarchy, to vent their basic feelings of resentment for the Establishment.

However it is doubtful if many of them shared his views on anything more than the desirability for a vague and notional socialist republic. As far as the available evidence goes, Muna did not urge on his listeners the need for a new form of party organization. Indeed not until his arrival in Kladno did he make references to a revolutionary vanguard composed entirely of proletarians to the exclusion of all other classes.[50] His response to spontaneous violence was equivocal in that he was willing to accept it as a practical need for his own protection. But in the long view it offended his belief in the necessity of disciplined party organization governed by professional revolutionaries of which he regarded himself as one. Muna at this stage presented no direct challenge to the state for his success in winning over a considerable part of the proletariat in Moravia was seen to be transient once the specific issues of freedom of speech and assembly had passed. The workers did not hesitate to turn on him for his stand on the Hungarian invasion of Slovakia.[51] However, in a few cases his appeal to violence as the means of change was taken up principally by miners in the Ostrava-Těsín-Karvina regions who expelled pit-owners and for a short time occupied and ran the mines for themselves.[52] While Muna acted as a trigger, these currents were largely semi-spontaneous expressions of opposition initially to their own local union and party officials whose discharge of the instructions of the Orthodox SDs left unsatisfied the basic needs of the working masses to participate in the organization from which they felt themselves shut out. It served also as a warning that they were not disposed to leave everything to the vagaries of representative government.

The issues Muna's case raised went further than democratic freedoms. They concerned the relation of the Czech Communists to the Orthodox SDs and of social democratic tactics to those of Russian Bolshevism, two questions left unanswered at the XII Congress. The entry into the party of Czech communists infused with a revolutionary spirit and political and organizational values at odds with those of the Orthodox SDs could not fail to have an affect on a politically unstable population and, through party and coalition, on the state itself. When confronted by the competition deriving from ideas more attractive to a large section of the people, the Orthodox SDs made every effort to deny the communists a platform. They attempted this in two ways, initially to block or reverse their admission into the party and secondly, to withdraw facilities for agitation either in party institutions or the party press. This provoked great resistance in different sections of the party and proved unworkable, not least because the Executive of the SDP was split on the matter.[53] Further, the left-wing of the Executive, which controlled the Central Secretariat administering and coordinating the SD organizations in the provinces, refused to comply. This state of affairs sat uneasily beside the claim of the Orthodox SDs that they were there to serve the people[54] when there was reason to believe that the people's desire to hear at first hand something about the Russian experience of socialism was being ignored. The alternative conference in Kladno suggested that the Orthodox SDs had already lost Zápotocký, although he temporized on the matter arguing that the Czech communists would accept party discipline if allowed entry.[55] Burian and the Centralists in Brno followed suit.[56] Of the other groups who opposed the Orthodox SDs, Cingr in Ostrava was almost wholly engaged in circumventing the strict security arrangements applied to the border area and was effectively isolated. In Plzeň, the alternative trade unions still had

## THE CHALLENGE OF RADICAL SOCIALISTS 89

not shaken off the domination of Pik and Habrmann. The Prague Left which began to form around the Committee for Defence against the White Terror demanded that Muna be allowed to address the party. They first urged him to throw over his imitation of Bolshevik methods, which Stivín asserted, rested on his mistaken view that the proletariat regarded the Czech bourgeois classes as co-responsible for the war, and, as in Russia, they could only be removed by armed conflict.[57]

In practical terms, Šmeralism began to evolve more rapidly when the Orthodox SDs refused access to the organs of the party to all opponents disseminating alternative ideas and policies. In so doing, they forced a reaction most noticeable in the activities of the Czech communists working on the fringes of the party, who were more or less interested in remaining in it for the advantages deriving from ready-made institutions. These could in time be turned to a split and the birth of a new party. Šmeral on the other hand, fresh from his meeting with Liebknecht in Berlin,[58] set about the task of forming alternative means of propaganda. He was intent on forcing the Orthodox SDs to keep their renewed promises of inner-party democracy in the interests of maintaining a mass party in which the voice of the rank and file would not only have its place, but in time would by popular consent achieve the removal of the old party secretaries, relics of the pre-war period, and firm up the class dimension of SDP policy. With this in mind, the old party organ *Sociální demokrat* was revived which, though it specifically distanced itself from Czech communists,[59] renewed its opposition role to the bourgeois character of the state and sought to correct the bias in reports of the revolution in Russia. Other groups hailed to the colours of radical social democracy, notably a section of the workers in Škoda Plzeň who abandoned the Plzeň organ of the Orthodox SDs and founded the publication *Pravda*[60] and Koutný in Hodonin where *Slovacko*, according to police reports, achieved great success n winning supporters for Šmeral.[61] Neither did the Czech communists rely on the party organs nor even those of Šmeral. Rydlo, rather ironically, settled Třebič and founded *Jiskra*, through which a stream of Lenin's writings and speeches made their way into the Czech Lands.[62] Another Czech Red Guard, Pergl, played a prominent part in the new radical political club "Spravedlnost" and newspaper in Ostrava which was more strictly censored than any other.[63] Muna, Hais and Koníček meanwhile attempted to bring Kladno over to Leninist forms of struggle which, in the light of its traditions, particularly Zapotocky's connections with the founding fathers of the SDP, was not an easy matter.

The Orthodox SDs and the government both interpreted the call of the radical socialists and the communists for a socialist republic as a sure sign not only of unanimity of purpose but also of a mighty socialist front directed to the violent overthrow of the state. Much was made of the riots in Kolín and Poděbrady, in which the police estimated a third of the rioters were ex-legionnaires, while a number of Russian and Czech Red Guards had helped organize armed raids on shops in Přerov.[64] The scandal over Mlčoch and the activity of the radical socialists among the ultra-nationalist "Stráž svobody"[65] seemed to indicate their penetration at many different levels of official and civil society. At the same time, the withdrawal from the National Assembly of prominent radicals like S.K. Neumann, whose old anarchist convictions reasserted themselves, and Stivín, who characterized voting as "parliamentary cretinism,"[66] was clear evidence of a disillusion with parliament as an agent of change and also of a hardening of attitude towards bourgeois society in general. Finally, the emergence of radical socialist sects bent on armed revolt, for example Kostyál's "Organization of Ex-Soldiers" in Moravia[67] and the "Movement of Un-compromising Legionnaires"[68] led by Franta Němec, a former member of the "Stráž svobody," put Modráček's claim of the imminence of a civil war in a new light.

The spectacle of a militant and powerful labour movement however concealed the poor prospects of a violent revolution. The most conspicuous and dramatic evidence of popular rebellion lay in strikes and hunger riots in which the government invariably saw the spore of the radical socialists. In fact, most were spontaneous and unorganized and the aims and, to a degree, the character of the people involved were of such a kind that Šmeral did not believe that their allegiance could be won to the degree required to form a coherent fighting force. The failure of the Spartacists, too, had confirmed him in his view that violence of this kind offered no lasting solution. He had reluctantly to accept the fact that he was unable to control or lead the spontaneous movement outside the party, not least because its members were beyond any institutional framework. In all likelihood it would have anyway rejected any close superintendence on the lines Muna envisaged. On the other hand, he firmly opposed Muna's initiative to set about an immediate foundation of a communist party in the early Spring of 1919. Lenin, who through Bela Kun maintained contact with Muna until the Hungarian venture changed all that,[69] believed against a back-drop of severe civil unrest, strikes and the SDs' Ultimatum which threatened to bring down the government, that a revolution was imminent. He pressed for the disciplined party organization in Kladno to form the basis of a communist party which he fondly imagined would transform the popular movement into an overwhelming force. Šmeral however was justifiably sceptical.

The founding of a communist party could only devolve to the advantage of the Orthodox SDs who, finally given the proof of a connection with the Bolsheviks whose material help would inevitably be construed as an attack on the state, would be enabled to close all party institutions to the Czech communists. They in turn would be compelled to set up their own, a lengthy and costly process losing the movement momentum at a vital moment. Radical socialist slogans were quite acceptable, but revolutionary ideology based upon proletarian internationalism, world proletarian revolution and appeals to the Czech working class to accept the Russian proletariat led by the Bolsheviks as its only reliable ally, was not realistic. Šmeral was indeed an internationalist, but he knew well that the continuing nationalist struggles in the Czech Lands led the workers away from the real causes of discontent and helped to neutralize the labour movement's challenge.[70] This could not be solved simply by the radical socialists' leaders of the various nationalities getting together to form an internationalist party by agreement when internationalism was conspicuously lacking in practice. Muna paid no heed to these specific national conditions and although, with outside help, he won the argument, from a genuinely internationalist perspective, it was a hollow victory which quickly turned sour if we take into account the decline in party membership after November 1921. This Šmeral was anxious to avoid as it led only to the isolation of the party from the mass of the people and to the formation of a relatively small avant-garde who would seek to impose a revolutionary solution from above, more or less without reference to the wishes of the people. In the long view, this would tend to alienate the workers in much the same way as had the elitism of the Orthodox SDs. Šmeral's way opposed the splitting and, ultimately, the isolation of the party. His slogan, "always with the masses", reflected his faith in the roots of the movement, from where popular discontent and unrest originated and was subsequently channelled into the local organs of the SDP. It was imperative therefore to stay within the party and guide the volume of protest through it, taking account of the demands of individuals and groups and fusing them with the overall drive for a socialist republic. His revolution was not then to be a violent seizure of power, like Muna's, but a revolution deriving from the power of the masses whose participation in winning the party from within would not contravene democratic values and whose ultimate success in implementing a revolution from the sheer size of its opposition to a weakly established order would maintain the movement within the bounds of political legitimacy. Any stress on proletarian internationalism would have made Šmeral's plan to gradually woo the party away from the Orthodox SDs a dead letter when the Republic was threatened on its external fronts. In contrast to Muna, he tended to blur the lines of ideology and, instead of appealing to the model of the Soviet Revolution, harked back to the founding principles of social democracy, thereby invoking the values of Czech traditions yet specifically repudiating the variety preached by Scheidemann. In the summer of 1919, Šmeral's reservations relating to Muna's doctrinaire stand on proletarian internationalism were seen to be wellfounded. The Hungarian invasion of Slovakia caused two mainstays of the radical Prague Left, Stivín and Brodecký, to abandon the movement and go over to the Orthodox SDs.[71] Muna finally accepted Šmeral's point and temporarily severed relations with Moscow. Other areas of dissension emerged, principally regarding money and the introduction of inflexible organization into the unintegrated fabric of the radical left. Quite apart from the inevitable clash which developed from their differences in strategy, there was tension reflected in the competition between Prague and Kladno for leadership of the movement which found expression in the literature of the time.[72] The Czech communists regarded themselves in some way as slightly superior in that they had actually taken a greater or lesser part in a successful revolution, had set up a rudimentary but effective system of revolutionary newspapers and cells outside the SDP and, the trump card, could count on the support of Lenin and the Comintern. Šmeral had still to be listened to because his popularity among the working class was undeniable, but as an ideologist he was in competition with Lenin which could, in their view, have only one result. Muna, Rydlo, Friedrich and Pergl, hence, had no hesitation in accepting financial and other support from Russia. It simply continued the practice begun in Kiev and Moscow. Šmeral however was loath on principle to allow the movement to be based even in the smallest degree on foreign money. Tactically it was a mistake, for it would inevitably come out and give the Orthodox SDs further opportunities for counter-agitation. Secondly, he remembered the experience of the pre-war years in which the domination of the party by the Austrian SDP had seriously hindered the development of the Czech section. Thirdly, he felt bound to raise the question of the survival of the radical socialists if Soviet Russia were destroyed by the Whites or Allied intervention. Finally, his cautious nature compelled him to bide his time until the consequences of accepting aid became clear.

The differences between them were accentuated after the sweeping victory of the SDP in the local elections which, though it hoisted the Orthodox SD, Tusar, to the head of a new government, brought few significant changes in either its composition or policies. The party political and governmental institutions were held to be incapable of achieving the objectives of the radical socialists. Alienated from the National Assembly for the way it had set itself up and also for its continual postponement of a general election, the Kladno radicals at Muna's instigation[73] precipitated a conflict between direct and representative democracy.

The most conspicuous sign of this trend was an attempt in Kladno to organize elections to a Workers Council. As a proletarian institution, it had a dual purpose. It was first a weapon against profiteering, a problem which the government was incapable of solving. Secondly, it was expected to provide an alternative to the SD unions which were still more or less loyal to the Orthodox SDs. Although the results of the Kladno election showed that much had still to be done to gain general acceptance,[74] it posed a significant threat to the Orthodox SDs to the extent that the repudiation of Workers Councils became one of the Eight Conditions by which the Orthodox SDs expected to achieve the proscription of the radical socialists from the party.[75] Workers councils as a form of political struggle were more closely associated with the Kladno radicals than with Šmeral, particularly after September 1920. However, he agreed with Zápotocký's view that all workers irrespective of political persuasion and members of the intelligentsia should take part in their formation at local, district and regional levels. He valued them as institutions free from the influence of the Orthodox SDs and the bourgeois parties and a solution to the problem posed by sympathizers of radical socialism who felt unable or unwilling to make a formal commitment to the party. To a significant degree then, this was part of his plan to exert continuous pressure on the institutions of government at all levels of society which would gradually crumble under the volume of protest. The main attack would of course be led by the SDP organs once the Orthodox SDs had been removed. But he reserved an important role for the councils as essentially non-party institutions helping to harness and organize the spontaneous social movement which would go far in meeting the demands of urban and local administration at the onset of the transition to a socialist state. He was also positively disposed towards them as they offered the germ of a solution to the nationalities problem, as the Bohumín workers councils jointly run by Poles and Czechs appeared to indicate.[76] Not least, he recognized their value as organs allowing the direct participation of the masses in the regulation of those aspects of their daily lives which were deeply affected by the Orthodox SDs' failure to solve their economic and social problems. To that extent, they would be willing assistants in the administration of socialized industry and agriculture.

Šmeral did not entirely agree with Muna and Zápotocký, who in 1919 had purveyed councils as a control organ on parliament with the power of veto[77] but in reality regarded them as the active organ of the revolution providing the organizational basis for a seizure of power.[78] His personal acquaintanceship with the Spartacist movement led him to conclude that councils of workers and soldiers when armed tended to give an enlarged significance to those revolutionaries who were tempted to achieve a revolution by the shortest route. Historically this often did not accord with the aspirations of the radical socialist workers and sent the uncommitted over to the side of the reaction. In any case, the tales of revolutionary councils obliterating society in Berlin and Budapest were having their own effect.

The government believed the radicals in Kladno could mobilize 50 to 60,000 strikers in a few hours[79], though the same could not be said of other areas. Indeed the level of radical agitation was intense everywhere, but it was characterized as much by its spontaneous and haphazard nature as by its magnitude. Partly to rectify these matters and partly to introduce some degree of coordination in the movement nationwide, the Marxist Left emerged. This marked the onset of the radical socialists' severest test for the Republic, the culmination of which gave Šmeral little choice other than to resign himself to the Czech communists view of the party and its role in the revolution. This marked a basic shift in Šmeral's opinion. His ultimate aim of socialization was in his view realizable only by legislation or by the workers own initiative.[80] The former had failed. It remained then to introduce a new Commission for Socialization based on the organizations of the working class and factory- and workers-councils, which however gave no place to union, cooperative and party organizations as their roles obstructed the intensification of class struggle, the precondition for a social revolution. Šmeral distanced himself from haphazard violence as the method of the political struggle of the workers councils and saw in them rather the basis for the education of the proletariat to its own mass, revolutionary action.[81] Unlike Muna, he made no attempt to impose a rigid and narrow command structure on them. On the contrary, he urged the widest supporters of the movement to decide their own future political line. He insisted that only a democratic dictatorship of the proletariat could gain and hold power in the state while Muna's solution, which depended on a small minority of individuals imposing their will in historical conditions often not lending themselves to a revolution, was from the beginning anti-democratic and if successful would lead only to a society based on the values of the army.

## THE CHALLENGE OF RADICAL SOCIALISTS 95

By the end of 1919, the radical socialists had a majority in the SDP insofar as fifteen regional organizations from the total of 26 in Bohemia, Moravia and Silesia fully endorsed the Programme of the Marxist Left.[82] The Orthodox SDs did not feel strong enough to expel the majority and anyway, one of them, the Prime Minister Tusar, was against a split which would have likely led to their enforced withdrawal from the coalition. What was worse, a government made up entirely of bourgeois parties would ultimately have favoured the radical socialists, perhaps even provoking a putsch. Šmeral too was against a splitting of the party. It would not only confuse the masses if two parties were in existence both claiming to be the heirs of social democracy, thereby decisively affecting his tactic of winning over the great majority of the industrial workers. But it would tend to give the initiative to the Czech communists, recently reinforced by the Hungarians who had played prominent roles in Kun's government,[83] strengthening their commitment to violent revolution and the Comintern. On the other hand, his agitation policy depended on maintaining access to the largest number of local organizations. This however was a mixed blessing. Initially, it helped to bring the anarchists into the movement who supported Muna in pressing for the early founding of a communist party.[84] Secondly, his open-arms policy allowed many people entry, who more properly belonged in other parties or indeed in none at all.

Šmeral went into the first national election in the Republic with the Orthodox SDs. However this did not imply a change of heart on his side nor even support for parliament as the ultimate means of change. He had earlier given notice that on no account would he tolerate the participation of the SDP in a coalition.[85] The national election was rather a useful device allowing the people to pass judgement on the previous tactic and policy of the Orthodox SDs, although the continued existence of the radical socialists in the SDP does not make it easy to discern whether SD voters cast their votes for the Orthodox SDs or the radicals. Nevertheless, the Czech SDP emerged as the largest party in parliament with 74 mandates in the Lower House. The Orthodox SDs were surprised by the result as they believed their commitment to coalition government would cost them many seats. Their success was put down to the effective agitation of the Marxist Left, who indeed gained 24 mandates on their own account.[86] The relative decline of the CSP suggested that the radicals had won over some of their supporters, but they had had greater success in the army. They had successfully played on the soldiers' fears of becoming embroiled in a new war, this time against Russia.[87] But parliament remained only secondary to the tactic of class struggle expressed through the mass strike which was expected to be the most powerful weapon in the armoury of the radical socialists once the Orthodox SDs had acceded to the legitimate demands for a party congress. The final stage of Šmeral's challenge was the attempt to achieve the democratic change of the party leadership which, having failed, placed him squarely in a situation where he was caught between his own democratic socialist values and the revolutionary attitudes of Muna, which, if they had been applied nationwide, might for a time have brought some success. As it was, Šmeral was caught unprepared, surprised at the Orthodox SDs refusal to accept that they were in a minority yet unable to counter their manoeuvres in any way which gave the radical socialists a chance of taking power.

Pressure on the Orthodox SDs did not abate after the general election victory of the SDP. The new government, despite being under the nominal control of SD ministers, bore a close resemblance to previous governments and was unable to maintain its popularity among those who had voted for the SDP in expectation of immediate solutions to their economic problems. Quite apart from a wave of strikes which coincided with Muna's release from prison under a general amnesty, there were signs that the Orthodox SDs had lost overall control of the party to Šmeral. Němec and Soukup broke with them as they were convinced it was only a matter of time before the Party Congress turned them out of the Executive and government. They formed a centre caucus with Stivín and Brodecký against both the Orthodox SDs and Šmeral. In effect it was a reflection of their opposition to Tusar who, while they accepted his stand on the necessity of coalition, had badly let down the proletariat on many basic economic questions.

On the other hand, this centre group attacked Šmeral for his reliance on mass action. They regarded this as an inherently unstable and undesirable method for a predominantly proletarian party which could take the initiative away from the more or less bourgeois party-intelligentsia on whom its organization was normally dependent. Stivín saw in the massive influx of inexperienced urban youth into the radical socialists a grave threat, not only to himself as an old party worker in danger of being pushed aside, but also in the new emphasis on ideology.[88] Many of them he classified as bourgeois dilettantes inspired by fashion or place-hunting. However, the new centre caucus could do little to halt the progress of the Marxist Left particularly in the light of its success in Moravia. The movement in defence of Russia brought new defeats for the Orthodox SDs not simply in the refusal of Škoda workers to make weapons but also in the paralysis of the main west-east railway artery. The winning over of Hybeš and the old Brno Centralists to the cause and the introduction of workers councils in the largest towns in Moravia indicated their declining authority, although the calls of the Czech communists in Prostějov to arm the proletariat[89] with the weapons railway workers had seized in Břeclav and Přerov[90] were clear symptoms that the radical socialist movement was neither united nor under Šmeral's control. However he maintained his stand on winning over the party from below and his policy was to a degree justified by the popular mood which forced Tusar to take no part in the convening of Second International.

The Orthodox SDs meanwhile were forced to address themselves to the problems posed by the expected success of the Left at the September Congress. The claims of Šmeral to have an absolute majority in the party appeared to be well-founded. Bechyně had discovered that the Brno workers overwhelmingly supported the radical socialists who were in control of the Regional Executive.[91] Apart from the city and district of Brno, the Marxist Left had a majority support in most of western and central Moravia. Ostrava was a notable exception where Prokeš secured the rejection of the Programme of the Marxist Left by attacking both Šmeral and the Orthodox SDs for attempting to split the party. He argued for the way of the centre caucus represented by Stivín.[92] Regional and local SD conferences had also discussed the question of sending delegates to the Congress which reflected the numerical preponderance of Šmeral's supporters. There seem to be few grounds for disputing Peroutka's estimate that two-thirds of the delegates were in the radical socialist camp.[93] It came as no surprise when the Orthodox SDs resigned from the government apparently in response to the opposition in the lower echelons of the party and outside it. However the real thrust of their challenge to Šmeral lay in forcing him to show his hand with an unambiguous statement of his aims. These were felt to be too radical for a large part of his support and bound to alarm them. The real struggle hence was about the party whose unity Šmeral had tried religiously to maintain despite the opposition of Muna and Lenin. He and his supporters were declared to be withdrawn from the party and the party Congress postponed.

Šmeral was expected to found a new radical socialist party in conjunction with the new Central Council of the Union of Communist Groups.[94] However Šmeral regarded the Orthodox SDs' act as a flagrant breach of democracy. Quite apart from the contentiousness of an unelected Executive representing a minority claiming authority to exclude or otherwise expel the majority, there was the question of the Orthodox SDs arrogating to themselves powers properly those of the Party Congress. Secondly, their resolution asserted that Šmeral's programme was communist, when in reality the bulk of it was drawn from the party programme of May 1918. The Orthodox SDs hence could not claim to be the legitimate heirs of social democracy as they had abandoned the old programme of the party. Finally, it was clear that the decision to postpone the Congress was not, as the Executive insisted, intended to allow regional organizations more time to discuss the conditions of entry to the Comintern, but an adroit move placing the ball in Šmeral's court. In effect, it was an invitation, either to a violent reaction, which would have given substance to their claims that he was a Bolshevik, or to found a new party, which would have taken the problem away from the confines of the party altogether and likewise from the government. Whatever the rights and wrongs of the argument, the demands of the state supported the Orthodox SDs and whatever happened, Šmeral could not avoid the squeeze between the Czech communists, to whom arguments about democracy and legitimacy were more or less irrelevant when a situation offering an opportunity to achieve a revolution was emerging before their eyes, and the radicalized masses who in the vital moment were paralysed by doubt and sensitive to the charges of lack of patriotism explicit in the Orthodox SDs' assertion that a revolution was the negation of the state.

Although there were elements in the radical socialist movement which were new in terms of the traditions of social democracy, most notably workers councils, support for III International and the presence of the Czech communists, the greater part of the Marxist Left had won its support on the old programme of social democracy and even maintained the old statutes of organization. The Orthodox SDs had placed themselves in a position which displayed a more or less contemptuous attitude to Šmeral's essentially democratic values. More important, their relation to the state insulated them from removal from their leading positions in the party. This placed Šmeral in a quandary. He had the option of maintaining his policy of uniting the rank and file and the local organizations without the Orthodox SDs, in the hope that within a short time they would accept the will of the majority members and resign, leaving him in outright control of the party. However given the support of their allies in the bourgeois parties, there was no reason to expect them to succumb quickly. Notions of democracy and political legitimacy flew out of the window when the state was perceived to be under a more or less direct challenge.

In Šmeral's view, it was imperative not to split the party thereby giving the initiative to the Orthodox SDs who had maintained that this had been his ultimate purpose all along. The problem therefore lay in organizing the majority of the party in such a way as to be able to remove the Orthodox SDs without giving in to the Czech communists whose violent solution grew daily more attractive among the frustrated and tended to strengthen their

THE CHALLENGE OF RADICAL SOCIALISTS 99

hand. Šmeral was by most democratic norms justified in going ahead with the Congress as planned, although it clearly would not be attended by the Orthodox SDs and neither would it solve his basic problem of how to remove them and the other vital question, the winning of the allegiance of the significant proportion of waverers in the party and SD unions. While he could reasonably claim that the Orthodox SDs had forfeited their authority within the party and hence were in no position to insist on pledges disclaiming support for the Third International nor on special conditions on members acting as Congress delegates,[95] another apparently arbitrary ruling which attempted to cut at the root of Šmeral's support by excluding "the recruits of socialism" as Stivín dubbed them, it was a different matter when it came to imposing the will of the radical socialists on the state.

The tactic of the Orthodox SDs gave rise to a more resolute approach on Šmeral's part which involved the property of the party. The radicals took control of the "People's House" in Prague and thereby embarked on a course of action which brought them into conflict with the law. It appeared that Šmeral had won the argument over democracy and legitimacy in the party, but his tactic was found to be wanting when he attempted to wrest control of the party organs from the Executive. His majority in the party gave him the moral right to take control of *Pravo lidu,* but there were no legal means of achieving it, so he simply occupied the building. Yet not wishing to break the bounds of legality, he accepted a change in the newspaper's name. The whole tenor of his strategy indicated that his primary interest was to retain the old familiar ways in the party. He tried to avoid precipitate leaps which would only tend to alarm his supporters who were in the main not at all Bolshevik but more intent on rectifying the Orthodox SDs' revision of the party programme and destroying the élitism in the SDP. Šmeral therefore went ahead with the Congress observing all the organizational and procedural regulations of the party with meticulous care. Of the 527 delegates present, most of whom had received their credentials from the Orthodox SDs well before the Congress, 321 supported Šmeral and the Left.[96] His admirable display of democratic rectitude was not only an important part of his personal philosophy. It was also intended to win over the marginal proletarian adherents of other parties, especially in the CSP, and also medium peasants and small tradesmen whose fears about nationalization Šmeral stilled at the Congress.[97] In pursuit of this aim, he adopted a new slogan "By degrees!" which excluded any recourse to revolutionary violence and he also rejected the strong minority support favouring the founding of an international communist paty. The real enemies were, in his view, not the Orthodox SDs but the Agrarian party which had dominated the political system of the Republic since its inception.[98]

Yet the Orthodox SDs did not allow the radical socialists any more time and space to conduct the conflict as they wished. Their recourse to the law on the question of the party's property laid down the lines of struggle which caught Šmeral unprepared. The legal judgement went against him and, although the moral outrage whipped up by the ruling added to the unpopularity of the Orthodox SDs, he was unable to mobilize opinion in effective defence. It was irrelevant to suggest that the size of his movement was evidence that Šmeralism corresponded more closely than any other party to the Czech social environment in that its solutions were perceived to be more realistic. When the chips were down and he had secured the isolation of the Establishment MPs, he was nevertheless still confronted with the problem of removing them.

To this extent, his real political strength was not all as it seemed. It is fair to say that he had been surprised by the tactic of the Orthodox SDs whose resignation from the government and attempts to proscribe the majority in the party came at a vital moment arresting the flow and growth of the mass movement. It affected Šmeral's challenge in at least two important ways. The resignation of the Orthodox SDs from the government had not affected the positions of the large minority of functionaries loyal to them in regional and local party secretariats. Šmeral hence was only in a position to carry out his revolution through the party organizations controlled by the radical socialists. Yet these were not sufficiently well-organized for that purpose nor were the leaders of the various sections in agreement on what tactics should be. While Burian and the old Brno Centralists stood closest to Šmeral, the preponderance of Czech communists in leading positions in the towns of Western and Central Moravia together with their strong influence in Kladno and parts of Northern Bohemia indicated conclusively that there was no unanimity on this point. Šmeral was unwilling to preach open rebellion, as Tusar predicted. Rather, he relied on workers gradually taking over a decaying state organization from the regions and working towards the centre. In the light of the unsolved Czech-German nationality problems, which erupted again in November 1920, and the workers' suspicions of the connection between communism and revanchism, rebellion was out of the question. Šmeral was in an almost impossible position in that his power to determine the course of events measured against the results of the legal judgment on the "People's House" affair was neither adequate to prevent the Orthodox SDs winning the argument nor was his overall strategy seen by the Czech communists as convincing enough to warrant another chance, and after the failure of the general strike in December 1920, they lost all patience. The mass movement was not given time, as Šmeral wanted, to mature to its own forms of revolutionary action. A conspicuous failure was the institution of workers councils which did not provide an effective basis for mass political struggle. Though many were founded before and some in the aftermath of the strike, there was no agreement about their role, some viewing them as in competition with trade unions, others as revived local national committees. At all events, they did not come up to expectations as the Brno police director noted.[99] Šmeral's insistence that the revolutionary movement had to come from below reflected his democratic values. Yet in late 1920 before the strike, it engendered a passivity which turned out to be fatal. The radical socialists' consciousness of their own numerical superiority led only to a mood of great tension and expectancy,[100] but when the conflict broke out, it was expressed, with exceptions, only in more or less violent strike action. In Kladno and the environs of Brno, it went as far as an armed revolt. Yet Šmeral was right in predicting that the threat of violence would induce the unions to proclaim their neutrality. This was of decisive importance in the struggle. The transfer of leadership to Kladno where the communists resorted to arms had a similar affect on the workers of the CSP and of other parties. The SD unions' neutrality alone took some 750,000 workers out of the struggle[101] and, although the rebels for a time made serious breaches in the continuity of state power, they were unable to construct a lasting basis on which a revolution could have survived.

To a degree, Šmeral was successful in the December events. The strike had not been organized nor led, as the communists observed. But Šmeral's main interest, a revolution from below, had been shown to be possible. The immense number of small rebellions which broke out in town and country[102] seemed to indicate that a mass democratic revolution was not in the realm of fantasy. In the conditions of the time, nationally and internationally, it would have been anyway unlikely for an armed revolution on the Bolshevik model to have survived. His mistakes then were not in having resisted the Leninist model of party organization and discipline, but in not having found a way to buy sufficient time so that the inherent difficulties posed by the winning of proletarian allegiance and the working out of the nationality problems in benefit of his movement could have been solved. As it was, he was left with no other alternative than to resign himself to the tutelage of the Comintern and accept that his special road was at least for the time being redundant.

*Chapter 4*

**The Economic Demands**

Radical socialism derived considerable support from those sections of the population in the Czech Lands who experienced a drastic decline in living standards in the war-years. This economic background was of great significance for Šmeral's movement as it provided the setting and illustrated the environment in which it developed. It is not suggested that all groups in society pauperized or otherwise reduced economically by the war and its aftermath sought redress in or through the radical socialist movement. Certain classes perceived their plight to be due to causes quite at variance with those the radical socialists regarded as the source of economic deprivation and turned towards other forms of radical political organization, for example, the conservative German National Socialists. Yet, the bleak outlook deriving from the economic situation suggests that there are grounds for believing that discontent could be expected to develop in those classes or groups in society who found themselves in conditions of poverty or relative impoverishment.

Their responses to the situation depended on a variety of factors, not least their class allegiance and their view of the nature of their penury. Often their perceptions of solutions met and influenced those proposed by the radical socialists and the organized exponents of these demands, in all likelihood stood to gain as they provided the most effective channel through which discontent could be expressed. Yet although they were well-placed in party and state to give voice to popular resentment, the situation was exceptionally fluid and support for them was uneven. This ultimately had an important bearing on the real relations of power in the state. Although expressions of defiance for the government were often focussed on issues of local significance—many strikes, for example, were organized to remove unpopular factory-and-estate-managers or were struggles for the reinstatement of dismissed workers—the great majority were called in response to the economic situation in which employment, wages and prices occupied a central position. Those on the economic margins of society did not simply respond with petitions to party or government. Most dramatic were the riots or breaches of the civil order which were frequently spontaneous and only occasionally initiated by organized radical socialists. Most frequent were strikes, whose extent often led the government to the misleading conclusion that Šmeral's movement was more powerful than in fact was the case. Nevertheless the economic demands of the popular movement provide an important insight into the character of the support for the radical socialists and help to explain why in the conditions of the time, they could not be realized.

The war brought great hardship to many people in the Czech Lands as indeed it did to the other succession states. However, it did not affect all classes equally. Side by side with the impoverishment of certain classes of people went varying degrees of enrichment. Both aspects affected the configuration of class forces. With the exception of certain border areas, Czechoslovakia did not form a major arena for military action in wartime. Nevertheless, the departure of men to the front had in the medium-term an important affect on the post-war supply situation. It affected agriculture more than industry where labour, especially in the war industries, was more urgently required and was left more or less untouched.

In the countryside, the family economy of the small, landless and poor tenant farmers was hardest hit and many indeed were ruined as they had neither the necessary tools nor labour to maintain their small plots of land as going concerns. Agricultural production on these settlements was barely enough to keep them alive. The overall level of production was influenced too by the necessity to supply food for the war effort and the orientation of industry to war production which led to a sharp decrease of agricultural machinery and tools. This was reflected in the gradual reduction of sown land for cereals, the growth of meadows and uncultivated land and in the visible decline of yields per hectare. Production of basic agricultural goods also fell, most by at least a third, and in one case, barley, by nearly two thirds. This had its affect on animal husbandry and there was a distinct move away from traditional livestock to goats and sheep in Bohemia and Moravia, which reflected the turn towards an animal economy based on smaller economic units using less labour. Not all farms were affected to the same degree. As regards requisition, for example, the larger peasant owning farmers were often enabled to shift the major burden onto the medium and small peasants. With their horses and oxen requisitioned, the small peasants in particular were removed of the possibility to till their land. The medium farmers with the necessary land, the means to employ labour and their working animals more or less intact were able to maintain production, a significant part of which found its way onto the black market. Those medium and small peasant farmers who contrived to save some produce from the requisitioning agents also made money in this way but to a considerably lesser degree.

Two aspects of the situation in particular contributed to the formation of the two sets of economic demands in the countryside which in the post-war period worked themselves out in the confrontation between the Agrarians and the SDP. The worsening of the economic condition of the landless and poor peasants led to their radicalization, although it was more gradual than in urban areas where hardship was more intense. Their demands were directed against the war and for a piece of the land in the hands of the foreign and aristocratic great landed magnates. Part of the wealthier peasants but mainly the larger owning farmers, having gained from the lack of food and resulting high prices, had the means yet were prevented by fideikomis from buying these lands. The interests of the landless and the medium farmers hence collided head-on after the war when the nationalization of the great estates made land available.[2]

On balance, the urban industrial workers were harder hit by the worsening supply situation, price inflation and the fall in real wages. In addition, they were affected by factors of a non-economic nature which nonetheless had some bearing on their economic position. The introduction of a semi-military regime in factories producing war materials had led to an increase in working hours. The end of the war released the working class from the worst evils of this system which the unions had felt powerless to obstruct as resistance was treated as tantamount to mutiny and dealt with accordingly. The expected immediate improvement in the workers' economic position did not materialize in the early post-war years. The supply situation remained as critical as it had been in the last stages of the war. Chronic under-nourishment was at least partially a cause in the abrupt increase in the illness and mortality rates. The most common cause of death in Prague at this time was tuberculosis of the lungs[3] which typically is related to poverty. The supply system tended to break down as a result of the government's inability to collect quotas and transport them to retail outlets. The poor harvest of 1918 and the export of a considerable part of it to the German parts of the Empire or to the war fronts by the Austrian authorities aggravated the situation. The rapid import of food was impossible as a consequence of the railway system's inability to cope with it and of the continuing link between Czech and Imperial currency. Indeed, four months elapsed before the first supplies of American flour arrived. Government appeals mainly to medium peasant farmers not to hoard food went largely unheeded.[4] Their refusal to sell at official prices provoked widespread urban resentment against them as a class and this in turn hardened the peasant farmers' attitudes to the controlled economy which many regarded as socialism through the back-door. The grimmest period lasted from the liberation until Spring 1919, yet even in Summer 1920, when 1,200 wagons of corn were loaned by Austria, there was little to suggest that a basic improvement had taken place. This was due in large measure to the Ministry of Supply which was unable to enforce supply quotas for requisitioning of which, in the first quarter of 1919, only two-thirds were filled.[5] Martial law too was introduced in border areas, among other reasons, to prevent illegal exports of food.

Apart from the lack of goods, other factors gave an impetus to price inflation notably the government's decision to overstamp all Imperial banknotes. This was an attempt to check the flood of newly printed Austrian money into the country, which was chasing the lower price level. The immediate effect of the overstamping was a fall in the internal value of the Czech crown by 50%. The lack of money on the side of more or less impoverished urban industrial workers and the lack of confidence displayed by agrarian sellers of goods gave rise to a system of barter. The departure of large numbers of the urban poor into the countryside in search of food caused a shift of wealth and other forms of property from town to country. Not only did local shopkeepers benefit from this situation, so too did the great estate owners. The popular urban reaction to their role in black-marketeering was reflected in part in demands for their expropriation and socialization. Profiteering was not restricted to the countryside. The black market flourished in the towns where industrialists, wholesalers and middle-men of all manner of size and description took the opportunity to enrich themselves. As small-scale price speculation was more clearly visible in smaller towns and villages, it was not infrequently characterized as an essentially petty-bourgeois preoccupation and one associated with the medium peasants and village and urban small tradesmen. This impression was strong especially among the urban workers and it was reinforced by stories of violent peasant resistance to requisitioning. Yet attacks on small commercial properties tended to disguise the fact that the supply of over-priced goods came largely from the great industrial and landed magnates.

The war brought about an exceptional process of social differentiation. One feature was an increase in the ownership of property. The official figures[6] below are not without fault. Nevertheless they indicate certain shifts of wealth which affected various social classes in different ways. The political expressions of these classes reflected a hardening of their attitudes particularly towards the property-less. (see Table 1)

## Table 1
## Ownership of Property

| Property in 1000s of crowns | Number of people with property | | | | Property in millions of crowns | | | |
|---|---|---|---|---|---|---|---|---|
| | 1914 | % | 1919 | % | 1914 | % | 1919 | % |
| up to 10 | 1,408,212 | 66.15 | 2,237,871 | 61.18 | 5,449 | 14.36 | 5,598 | 6.75 |
| 10–20 | 342,578 | 16.09 | 563,881 | 15.42 | 4,815 | 12.69 | 8,015 | 9.67 |
| 20–30 | 134,977 | 6.34 | 264,503 | 7.23 | 3,299 | 8.70 | 6,472 | 7.81 |
| 30–50 | 121,079 | 5.69 | 241,825 | 6.61 | 4,656 | 12.27 | 9,314 | 11.23 |
| 50–100 | 82,439 | 3.87 | 205,107 | 5.61 | 5,589 | 14.73 | 14,326 | 17.28 |
| 100–250 | 29,083 | 1.37 | 115,811 | 3.17 | 4,267 | 11.25 | 16,998 | 20.50 |
| 250–500 | 6,475 | 0.31 | 19,723 | 0.54 | 2,210 | 5.83 | 6,630 | 8.00 |
| 500–1000 | 2,389 | 0.11 | 6,072 | 0.16 | 1,622 | 4.28 | 4,098 | 4.94 |
| 1000–2000 | 912 | 0.04 | 1,987 | 0.05 | 1,240 | 3.27 | 2,687 | 3.24 |
| over 2000 | 655 | 0.03 | 1,154 | 0.03 | 4,788 | 12.62 | 8,774 | 10.58 |
| TOTAL | 2,128,799 | 100.00 | 3,657,934 | 100.00 | 37,935 | 100.00 | 82,912 | 100.00 |

In 1910, the population of the Czech Lands with Slovakia was recorded as 13,669,259[7] of whom 2,128,799 were classified as having property, excluding personal articles, i.e. clothes and furniture, likewise precious metals and objets d'art. By 1919 with a slightly lower population (13,613,172 - October 1918 figure) this number had risen by over a million to 3,657,934. Even allowing for inflation which we shall consider shortly, the lowest group had expanded by more than half. However, as the upper borderline is 10,000 kč, just above the average yearly wage of an industrial worker which stood at 8-9,000 kč, there are no compelling grounds for assuming that, at this level, there was a significant degree of social and economic mobility upwards. Of all property owners, those with assets under 10,000 kč experienced the lowest percentage increase. From the group owning 20-30 thousand kč to those with 1-2 million, there was roughly a 100% increase in each group. Yet the greatest increase was seen in the groups from 50,000 to 1 million kčs, especially 100,000 to 250,000, who recorded a percentage rise in terms of total wealth of the nation, from 11.25% to 20.50%.

As fortunes were made in the war most conspicuously by medium farmers and by businessmen engaged in the food industry, in which Czechs played the dominant role, it may be safe to conclude that their wealth was generated by the scarcity of goods and their overall control of the flow of agricultural production. Great wealth was also made by industrialists engaged in production for the war effort. But until 1921, when Czechs came to predominate in heavy and allied industries,[8] these fortunes were made more by the Germans, who were given advantages when a shift in industrial production brought the Czech Lands an increased share of heavy industry to fulfill the demand for war materials. The primary characteristic of Czech industry after the war was the predominance of light over heavy industry.[9] Except for food and leather goods, the Germans controlled the production of light industrial consumer goods and we may have legitimate reasons for supposing that they would be well-represented in the burgeoning middle property groups.

At the top of the scale, we find in 1919, 1154 millionaires whose total assets exceeded by more than one-half those of the lowest group numbering some 2.3 million individuals. This latter group, while not of primary interest to Šmeral who appealed to the urban property-less and especially skilled worker proletarians to provide the backbone of his movement, did have the potential of being drawn into the political struggle whose principal aim was the destruction of the powerful bourgeois interests in medium and large-scale industrial and agricultural concerns. Unlike other radical socialists, he did not dismiss small property owners out of hand but, perhaps mistakenly, believed they would aid the movement, given the protection of their small financial interests, without bringing to it the values harmful to proletarian interests associated with the medium property-owning classes.

At the other end of society were the urban industrial poor. In general, they were worse off than their counterparts in the countryside, an environment which afforded greater possibilities for obtaining food if not much else. The question of prices and wages was a vital concern for the urban workers, as was unemployment benefit for those without gainful employment. The directive from the Ministry of Supply to all local administrations in Bohemia and Moravia to fix and publish maximum prices for subsistence goods[10] proved to be ineffective as a means of checking the rise in prices. Quite apart from black-market prices, over which it had no control, the index of official prices continued to rise until its peak in 1921. Exact statistics of the cost of living were not kept in the war-period, but an approximate guide to the movement of prices of basic goods can be gleaned from retail prices published by the Ministry of Supply in 1920.[11] These figures, which are reproduced below, place official and black-market prices side by side and, it should be added, were drawn only from prices in Prague as a result of the difficulties in gaining reliable and complete information from other areas. One major

Table 2
Retail Prices in Prague, 1913–1921 (1913 = 100)

| Year | Unweighted index of official prices of 38 kinds of goods. | Unweighted index of black market prices for 24 kinds of goods. |
|---|---|---|
| 1913 | 100 | 100 |
| 1914 | 112 | 194 |
| 1915 | 192 | 425 |
| 1916 | 248 | 796 |
| 1917 | 389 | 1,495 |
| 1918 | 660 | 2,373 |
| 1919 | 990 | — |
| 1920 | 1,750 | — |
| 1921 | 1,914* | — |

*Estimate based on calculation of the Index of the Sús from 1921 using the methods of the Ministry of Supply.

deficiency of the indices is that they are not weighted. Nevertheless they form a useful guide, when set against income, of the likely constraints on consumption placed upon urban industrial workers which contributed to their resentment and led a part to radical socialism. (see Table 2)

It is clear that official retail prices in 1918 were 6 or 7 times higher than the year before war broke out. By 1921, the figure had reached 19. Black market prices recorded only until 1918 rose by at least 23 times compared with 1913 and it is tenable to assume a further rise until early 1922 when prices began to fall. It is in addition of importance to note that coal, a basic means of heating and cooking, rose by 7 times on the black market. The table reproduced below[12] gives a helpful overview of the rise in prices until 1921 and the stabilization which followed in subsequent years. (see Table 3)

In a situation of constantly rising prices, both on and off the official markets, the buying power of workers' wages was also progressively reduced. Nominal wages rose twice over between 1913 and 1918 but the yearly increase in peace-time was greater: in 1919 — 69.7%; 1920 — 71.2% and 1921 — 60.5%. Indeed in 1921 the average Czech worker with all allowances and emoluments earned 30.97kč daily and 7,741.50 kč per annum, the highest annual average worker's wage until the Second World War. A caveat however should be added to these figures set out in detail in Table 4.[13] For their own purposes, the data collecting body set the upper figure of wages at 12,000 kč per annum when it was known that a greater proportion of the workers than before earned over 12,000 kč. There were in all likelihood fewer in this category in 1919 and 1920 when the average wage level was well beneath this upper limit. It does not seem unreasonable to conclude that the average industrial worker earned in 1921 about 32-34 kč per day or 8000-9000 kč per annum.[14] (see Table 4)

The relation between wages and official prices drawn from the quoted figures is presented below. (see Table 5) It does not take into account black-market prices. At the end of the war, the buying power of the Czech crown fell roughly to a third of its pre-war level and, in 1921 when conditions began to pick up, it reached about 55%-60% of this level. No account is taken of the differences in quality of goods or food between the pre- and post-war periods which had some affect on living costs and standards.

The sharp fall in real wages meant considerable hunger and want for most of the working class. Although there are no records of their patterns of consumption in the post-war years, it seems reasonable to assume that their diet was more or less restricted to the most basic kinds of food. Meat and

## Table 3
## Cost of Goods

| Kind of Goods | Prices in Crowns VII 1914 | Prices in Crowns 1921 | I 1921* | Index (July 1914 = 100) 1921 | Index (July 1914 = 100) 1922 | Index (July 1914 = 100) 1923 |
|---|---|---|---|---|---|---|
| Wheat flour (kilo) | 0.42 | 8.45 | 2478 | 2012 | 1149 | 757 |
| Pork (kilo) | 1.86 | 23.03 | 1544 | 1238 | 1203 | 994 |
| Pork fat (kilo) | 1.88 | 35.67 | 2264 | 1897 | 1332 | 1049 |
| Butter (kilo) | 2.70 | 48.81 | 1725 | 1808 | 1477 | 1006 |
| Milk (litre) | 0.23 | 3.31 | 1487 | 1439 | 1365 | 913 |
| Egg (per 1) | 0.07 | 1.21 | 2185 | 1729 | 1586 | 1157 |
| Sugar (kilo) | 0.85 | 9.07 | 1840 | 1067 | 811 | 595 |
| Potatoes (kilo) | 0.10 | 1.60 | 1240 | 1600 | 1440 | 510 |
| Beer (litre) | 0.36 | 3.20 | 800 | 889 | 964 | 781 |
| Brown coal (100 kilos) | 1.98 | 33.21 | 1905 | 1677 | 1553 | 1325 |
| Kerosene | 0.36 | 6.96 | 3711 | 1933 | 1061 | 717 |
| Soap | 0.73 | 19.90 | 3400 | 2726 | 1865 | 1171 |
| Woolen dress material (per metre) | 1.73 | 44.52 | 3206 | 2573 | 1799 | 1076 |
| Flannel (per metre) | 0.53 | 17.10 | 4600 | 3227 | 2013 | 1226 |
| Men's shoes (pair) | 13.68 | 215.75 | 1755 | 1577 | 1158 | 778 |
| Women's shoes (pair) | 11.87 | 195.27 | 1304 | 1649 | 1250 | 836 |

*Period of greatest scarcity.

## Table 4
## Average Wages Earned

| Czech Lands only (until 1920) | 1913 | 1918 | 1919 | 1920 | 1921 Czech Lands | 1921 Slovakia | 1921 Czechoslovakia |
|---|---|---|---|---|---|---|---|
| Average number of insured in 000s | 1119.2 | 662.9 | 810.1 | 994.7 | 1068.1 | 134.6 | 1202.7 |
| Index | 100.0 | 59.2 | 72.4 | 88.9 | 95.4 | — | — |
| Total of days worked | 299.6 | 162.0 | 200.2 | 252.3 | 267.0 | 29.0 | 296.0 |
| Average number of working days per insured person | 267.7 | 244.3 | 247.1 | 253.6 | 250.0 | 215.5 | 246.1 |
| Total wages for all insured persons (millions of crowns) | 911.1 | 1074.8 | 2255.7 | 4867.3 | 8269.0 | 833.0 | 9102.0 |
| Index | 100.0 | 118.0 | 247.6 | 534.2 | 907.6 | — | — |
| Average daily wage per insured person in crowns | 3.04 | 6.64 | 11.27 | 19.29 | 30.97 | 28.75 | 30.75 |
| Index | 100.0 | 218.4 | 370.7 | 634.5 | 1018.8 | — | — |
| Average yearly wage per insured person in crowns | 814.1 | 1621.2 | 2784.5 | 4893.2 | 7741.5 | 6191.6 | 7568.2 |
| Index | 100.0 | 199.2 | 342.0 | 601.1 | 950.9 | — | — |

## Table 5
### Relationship Between Wages and Prices

| Year | Index of retail prices of 38 kinds of goods in Prague | Index of average wages insured at Accident Insurance Companies | | | |
|---|---|---|---|---|---|
| | | Daily wage | | Annual wage | |
| | | nominal | real | nominal | real |
| 1913 | 100 | 100.0 | 100.0 | 100.0 | 100.0 |
| 1914 | 112 | 104.6 | 93.4 | 94.2 | 84.1 |
| 1915 | 192 | 111.2 | 57.9 | 104.0 | 54.2 |
| 1916 | 248 | 124.0 | 50.0 | 122.8 | 49.5 |
| 1917 | 389 | 161.1 | 41.4 | 154.9 | 39.8 |
| 1918 | 660 | 218.4 | 33.1 | 199.2 | 30.2 |
| 1919 | 990 | 370.7 | 37.4 | 342.0 | 34.5 |
| 1920 | 1750 | 634.5 | 36.2 | 601.1 | 34.3 |
| 1921 | 1914 | 1018.8 | 53.2 | 950.9 | 49.7 |

animal fats, which they had been accustomed to eating before the war, were for most people out of the question. There are no figures for agricultural workers for this period, but their general economic position in 1928[15] gives us grounds for assuming that it was hardly any better. Their monthly income ranged from 80-155 kč in Bohemia, 71-166 kč in Moravia and 79-100 kč in Slovakia. Allowances however should be made for certain benefits, notably some free food (60 kilos of flour or 80 kilos of wheat; 80 kilos of potatoes; 1 kilo of fat; 30 litres of milk), accommodation (a room in a cottage usually 12 square metres), fuel (4 cubic metres of firewood annually and 25 q of brown coal = 2400 kilos). In contrast to the average industrial or agricultural wage worker, were those at the top of the so-called "workers bureaucracy," leading officials in unions, social and educational institutions and workers sickness and pension insurance companies who by 1928 earned in the region of 3000 kč monthly.[16] Even further removed were the career politicians of the SDP, one of whom, Soukup, came in the course of time to own a great estate near Poděbrady and five apartment buildings in the centre of Prague.[17]

Unemployment was a problem which afflicted the Republic almost from its inception. In February 1919, the number of unemployed supported by the state stood at 267,000 for the Czech Lands.[18] This declined slightly in 1921 due to the renewal of production especially in light industry but by the cusp of 1922-23 had risen to about 440,000 people.[19] A significant part of the unemployed were, of course, demobilized soldiers who were allowed benefit of 4 kč per day. All others received from 60 hallers to 5 kč per day with an allowance of 1 kč for every dependent.[20] The law providing for unemployment benefit introduced in December 1918 was amended in February 1919 and as a result the level of support was lowered by 50%.[21] Although data from 1918 to 1920 is lacking, evidence from 1921 suggests that not all of the registered unemployed for one reason or another received benefit. For example, in May 1921, there were 108,600 unemployed of whom 47,200 received benefit. October's figures were 62,900 and 19,700 respectively.[22] In certain industrial areas which coincidentally were centres of militant socialism, notably Kladno, benefit was stopped completely.[23] Attempts to suspend payments in Trhové Svíny[24] and in towns in Moravia provoked serious riots forcing the authorities to abandon their plan.[25] In the countryside, the situation was worse. Day-labourers in agriculture were effectively reclassified and no longer deemed to be workers. Consequently, the government ceased to pay benefit altogether in 80 rural areas and reduced it in a further 103.[26]

Given the economic environment, there are grounds for believing that there was a good deal of poverty and that this affected the actions of the industrial working class more than, for example, the agricultural workers. Unlike the latter, the industrial proletariat did not enjoy the degree of economic protection regarding food and accommodation as the agricultural labourers did. Neither could they benefit from the opportunities deriving from social relations in the village and it is a moot point whether the higher wages in urban industrial areas compensated for this purely in terms of living standards. On the other hand, the consciousness of the urban proletariat that there were powerful union and party institutions to put their case made their reaction to their own impoverishment considerably more militant than was the case in the countryside. Here relations between the classes were more patriarchal and proprietorial and agrarian consciousness was in any case more readily influenced by the traditional notions of authority and respect associated with the Gemeinschaft.

Urban discontent among industrial workers manifested itself in a number of ways. There was a strong movement in favour of organization and from 150,000 members in early 1918, the SDP membership grew to 460,000 in September 1920.[27] Perhaps more significant for the daily economic struggle of working people was their decision to join unions, which grew enormously as a result and gave point to Šmeral's view that no armed revolt was necessary if the working class organized in the party and unions could be mobilized at the appropriate moment. In conditions of war and strong discouragement from the Austrian authorities, the trade union association, Odborové sdružení československé (hereafter OSČ), which was in a more or less close relationship with the SDP, had in wartime conditions (1917) about 43,000 members. By 1919, the membership had risen to 650,000 and in 1920, shortly before the split in the party, reached a peak of 856,305.[28] Discounting the Union of Agricultural Workers (115,000), this figure represents just under half of the 1.8 million workers organized in trade unions and about a quarter of all industrial workers. It included 180,000 women industrial workers who played a significant role in the SD election victories in 1919 and 1920 and likewise were active in organizing demonstrations against black marketeers, often without party or union approval. The SD unions nevertheless had the ability to exert popular pressure on governments of a kind hitherto unknown in the Czech Lands.

The forms of struggle adopted by the unions varied. In the early stages, their tactics were directed to gaining more members, first among those not organized in unions at all and then among workers organized in trade unions linked with rival political parties. In the conditions of the time, it was more or less impossible to win over the union members in the German union (ZDG). Efforts were made however among workers in the union of the CSP, Československá obec dělnická (ČOD) which in the chemical industry at least were conspicuously successful. However, their methods of conversion relied more often than not on intimidation. The public and proletarian opposition which this aroused contributed to the noticeable increase in the size of the ČOD.[29]

The most emphatic and wide-ranging form of popular discontent was expressed in the strike movement which from 1919 until 1922 attained hitherto unseen proportions. During this period when the pressure of the masses was at its height most of the important social reforms of the Republic were enacted. The last great strike of the war period organized by Šmeral had shown that specifically political aims could be combined with a general economic protest and to significant effect. Yet with the exception of the mass strike in Ostrava in early 1920 and the December General Strike, the mass mobilization of the workers was conspicuously lacking. The course and conduct of the strike wave gave Šmeral few grounds for optimism as far as the role of the unions was concerned. He was not so concerned by the fact that economic protest was regionalized and to that extent not so conspicuous. Nor was it that strikes were too few in number to exert any real pressure. As evidence below suggests, there was a considerable number. There are few, if any, indications in the official statistics of the incidence of unofficial strikes or of the size of the productive units in which they took place. Šmeral knew however that in many places union officials conspicuously failed to work for the achievement of the workers' economic demands and ignored their political demands altogether.[30] Workers from Karlín and Žižkov had joined the hunger riots in Prague in May 1919 complaining that their union leaders failed to represent them and indeed disregarded their instructions to turn back.[31] Šmeral was correct in his assertion that the union officials' management of strikes actually obstructed the intensification of class struggle. Their cautious attitude to strikes was governed by their fear of the mass movement getting out of hand. Yet while the divergence of opinion between rank and file workers and the worker bureaucracy gave strength to his movement, he could not effectively mobilize the masses until he had won over the union leaders. This was ultimately seen to be impossible as it was conditional on Šmeral first winning over the institutions of the party. The unions, both the OSČ and the ČOD, displayed great reluctance to be drawn into the political struggle. Strikes were called by them in which political demands were at the forefront, but most of these concerned the political freedoms which Muna's case represented.

## THE ECONOMIC DEMANDS 117

In general terms however, it seems, although statistical evidence is lacking, that small factories and workshops employing under 50 persons felt the brunt of the strike wave. This is not to say that the great concentrations of industry were free of strikes. Many were called in the factories of the "Red Ring" (Karlín, Vinohrady, Smichov and Žižkov) which began to form around Old Prague in 1920. But mass strikes were not the order of the day, neither there nor in Plzeň and Brno, until the December General Strike. It was called with specific political aims in mind yet Šmeral did not feel them to be compelling enough to attract the support of the unions to whom the workers still looked for guidance. He was hence forced to combine them with economic aims to win support from the unions who were ready within bounds to seek redress for the social and economic ills of the system, but unwilling to be a party to a movement directed more or less explicitly against the capitalist organization of production. (see details of strikes from 1919 on Table 6)[32]

From the available figures[33] giving the motive for strikes, 42% supported a demand for an increase in wages. A further 9.2% were against a lowering of wages. All others were classified as political strikes, although their aims, appear not to have been significantly different from strikes of a predominantly economic character. The length of the strikes in question on average 4.4 shifts (compared with 24.6 in 1923) is officially assumed to be an indication of their primarily political character. This seems to be questionable.

On the balance of the evidence so far presented, it is reasonable to assume that the economic environment forced certain classes, above all others, to address themselves to basic problems of economic survival. This led directly to the burgeoning of the unions who, for better or worse, occupied a leading position in the frontline struggle and through which the fight for higher wages and better conditions was fought. It also led to a radicalization of the mass of industrial workers which was expressed in the rapid growth in the SDP and in the number of votes cast for the party at elections. The pressure of the mass movement played an important part in inducing the government to introduce certain of the radical socialists' political demands onto the statute book. The May 1918 programme of the SDP formed the basis of the Minimum Demands of Škoda-Plzeň[34] and cropped up in the many other petitions to the government which emanated from all parts of the Republic.[35] Many of their political demands were acceded to. The form of the state was republican. Universal suffrage was the normal method of electing governments, even if in practice the most powerful parties at the polls were sometimes excluded from a share in government. The radical socialists' plan for proportional representation for national minorities had gone awry, but in the conditions of the time, that was not unexpected. Fundamental political

## Table 6
## Strikes 1919–1923

|  | 1919 | 1920 | 1921 | 1922 | 1923 |
|---|---|---|---|---|---|
| Number of strikes (excl. lock-outs) | 242 | 590 | 424 | 263 | 225 |
| Number of factories affected | 744 | 4080 | 1693 | 7894 | 1078 |
| Number of strikers (in 1000s)* | 177.4 | 491.8 | 183.7 | 437.7 | 181.3 |
| Number of shifts lost (in 1000s)* | 574.5 | 2148.3 | 1846.8 | 3679.8 | 4468.3 |
| Average number of shifts lost per striker | 3.2 | 4.4 | 10.0 | 8.4 | 24.6 |

*Not including workers prevented from working by the strike. This applies similarly to number of shifts lost. (32)

freedoms were guaranteed by the constitution although, as in all types of state where political opposition takes on too threatening a countenance, these were often hedged about with restrictions. A start had been made with the secularization of society particularly in respect of marriage and education.

The realization of certain of the economic demands too, compared with the situation under the Empire, was a significant step forward. These however were peripheral in relation to the central aim of the socialization of the means of production. Nevertheless, popular pressure for the eight-hour working day for example was so strong that in many places it was forced on factory owners and the government recognized this situation juridically only after the event.[36] Unemployment benefit was introduced in December 1918, and although it was inadequate in terms of providing anything more than the bare essentials it did in all likelihood help to prevent people from swelling the ranks of the hunger rioters and, on the other hand, weakened the impact of Muna's appeal to revolutionary violence. However the crux of the radical socialists' economic demands was the socialization of the great estates, railways, mines and great industrial concerns. Public feeling at nearly all levels of Czech society supported a partial revision or reform of property relations, but certain conditions existed which watered-down and ultimately shelved the demand for the socialization of industry and agriculture.

The system of a controlled economy inherited from the Empire grew stronger in 1918–1920 responding to popular pressure for a share in consumption at equitable prices. This system with the law for the protection of tenants[37] provided a possible springboard to the abolition of productive private property. It was based on a law which made it the duty of every manufacturer and farmer, irrespective of size, to register the amount of goods produced, which, with the application of the price laws, provided some defence against the excessive prices on the black market. On the one hand, it restrained the rise in prices, which otherwise would have been higher, and the profits derived from the low, fixed price exports of goods helped subsidize the domestic price of flour. On the other, as Švehla observed [38] the centres administering the controlled economy in principle knew down to the smallest details the size and shape of the means of production and his hints that certain trade syndicates should be brought under the control of the nation caused apprehension among certain classes of the imminence of nationalization.

In reality, the degree of control was not as tight as he suggested. In the first four months of 1919, some 3,500 warehouses were discovered containing unregistered goods.[39] There were also some 7,500 prosecutions for profiteering from January through March 1919 which represented only a fraction of those engaged in black market activities.[40] There was widespread corruption in the local offices administering the system, which were frequently staffed by local businessmen, whose dishonesty Švehla put down to a mentality inherited from the Austrian civil administration. Vrbenský, the Minister of Supply, made himself unpopular by his committment to supply the poorest first which resulted in administrative obstructions to his policy[41] and likely contributed to him being dropped from the subsequent government. Finally, the controlled economy had an affect on nationality relations. German manufacturers in particular were intensely resentful of the fact that part of the product of their factories and workshops found its way on to the black market via the "Centraly" and augmented the income of the Czech officials who staffed them.

Already before the destruction of the Monarchy, the SDP had demanded the expropriation of the great capitalists. Their demand was supported by the all-union Congress held in early October 1918. This was confirmed as official SDP policy at the XII Congress in December 1918 where it was explicitly stated that the party would work for "the expropriation of the great estates, mines and great industrial concerns." In smaller capitalist economic undertakings, it was envisaged that the employees would participate in running the organization and also draw a share of the profits.[42] This view was not restricted to the workers and their political and union representatives. Kramář, in the first government programme of 9th January 1919 spoke of the expropriation of the landed magnates and complete control of the mines whose owners were not to be allowed to keep them at their disposal.[43] The President's Club had also accepted a recommendation to nationalize all mines and factories of a monopolistic character.[44] The temper of the times was so strongly in favour of expropriating the great industrial and landed interests in the state that the demand for socialization found a place in the programme of all the governments from 1919 to 1921.

Yet the popular view of the statements of politicians and governments on expropriating industrial and agricultural assets in benefit of the whole nation was misconceived. The slogans of the government appeared to support the socialization of a good part of the productive means, but in reality they were empty of content. In early 1919, a commission of enquiry was set up to prepare the ground for the nationalization of the coal mines and steel-works. Yet the nationalization envisaged was not intended to be carried out in a socialist sense rather to reverse the dominant position of the German bourgeoisie who controlled the majority of heavy industry, particularly in mining, steel and chemicals. To that extent, the talk of nationalization did not refer in any sense to workers' control or even to the erection of quasi-governmental bureaucratic organizations to run these concerns. Nationaliza-

# THE ECONOMIC DEMANDS 121

tion in this context meant the safeguarding of national assets as a condition of the continuity of national economic life and, with certain aspects of the Land Reform, was a fundamental step towards strengthening the territorial integrity of the state. While radical socialists impatiently awaited some evidence from the government that nationalization or socialization was on the way, which in their sense of the word had never been made, the government gave their fullest support to private enterprise insofar as it supported the interests of state.[45]

This was not clear in the conditions of 1919, partly because of the manner in which the government was dealing with the economic crisis. The vulnerability of the lower sections of society had increased pressure for a reorganization of the controlled economy in the direction of the complete control of supply by the government. It seemed but a short step to the nationalizing of all productive concerns, particularly in view of the fact that the imminent local elections promised to give the local administrations large SD majorities. These were admirably placed to carry out a policy of this kind. Another aspect informing popular attitudes was the determination to avenge the long period of national oppression and it seemed just and natural to make a start with the nationalizing of the great estates vacated by the Habsburgs and other foreign magnates. This principle could equally be extended to heavy and large-scale manufacturing industry, the majority of which was in non-Czech hands.

These were then compelling reasons why the Czech bourgeois classes could not reject outright the popular demands for nationalization without running the risk of stirring up further discontent. On the other hand, to initiate some form or degree of nationalization would have meant some curb on their own economic and political power. Their strategy was to gain time, trusting that the economic crisis which gave body to Šmeral's movement would be quickly solved by a renewal of production.

In the interim, commissions of enquiry were set up to examine the feasibility of nationalization and these in conjunction with the uniformly radical social slogans of the parties contrived to create an atmosphere in which it was regarded as more or less inevitable. This had an important side effect. The sense of the impending appropriation of the means of production which applied to the sympathizers of all the major parties prevented a flight of support to the radical socialists. The CSP too was at the forefront of the popular movement for nationalization. Yet the programme of the party regarding socialization was changed after the wave of popular radicalism had receded, yet their supporters did not switch to the radical Left, partly however for national reasons. Even the National Democrats, typically the representatives of the financial and industrial circles, endorsed the necessity for radical change in the social and economic order.[46] In all likelihood, this was a reaction to the clamour from the street. Yet it made a significant contribution to the fluidity of the situation in that, the appearance of the economically most conservative section of society agreeing to this demand removed the need to organize or otherwise mobilize politically for its achievement. The mood was also influenced by the terms bandied about which reflected the different party views of nationalization. The properties of the Habsburg family were among the first to be taken into the ownership of the Czech nation. The term applied to this *vyvlastnění* (lit. expropriation) was attractive in that it combined a reference to dispossession in favour of the nation as a whole without payment of compensation. Despite the special conditions attaching to it, this was seen as a step towards the abrogation of the capitalist order of private property. This term was used more or less indiscriminately with those such as *znárodnění, zestátnění* and *socializace* by even the bourgeois parties. It appeared that the demand had been accepted and it only remained to agree on the form of nationalization.

As far as the nationalization of land was concerned, the radical Left, as we shall see,[47] were, in the conditions of the Czech countryside, unable to meet the needs of a section of the peasantry who provided a potential pool of support. It must be said also that the Left regarded their demands for land as dependent on the proletarian revolution in the towns and secondary to it. The driving force of the revolution hence lay in unemployment, the crisis in production and the response to extortionate prices which afflicted urban areas more deeply.

Šmeral's position regarding socialization was significantly different from Muna and the Kladno radicals.[48] He also opposed the Orthodox SDs who qua Kautsky argued that socialization or nationalization was impossible where there was nothing to socialize. Šmeral's solution however took this implied criticism into account insofar as it addressed itself to the resolution of the food crisis, a principal source of objection for the Orthodox SDs. Initially, he drew a distinction between heavy and light industry. In respect of the former, he favoured socialization for, despite the general disorganization of production nationally, the war had paradoxically created favourable conditions for the development of coal mining, iron and steel and the chemical industries and also in certain areas of light industry which had supplied the army, notably textiles.[49] The socialization of these industries would not have meant "the socializing of chaos," as Masaryk characterized it, for industrial production across the board was about 50% of its 1913 level.[50] However, socialization could in the final analysis only be predicated on the agreement of the Allies who were only antagonized by it. Yet leaving aside this dimension until later,[51] conditions were not unfavourable for socialization in this area of economic life. About a third of the industrial working class were employed in heavy industry and this provided the motor of Šmeral's movement, although it should be added that he failed to translate his popularity among them into institutions, like the unions for example, which would have helped put them on the offensive.

As regards light industry, Šmeral did not, like Muna, demand wholesale socialization. His attitude was influenced by the presence of the food crisis and also by his belief that great capital was the principal enemy, not small-scale producers. For this reason, he proposed to specifically exclude from socialization small and medium peasants in the countryside likewise those who had benefitted from the shifts in wealth at the lowest end.[52] This also applied to small producers in light industry, whom the war had hit hardest and who could more readily achieve a more or less rapid renewal of productive activity thereby increasing opportunities for employment. His policy hence was addressed to those home production units employing up to five workers who made up between a fifth and sixth of all concerns in light industry. It embraced also similarly small concerns which concentrated half of the total number of workers employed in the food industry[53] and, given the food crisis, was necessary to stimulate confidence as a pre-requisite for the revival and continuity of food supplies.

The industrial workers and the small producers (town and country) formed the two most numerous social groups. Figures are lacking for 1919, but in 1930 there were 573,000 small businesses employing up to 5 persons (without home production) having 1,024,000 workers. Two-thirds of these employed no wage workers.[54] Šmeral's demand for socialization was framed in such a way then as to appeal to both industrial workers and small producers, who if they could not be won over entirely could be at least neutralized in the struggle with the main enemy. Yet it is a moot point whether he won over many of the small traders and producers. The only more or less reliable indication we have is the number who joined the party. This of course gives no clue to those whose sympathies were with Šmeral but felt unable to make such a strong commitment as joining the party. The earliest set of figures relating to the social composition of the party is from 1924. By that time, conditions had changed and Šmeralism had been abandoned. The policy on socialization was also not the same as in 1920, given the existence of a Soviet dominated Communist Party and the absence of Šmeral himself. Nevertheless, shopkeepers, small businessmen, public employees and peasants together formed 9.75% of the total party membership numbering 93,470.[55] Of this total, 1.6% were said to be former members of the CSP.[56]

The structure of the economic environment tended to lead to popular discontent and ultimately strengthened the ranks of the radical socialists. It also helped to frame radical socialist demands. The income/unemployment axis appeared to indicate a trend determining the degree of support for Šmeralism. There were general indicators of this tendency principally the growth of the OSČ unions and likewise of the SDP. However there is a methodological difficulty in that it is more or less problematical to identify— the major centres apart—those party organizations which opposed the Orthodox SDs and hailed to Šmeral. The same thing applies to an examination of voting patterns. The SDP was the single most popular party in 1919 and 1920, if we accept the local and general election results. However to identify more closely the support for Šmeral would require a breakdown of these patterns by 1) ethnic group, 2) occupation (industrial and rural areas), 3) unemployment (by profession and by ethnic group), and 4) by district basis of income. It is unlikely that such data were recorded at the elections and if they were, they have not so far been made available. Their appearance or their reconstruction by other means would give a firmer basis for conclusions about the popular basis of Šmeralism.

*Chapter 5*

**The Social Problem—Town and Country**

Socialist movements in general developed as a result of the struggle between classes which became more differentiated in conditions of increasing industrialization. As such, they appealed in particular to workers in an urban industrial setting whose interests they sought to defend and expand. As a Marxist, Šmeral emphasized the role of the working class as the principal agent of change in society. His central aim to socialize large-scale industry was closely connected with a basic organizational principle of socialism. He wanted to abolish large-scale productive private property, but he was not dogmatic to the extent of regarding all property as theft. In practice, he left open the question of the socialization of smaller concerns as his peasant programme suggests. Nevertheless, the socialization of industry corresponded closely to the aspirations of workers in mining and heavy industry in relatively large industrial conurbations.

In Bohemia, these were clearly noticeable especially in Prague's industrial suburbs, in Plzeň and Kladno, and in Moravia, Ostrava, Přerov and the regions in and around Brno. These areas contained the great factories employing more than 250 workers who together formed about one-third of the industrial workers in the Czech Lands, a factor which helped to shape Šmeral's strategy. High concentrations of workers fostered the growth of proletarian class consciousness in which the workers' relation to the productive-means was more clear-cut and was reflected in the growth of and adherence to party and union organizations. Up to a point this contrasted with workers in light industry, whose subjective awareness of their position did not always correspond to their real relation to the productive process for two reasons connected with their conditions of life and work. A large proportion of them were concentrated on the ethnic marches or mixed nationality regions in North East and North West Bohemia.[2] This and the fact that many were employed in smaller concerns—40% of all workers

125

laboured in units employing up to 50 people[3]—created conditions placing constraints on the development of a purely proletarian class awareness which likewise affected organization. However, this did not necessarily exclude Šmeralism for many were still attracted by its social aims. Their support however was guarded and his internationalism caused them to give more support to other kinds of socialists who themselves claimed to share more or less his central economic and social concerns. A significant group to whom Šmeral appealed, the intelligentsia, also found their natural habitat in towns. Part of them came from the petty-bourgeois classes, like Šmeral himself, and their alienation from bourgeois society was not infrequently connected with university education and the shock of adjustment from small towns to life in the metropolis. University brought some into contact with the SDP where they found a haven as organizers, journalists or teachers in union and party centres. These combined with the members of the working class intelligentsia who availed themselves of opportunities provided by the union to find employment in its bureaucracy. Finally, the commercial and insurance activities of the party, where personal interest met a belief in social justice, also found an expression in support for Šmeral's revolution.

Most of the aims on which Šmeral based his appeal were those of a large part of the workers and a section of the intelligentsia in an urban, industrial environment. This created a division between the town and country which in its implications had a marked effect on political developments. While Šmeral could rely on the industrial proletariat responding to their economic circumstances according to a more or less developed class consciousness, he could not expect the same from the class of landless workers. This was equally valid for the semi-proletarian section of the small peasants who received their primary source of income, as we shall presently see, from an industrial environment. Yet, though they shared some of the interests of the working class, which to a degree provides grounds for believing that they approved of Šmeral, they were still inspired by the aspirations of the agrarian Gemeinschaft. Operating on the model of industrial society, Šmeral looked to the landless concentrated, in relative terms, on the great estates to provide the driving force of the revolution in the countryside. Their precarious conditions of existence suggested that they would be the radical element most ready to rise against the country establishment. Yet his solution to the problem of the land was drawn less from a considered analysis of the social forces in the Czech village and more from his strategy extrapolated from the opposition of classes in towns.

His failure can also be attributed in large measure to his overlooking or otherwise ignoring the significance of the land question. In this regard, he was not dissimilar to most European socialists for whom this problem had hardly merited serious attention before 1914. Conditions in the Czech Lands did not allow him to expect a repetition of the manner in which the Soviet Revolution had been carried from the cities to the countryside. Firstly, the Czech Lands did not have the enormous concentrations of industrial workers in a handful of cities, as for example existed in Russia. Secondly, he could not count on the links between the town and country derived from first-generation industrial workers drawn from the villages who had played an important role at the revolution's outset. Thirdly, there was no defeated army of armed peasant proletarians at his disposal. His priority of course was an urban proletarian revolution. Yet he hoped to avoid a full-blown civil war and to do this he had to address himself to the problem of breaking the power of the Agrarian Party. This involved winning the most numerous section of the countryside, the peasantry.

The problem confronting him had more or less two sides. He had to come to terms with the primary objective of the small peasants, the acquisition of a piece of land, and to free them from the constraints they had laboured under since the pre-war era. The post-war Land Reform hence was of vital importance. Despite the small peasants' contact with the towns, they were significantly less revolutionary in the terms demanded by Šmeral than the landless workers with whom, on a seasonal or part-time basis, they were to a degree in an employer–employee relation. The second problem then was to resolve the contradiction between the conflicting interests of these two groups, which collided centrally over the issue of the great estates, and bring them into a workable political partnership. This was not an impossibility for the unions of agricultural workers which began to emerge in 1907 were specifically directed against the rich peasants, medium and great magnates. The war years showed too that in special conditions, there was a basis for an identity of interests between the landless, the dwarf-holders and the small peasants on the one hand against the rich peasants and medium and great landowners on the other. These two aspects, roughly speaking, form the basis of this chapter which helps to illustrate a crucial area of constraint which conditions in the countryside placed on Šmeral. Agrarian dominance too was not a new departure, but the working out of a trend which had been underway since well before the war. Nevertheless how they seized their advantage ultimately became an important factor in Šmeral's defeat. In apparently satisfying the land hunger of the small peasants, they suborned his appeal. Had the peasants known however that the Agrarians' offer of a piece of land to all those who could work it only created conditions ultimately strengthening the medium peasants and the Agrarians' own financial institutions, then arguably Šmeral's programme might have been more appropriate. As it was, the small peasants' yearning for independence expressed through small-scale property ownership brought them within 10 years into close dependence on the Agrarian bourgeoisie. Whether the structure of the Czech village favoured the solution of the Russian Right SRs or indeed that of the Bolsheviks is an interesting point which merits some consideration. Some attention will also be paid to Lenin's persistent stress on a link between the urban proletariat and the landless agrarian workers as a condition of revolution and more particularly whether this notion had any practical significance in the Czech Lands.

Before the Land Reform, the economic and social configuration of the countryside in the Historic Provinces was characterized on the one hand by the preponderance of aristocratic estates, the latifundiae, and on the other by the dwarf-holdings of up to 2 hectares (in 1902, 47.1% of all agricultural units).[4] The other numerically significant group operating between these two poles were, roughly speaking, the small and part of the medium peasants who were engaged in a constant struggle with those economic forces which threatened to drag them down to the level of the dwarf-holders. They worked land from 2 to 10 hectares and represented 36.5 of the total number of farms.[5] Above them was a class who often combined cultivation on their own account with the provision of retail outlets supplying the needs of those who worked the land. This group, whose holdings of land were not inconsiderable, I shall refer to as the village bourgeoisie.[6] The origin of their wealth and present economic activity was not based exclusively on agriculture for they often had commercial or business interests in the village which set them apart from the rich peasants, some of whom were otherwise their financial co-evals.

In the early 1900s, the aristocracy represented 0.04% of all owners of land, yet held 30.81% of the total area of the Czech Lands.[7] The concentration of lands and the semi-feudal survival of fideikomis obstructed the easy movement of land by purchase. This was mitigated to some extent by the leasing of small and large tracts by a significant proportion of aristocrats who chose not to farm their own estates. At the other end of the scale of farmers and cultivators of the soil were the small peasants. Those who formed land up to 1 hectare represented roughly 28.6% of all agricultural concerns (1896 figure).[8] The pre-war situation was marked by a decline in the average size of peasant holdings which was most noticeable in the splitting of the holdings of the smallest peasants. This was caused largely by the increasing indebtedness of the peasantry,[9] which was a fair reflection of the degree of difficulty encountered in trying to make small holdings work. Most were hardly viable even within the restricted terms of economic self-sufficiency and as a result the peasants were drawn into a more or less close dependence on the village bourgeoisie. They became aware of the advantages to be gained from offering loans on a small scale locally and had set up their own credit institutions which helped to fill the gap left by the urban banks who more or less refused to serve anybody except the landed aristocrats. These credit institutions developed into provincial organizations and the fact they were run on national lines gave them the appearance of carrying the banner of national opposition and induced a sense of Czech separateness and, to a point, unity. This reached a high point in 1911 with the founding of the Agrarian Bank, the first all-Czech bank. It coincided with the emergence of a more or less novel form of Agrarian intensive agriculture free of the control of the aristocracy and based on forms ranging in size from 50 to 200 hectares.

Some detailed consideration will be given now to the various strata making up the social geology of the countryside in which, for our purposes, the peasantry occupied the most important place. However the problems and interests of the various peasant groups should not be allowed to conceal the fact that other classes were also significant in determining the power configuration in rural areas, not least the rich peasants and medium farmers whose political expression was the Agrarian party. At about the turn of the century, the medium peasant holdings were breaking down.[10] On the one hand, the total number of farms rose and this tendency was most visible in farmsteads not exceeding 2 hectares. However, there was an opposite tendency reflected in the gathering of part of these holdings into larger units in the hands of a relatively new class of farmer. In 1902, small-holdings of up to 2 hectares formed 48.3% of all agricultural concerns.[11] Farming at this level had a family and subsidence character. Some 94% were family concerns in which the woman was the most important worker on 51% of the holdings and where child labour was not uncommon (4.2%). This type of farming did not lead to self-sufficiency for there was a high degree of dependence on the wage-work of the menfolk either in industry or agriculture (46.1%) or alternatively in cottage industry (11.3%). The smaller the holding, the greater was the extent of this dependence, so that 51.5% of all units up to 0.5 hectare sent the males into permanent jobs elsewhere (no records were kept for part-time workers) and 12.6% relied on cottage industry. In this group, 39.8% worked their own land but this made no difference to the yield which merely augmented the Existenzminimum from paid labour.

Owners of small-holdings, market gardens or vineyards near towns and serving local markets proved to be exceptions to this general rule. In contrast to most small-holders, whose agricultural activity was founded on one or other forms of animal husbandry, they produced fruit and vegetables or what constituted more or less a cash-crop. Among the small-holders there was close contact with centres of industrial activity. As we have seen a significant number of the country population in this group lived in villages. In addition, the characteristic of the Historic Provinces, namely the distribution of small-scale industrial undertakings throughout towns and even villages, worked in favour of a part of the agricultural population coming into contact with urban industrial workers. No great distances were involved and these were not infrequently reduced by the growth of communications, especially railways. As a result the villages were not as isolated from each other and neither were the towns as was the case, for example, in Russia. Some contact at least was made with urban workers and their representatives in trade unions and the socialist parties, although the latter did not emerge in any numbers in semi-rural areas until 1918. This trend together with their experience of labour in a factory or work-shop helped at all events to initiate the breaking down of the rooted distrust for the towns in general and the urban workers in particular whose interests the Agrarian party had always described as opposing those of the rural community.

On the other hand, there was a large section of dwarf-holders who were tied more or less securely to the countryside by the conditions of their leases. In general, these were of two kinds. The traditional type involved the payment of a non-economic rent together with the legal obligation for males to work on the estates of the landlord. The dwarf-holder in this position was often unwilling to go and work in the towns even though his financial standing might have justified it. In addition, it reinforced dependence on the landlord who more often than not was a member of the village bourgeoisie and who carried a not inconsiderable degree of power and authority within the Gemeinschaft. Some 41.8% of the group farmed on this basis while only 18.4% had the second type of lease which involved the payment of an economic rent and placed no labour liability on the lease-holder. Of all categories of farms, these dwarf-holders recorded the only percentage rise over the period 1902–1921.[12] Using 1902 as base (=100), the index rose to 133 in 1921. The group cultivating a small-holding up to 0.5 h rose most sharply to 180. This was caused as we shall see by the disintegration of farms normally but not exclusively in the lower half of the medium category.

Nearly a quarter of the total number of farms, small-holdings and estates were made up of small peasants farming land from 2 to 5 hectares in size.[13] Family concerns predominated and women provided the staple of the labour force freeing their menfolk to go to the towns where more than a quarter were gainfully employed. Just under one in ten of these households was engaged in cottage industry. Of these concerns, 40% farmed on their own land while the remainder farmed as tenants. Rent-and-labour leases were only slightly less than in the previous group but rent only agreements fell sharply, compared with the dwarfholders, to less than 1 in 20. By 1921, the number of farms represented as a percentage of the total fell slightly.

The third group was represented by the medium peasants farming 5-10 hectares. They were still predominantly family concerns and two-thirds owned their own land. Most of them were more or less self-sufficient and, at the top end, a good few produced a surplus. At the lower end, 7.4% of the concerns sent their menfolk to work in industry to augment the family income. The incidence of rent-and-labour leases was high, but the most striking feature is that they were employers of significant numbers of permanent labourers. These farmsteads were in addition the smallest in which the employment of administrative staff was economically viable suggesting a sufficient flow of produce to require careful control particularly in respect of its transport to and sale in the towns. It was the stage in production more or less representing the beginning of intensive agriculture.

Farms of 10-20 hectares indicate a sharp fall in the number of family holdings, which accounted for just over one-third. It was the second highest group in percentage terms working their own land with the help of a permanent body of labour which was double that of the previous group. Despite the fact that none of the family concerns sent anybody to the towns to work in industry nor in cottage industry, this group experienced a significant decline over twenty years. By 1921, it fell more sharply as a whole than any other category. In general, this reflected a splitting into smaller units, although some were joined to larger farms. The group above them, rich peasants farming land 20-50 h in size, also suffered a decrease. On the other hand, the principle of ownership was most strongly entrenched in this group. A little over one in ten was a family farm but the fact that two-thirds employed permanent labour is an important indication of the strengthening of wage relations in this sector of agriculture in particular and of a significant increase in farming efficiency. It was also unusual in that it was the only category which lost concerns in all areas of agricultural production. Between 1902 and 1921, these farms as a percentage of the whole fell from 3.8% to 2.7%. Notwithstanding, the first decade of the century and especially the war years brought a great increase in wealth to a section of the great peasants[14] who extended their farms and moved into larger, more-efficiently organized estates. These ranged in size from 50-100 hectares and had two notable features. Initially, more than 40% of them employed managers and office staff and secondly, the number of units with permanent labour fell by a third over against the previous category. This is partly explained by the fact that up to one-third of these estates contained extensive areas of forest and woodland and partly by the relatively high incidence of electric-, steam- or water-powered agricultural machinery, the first to use them. The family character of farms so pronounced at lower levels of hectarage all but disappeared. Some 74% of farms were owned, but there was a relatively large increase in land rented on new leases.

At the top end of the scale were the farms exceeding 100 hectares of which the greater portion comprised the latifundiae. The clearest feature of these concerns was the very high incidence of estates employing managers and officials who maintained the flow of production in the customary absence of the landowner. Family farms were nowhere in evidence and seasonal labour had almost disappeared. The employment of permanent labour was characteristically low, indeed the lowest of all groups. This is partly explained by the custom of landed magnates who tended to use their tenants to provide labour which was cheaper than investing in farm machinery. Only 70% of concerns worked their own lands. The Agrarian great farmers who worked estates up to about 200 h in area favoured more intensive methods of cultivation than the latifundiae who were often uninterested in farming as such at all. Their more efficient and intensive use of the land enabled them to increase their profits and to expand. Yet often this brought them up against fideikomis. In the search to expand their estates, they could not buy and had to settle for renting holdings from the landed magnates, a tendency which was reflected in the doubling of concerns farming on rent-only leases as compared with the previous group. Tables 7, 8 and 9 give a summary of these figures.[15]

To recapitulate briefly, the most conspicuous feature of social stratification in the countryside visible from these statistics over the twenty years from 1902 to 1921 is the above average decline of farms in the middle group, 10–20 hectares. One way or another these agricultural units were either acquired by the capitalist medium-farmers or rich peasants who were thereby enabled to augment their holdings without reference to the primary source of land, the great estates. However most of these farms were broken up and one way or another filtered down through the system leading to a marked growth in the number of dwarf-holders. In all likelihood, this growth also masks an absolute bankruptcy of a section of the lowest group (0–0.5 hectares) who were forced thereby to join the ranks of agricultural labourers or contributed to the flight from the land or even to emigration abroad.[16] It is perhaps legitimate to classify about half of the dwarf-holders as semi-proletarian agricultural undertakings in that the main bread winner worked in semi-

## Table 7
## Number of Agricultural Concerns (Czech Lands Only)

| Groups of Farms by Area (hectares) | 1902 Classification of Farms | | | | 1921 Classification of Farms | | | |
|---|---|---|---|---|---|---|---|---|
| | all types of land | | agricultural land | | all types of land | | agricultural land | |
| | Number of Farms | | Number of Farms | | Number of Farms | | Number of Farms | |
| | Absolute nos. | % | Absolute nos. | % | Absolute nos. | % | Absolute nos. | % |
| 0–2h | 428,470 | 47.1 | 438,029 | 48.3 | 573,372 | 51.9 | 586,676 | 53.0 |
| 2–5h | 220,065 | 24.2 | 222,533 | 24.6 | 264,824 | 24.0 | 268,897 | 24.3 |
| 5–10h | 111,698 | 12.3 | 114,510 | 12.6 | 125,601 | 11.3 | 127,186 | 11.5 |
| 10–20h | 92,535 | 10.2 | 91,957 | 10.1 | 91,322 | 8.3 | 88,522 | 8.0 |
| 20–50h | 48,330 | 5.3 | 34,309 | 3.8 | 43,764 | 3.9 | 29,143 | 2.7 |
| 50–100h | 3,865 | 0.4 | 2,287 | 0.3 | 3,490 | 0.3 | 2,443 | 0.2 |
| over 100h | 4,587 | 0.5 | 2,838 | 0.3 | 3,363 | 0.3 | 2,869 | 0.3 |
| TOTAL | 909,550 | 100.0 | 906,463 | 100.0 | 1,105,736 | 100.0 | 1,105,736 | 100.0 |

Table 8
Pattern of Ownership/Renting, 1902

| Groups of Farms by Area | Family concerns as % of group | % of group owning lands | % of group Rent only leases | % of group Rent and labour leases |
|---|---|---|---|---|
| 0–2h | 94 | 39.8 | 18.4 | 41.8 |
| 2–5h | 84.6 | 41.3 | 4.7 | 54.0 |
| 5–10h | 64.2 | 62.4 | 1.7 | 45.9 |
| 10–20h | 35.9 | 77.8 | 0.9 | 21.3 |
| 20–50h | 13.7 | 83.9 | 1.0 | 15.1 |
| 50–100h | 1.8 | 74.2 | 8.3 | 15.0 |
| over 100h | — | 70.0 | 19.7 | 11.3 |

Table 9
Composition of Labour Force, 1902

| Groups of Farms by Area | % of group employing labour | | | % composition by gender | | | % of group receiving wages from | |
|---|---|---|---|---|---|---|---|---|
| | Perma-nent | Sea-sonal | Adminis-trative | Male | Female | Child | Industry | Cottage Industry |
| 0–2h | — | — | — | 44.8 | 51.0 | 4.2 | 46.1 | 11.3 |
| 2–5h | 8.1 | 5.4 | — | 44.8 | 48.0 | 7.2 | 27.4 | 8.6 |
| 5–10h | 22.6 | 7.2 | 1.2 | 44.9 | 46.2 | 8.9 | 7.4 | 2.8 |
| 10–20h | 46.3 | 11.1 | 1.9 | 44.6 | 45.6 | 9.8 | — | — |
| 20–50h | 65.0 | 14.9 | 4.7 | 45.8 | 44.1 | 10.0 | — | — |
| 50–100h | 42.5 | 13.7 | 41.7 | 53.9 | 41.2 | 4.9 | — | — |
| over 100h | 4.9 | 1.9 | 93.7 | 64.3 | 31.9 | 3.8 | — | — |

urban or urban industrial conurbations. On the other hand, their wives and families were involved in labour-intensive subsistence farming often based on a simple form of animal husbandry. They were not involved to any great degree in cash-crops or the production of a surplus nor even in a wage-relation with other farmers, unlike the agricultural workers. Semi-feudal survivals like rent and labour leases did however maintain a clear line of dependence on other classes in country society, most notably the latifundiae to whom for the use of their land, they were obliged to work and, in exceptional cases, for example on the Schwarzenberg estates, to give up part of their produce.

The single most important problem in the pre-1914 period was the lack of land caused by the concentration of estates in the hands of the landed magnates and the legal restrictions on their sale. This affected the thriving medium-estate holders in particular and prompted their representatives in the Agrarian party to initiate efforts to find a solution even before the war. Although the landless agricultural workers were not regarded as properly belonging to the family of the countryside as they were neither cultivators nor farmers, and hence their interests as wage earners placed them on a par with urban workers, the Agrarians did seek to legislate for their social and economic neighbours, the dwarf-holders. In support of their ideology stressing the mutual interdependence of all sections of the peasantry with the village gentry and the medium farmers, yet excluding all sections of German or foreign origin, they took some tentative steps to make land available to both peasants and independent farmers. Cooperatives formed by the village gentry rented large farms,[17] and long extensions of leases[18] were given to the peasants whose conditions gave the larger farmers a stable source of labour. Yet this was only regarded as an interim stage for the aim of the Agrarians was to bring land into private ownership.[19] These initiatives were attempts to purvey the interests of the village as common over against the towns and were something akin to class-cooperation based on the natural order of things and a kind of loose agrarian national coalition against foreign ownership of the land. However, this aspect did not come into prominence until the end of the war for the Agrarian bourgeoisie's emphasis lay on the economic necessity of a land reform. There was no appeal for a reform on a democratic and national basis, a cry which went up in 1918, for fear that the latifundiae might rescind the leases on rented holdings, the bulk of which were in their gift.

The war gave a special importance to agriculture. While it set the towns against the countryside, there was an analogous deepening of the divisions in the villages on both a national and social basis. The Czech Lands' traditional role as the granary of the western half of the Empire, among other reasons, more or less negated the import of food. Different sections of the countryside reacted differently to the gradually worsening supply situation. The war brought conditions affecting the landless and small peasants most visibly, both in the economic and social sense. Wholesale conscription deprived families of their breadwinners. The peasants' food stores disappeared under the weight of requisitions and their animal or tool inventories were often depleted leaving them with few means to cultivate the land. Women and children were driven into the arms of the medium farmers who gladly employed them, as much of their labour force based on male workers had gone off to the front. Wage rates however were lower and this together with machine cultivation enabled them to reduce their production costs. Prices on the other hand rose. The rich peasants and medium farmers were helped considerably by the Agrarians' influence on the controlled economy. Its principal executive bodies were the "war economic centres" which regulated the sale and purchase of agricultural produce and were dominated by Agrarians (Viškovský directed the Corn Institute; Bergmann, the Provincial Commission for the Sale of Livestock; Frankenberger, the Provincial Centre for Animal Feeds).

Great profits were made. For example, in one year alone, the cooperative of Agrarian landowners formed to control the movements of purchases made 1.5 million crowns in agents' fees.[20] This class of farmers had significant leverage in another way. Many had official capacities as mayors or public officials in towns and villages throughout the Historic Provinces. As such, they were responsible for levying requisitions and likewise entrusted with the purchase of food for the armed forces. They often managed to shift the requisitions away from the middle farmers on to the small and part of the medium peasants. Only towards the end of the war when it was clear that the dwarf-holdings had been too exhausted to support the scale of requisitions did the authorities turn their attention to the medium farmers. Many of these had meanwhile being enjoying the privilege of supplying food for the Imperial ordinance, the schedules for which were in the gift of the local public officials. When they were confronted with a situation in which they were forced to divert their supply of products at market prices to the demands of the requisition commission, they promptly placed themselves at the head of an anti-requisition movement. As such they strengthened their popular image as defenders of the countryside as a whole and all classes within it.[21] Nevertheless, the profits they made from the war were very large. This was reflected in the paying off of debts and in investment in Agrarian credit institutes. While on the one hand, loans fell from 229,709,000 to

173,894,000 crowns in 1918, deposits rose from 245,392,000 to 720,592,000.[22] A revealing index of this trend lies in the movement of the assets of the Agrarian Bank itself which rose 30 times over in this period.[23] War increased the demand for land but this did not come solely from those enriched by it. The deteriorating supply situation in urban areas prompted industrial workers to look for allottments to grow vegetables.[24] Yet the real pressure of demand emanated from the Agrarian bourgeoisie who were unable to increase production by investing in machinery or fertilizers and hence looked to an increase in the size of their holdings as the answer.[25] They turned to medium- and small-peasants for whom requisitions and a decline in productive capacity had made their struggle hardly worthwhile and had reduced many to penury. The selling off of their land reached such proportions that the authorities, fearful of its impact on requisitions and unwilling to shift them onto the medium farmers, restricted the sale and leasing of dwarf- and small-holdings.[26]

Of all sections of the countryside, probably the landless suffered the most. Many thought themselves to be twice cursed. Either they were subject to conscription, which the medium peasants and above were often in a position to avoid, or they stayed at home where wages were rarely if ever raised and which anyway maintained only a fraction of their 1914 value.[27] In addition, the opportunities for acquiring food were entirely restricted compared with peace-time conditions. There was not enough money to buy basic semi-durable goods like shoes and clothes and the progressive lowering of rations as the harvests went for export laid them open to disease and early death. There was here a basis for an anti-Austrian movement on a not inconsiderable scale, for the working dwarf-holders, though they had differing interests, felt the foundations of their existence to be threatened. They violently resisted the requisition commissions and took part in the hunger riots in towns. They were also prominent in the raids on mills and village shops and likewise on the estates of the Schwarzenberg, Clam-Martinitz and Fürstenberg families. Towards the close of the war, solidarity among the country classes was wearing thin. The great peasants and medium farmers had, it is true, also put up a stiff resistance to requisitioning, thereby giving their struggle a seemingly anti-Austrian character. They sabotaged supplies but it is questionable whether this was a protest against the war arrangements of the Monarchy, which had effectively enriched them. Judging from the state of the black market, they felt as little compunction in demanding high prices from the Czech landless peasants or dwarf-holders as from urban industrial workers. Yet this was to a significant degree lost on the landless and the small-peasants, principally because there were few political and union organizations in existence capable of mobilizing opinion or initiating any action against them. The absence of active and class-conscious workers, most of whom were at the front, also took its toll. In conditions of war, the national as opposed to the class enemy took the blame.

Despite their unhappy experiences in the war, which one way or another amounted to class oppression, the landless workers did not undergo any wholesale change in consciousness as a class, except as we shall see in one important respect. Once again, nationalism played its part in diverting them from the real causes of discontent and the Agrarians were enabled to pass off the Austrian state and its organizations, particularly the Catholic Church and the aristocracy as the source of their sorrows. The conditions of their existence however more or less ensured that they would play only a minor role if any in the revolutionary movement in the towns. Numerically they were powerful. In 1921, there were 583,000 registered males in the Czech Lands, which with day-labourers (classified separately as *nádeníci*) and apprentices, brought the total to 956,306.[28] This represented something under 20% of the agricultural population of 5.4 million, of Czechoslovakia, or over a quarter of the 3.158 millions in the Czech Lands.[29] The mainstay of this class of workers was the agricultural labourer (*deputátník*) who, in return for his work, received wages and usually a tied-cottage and supplies of food. The journeyman labourer (*nádeník*) on the other hand was frequently a day labourer and had nothing from his employer apart from his wage. Yet he had the advantage of a strip of land and the implements to work it and hence represented an intermediate stage between the wage workers and the dwarf-holder. Their consciousness derived from qualitatively different conditions even within their own "class" and their appreciation of their own interest was not the same. They were not concentrated in small areas except for the restricted numbers working intensively on the great estates or those of the medium farmers and the great peasants, mainly in South Western Bohemia and parts of Eastern Bohemia and Silesia. The dependence of the labourer on his employer for his bed and board quite apart from his income acted as a powerful constraint on association, not to mention the fact that it was discouraged by the whole ideology of the countryside. Access to light-industrial areas was not difficult from the country but the notion propagated by the Agrarians that the town and industry were opposite to and therefore enemies of village and agriculture combined with agrarian conservatism to forestall any genuine links. The journeyman labourer on the other hand was not tied so firmly to his employer, but his desire to work his land more efficiently and perhaps drag himself into the class of dwarf-holders overcame

# THE SOCIAL PROBLEM 139

any impulse to mobility which could have brought him into close contact with towns.

It must also be added that the SDP was at least partly responsible for their relative isolation. They were slow in erecting political and union organizations in the countryside. The relative lack of importance they attached to the land question is shown by the fact that it was put on the agenda of the Party Congress for the first time in the SDP's history in 1919 and this only as a result of the discussion prompted by the surprising news that they had polled 39.9% of the country votes in the 1907 national election. However, by 1920 the Union of Agricultural Workers affiliated to the SD OSČ had grown from almost nothing to over 110,000.[30] Yet although this was a major step forward in bringing agricultural labourers into a closer connection with the radical socialist movement in the towns, it had little effect on the journeymen who had already espied that the Land Reform would better serve their interests and looked to the Agrarian "Domovina" for their salvation.

The second and more numerous group to which Šmeral appealed and one which ultimately had a decisive influence on the course of events was based on the dwarf-holders and small peasants. Using the figure of Reich[31] who suggests a figure of 1.964 million as representing the total number of agricultural concerns in the Czech Lands in 1918, we can estimate, with the knowledge that the dwarf-holders represented about a half of all concerns, something over 900,000 (0–2 hectares). This however seems rather high. Official statistics in 1921 put the number of dwarf-holders at 586,676 (0–2 hectares) and small peasants (2–10 hectares) at 453,793.[32]

At all events, it was a large group of people which satisfied Šmeral on two counts. Firstly, it was capable of providing an agrarian counterpart to the industrial mass movement and secondly, its connections with the towns and its position in the scheme of productive relations was such that its interests would not conflict with industrial proletarian interests. We have seen that a significant number of dwarf-holders, especially at the bottom of the heap, were actually engaged in industrial production. It would however be stretching a point to suggest that they developed a new-found industrial class-consciousness in the space of a generation powerful enough to overcome the social and economic values they had derived from their position on the land. On the other hand, only a small proportion worked their own land and most had had the experience of failing in their attempts to achieve self-sufficiency. Rents for smaller pieces of land were pro rata higher than for larger areas and often led to indebtedness. They had few, if any, surpluses and were not involved in price exploitation, which was characteristic of the rich peasants and above, and indeed were often victims of the black market in the same way as the industrial working class. On the whole, as regards food supplies above, they were generally better off. Some indeed regarded their income from industry as primary and simply left permanently for the towns, though no figures are available. But most became aware that no other possibility existed for improving income from agriculture than an expansion of their holdings one way or another. They formed accordingly an important group in the struggle to expropriate the landed magnates, but did not carry the class struggle into the villages as Šmeral hoped.

It was not entirely different with the small peasants. A lack of land—an average 3.2 hectares per homestead—little permanently or seasonally employed labour, little surplus for market and anyway not of a kind enabling him to avoid buying products grown under conditions of large-scale production—all these factors tended to weaken his ability to withstand competition and, unless he was completely self-sufficient, would tend to force him into decline. He perceived his interests then to be in opposition to those of the rich peasants and the village bourgeoisie to whom he was financially indebted and who demanded high prices for food, seed and the hire of oxen and machinery. His ideal hence was land of such an area enabling him to shelter from the competition of the great productive units. As a result, small-peasant consciousness tended to oscillate between hatred for the great peasants and medium farmers, on whom they were to a significant degree dependent, as a consequence of which they gave general support to the revolutionary movement,[33] and suspicion of the urban socialists' solution to the land question which was not at all to his liking. He was uninterested in destroying capitalism on the land, only in satisfying his land hunger although this required not only the expropriation of aristocratic and church lands, but also, to a degree, those of the bourgeoisie's so that all interested members of the village community could have an opportunity to become independent and self-sufficient medium cultivators of the soil.

The dual character of peasant interests was perhaps seen most distinctly with the medium peasants. Nearly two-thirds owned their land, they were employers of significant numbers of permanent labourers and they were not subsistence farmers like the peasants with smaller holdings. On the contrary, they often produced a surplus to be sold on the market which, in conditions of war, gave them financial means well beyond those of the small peasants. As a seller, he supported the Agrarians' demand for the abolition of the controlled economy and for the introduction of a free market in agricultural produce. On the other hand, he shared with his smaller neighbours an inability to compete effectively with the medium and great farmers. Hence, they too opposed a collectivist solution to the land problem and with their profits from the black market were willing to buy land which in time they anticipated would raise them into the ranks of the village bourgeoisie. To gain the active support simultaneously of the four groups, the landless, the dwarf-holders, the small- and medium-peasants was in the conditions of the time more or less impossible. Even within the same class, there were basic differences of attitude and interest. It remained then for Šmeral to frame a set of demands which would correspond to the needs of that class whose support he thought most essential for the victory of the radical socialist movement and which would, at the same time, neutralize the opposition of the others. After the war, there was no resistance to the idea of a land reform. Apart from being an economic necessity, it was a completion of the national and democratic revolution and as such a demand common to all classes. However, in the conflict over how the expropriated land should be divided, the Agrarians won a victory which in its effects went far beyond the countryside. Their capture of the peasantry prevented the radical socialists from spreading their movement, an important factor in Šmeral's failure, and gave them a power base which enabled them to dominate the Republic politically for years to come.

The Orthodox SDs regarded the whole land question as little more than an economic problem. They were inspired by the need to renew production as quickly as possible and thereafter maximizing it, but in such a way that the agricultural workers received continuity of employment and a full return on their labour. Apart from this, they were interested in large-scale agricultural production which, according to Bechyně's plan, would be achieved by a state-collectivist solution based on the expropriated great estates. In the light of the experience from the war years, they were set on achieving an efficient supply of cheap food to the towns and at the same time allaying the apprehensions of the landless workers who feared that the breakup of the estates of the latifiundiae would lose them their jobs.

Another influential stream in the SDP existed however which rightly suggested that the maintenance of the great estates, while admirable from the point of view of achieving large-scale production, would be complicated by the opposition of the peasantry. Led by Modráček, it posited a system in which agricultural co-ops would take over these estates more or less intact and let out parcels of land within it to the peasantry on long leases enabling them to farm independently, yet if they wished, allowing them to take advantage of the benefits the co-op could offer as regards the provision of finance, wholesale purchase and even of community help for the more technically demanding kinds of work. Šmeral however rejected the Orthodox

SDs assumption that the land question simply concerned the confiscation and nationalization of the foreign aristocrats' estates and their transformation into one or other forms of large-scale production, which was assumed per se to be of a socialist character.[34] He regarded it first and foremost as a political question in the struggle to gain allies for the radical mass movement which was almost entirely an urban, proletarian phenomenon. It is reasonable to argue that by the time Šmeral addressed himself to the problem the peasantry posed for the radical socialist movement, it was too late. Despite the fact that the introduction of the law in May 1919 allowing the peasantry renting up to 8 hectares to buy their medium- and long-term leases (Záborový zákon) showed them to be all in favour of buying their land, Šmeral did not respond. Indeed in the first programmatic statement of the Marxist Left, largely his work, there is no mention of the expropriation of the great estates nor of the Land Reform. He had not considered the problem beyond referring to the socialization of all large-scale productive means.

Šmeral's thinking was dominated by the conditions in the towns where the mass movement of organized factory workers would first make the revolution and then carry it from there into the countryside. To that extent, he looked at the parallels between wage relations in an urban industrial setting and those in the countryside and insofar as he had considered a policy for the countryside, it hinged on the defence of agricultural workers whose working environments, the great estates, were one way or another about to be dismembered. He therefore demanded the nationalization of the great estates and the socialization of land. He favoured the maintenance of the great estates as the basis of some kind of collectivist agriculture, while the other land would be divided on long-term inherited leases or, through the intermediary of a co-operative, rented out to individuals.[35] This was not attractive to the small peasants who expressed their violent antagonism to both cooperative and state collectivist forms of agriculture and likewise to renting. There was little doubt that they could be won only by parcelling the land. Šmeral's specific exclusion of small peasant holdings from his plans for socialization[36] and the attempt to end their dependence on the village bourgeoisie by annulling their debts and giving them tax advantages[37] was not enough to achieve their neutrality, let alone win their cooperation. These provisions however tend to conflict with an attitude the radical Left displayed which was more than slightly dismissive of the aspirations of the small peasants. The limits of the land to be allocated depended on how much a family could reasonably cultivate. In effect, this implied a continuation of the unstable existence of the cottagers and dwarf-holders. The legitimate aim to operate in the relatively stable conditions of the medium peasants was treated as an expression of the selfishness of those aspiring to become rich peasants.[38] In addition, there was a reflection of class antagonism in their attitude to the Agrarians who were felt by 1920 to have the small- and medium-peasants already in their maw.[39]

Though the Left won great popular support in the towns, where the struggle of the classes was most clear-cut, they found it impossible to transfer the premises on which it was waged to the conditions of the countryside. There is little evidence of them winning over the small peasants working in industry and most of the radical activity in the countryside appears to have been sponsored by industrial workers. Yet the fulcrum of the struggle lay in the small/medium peasant class and they had to be won over, not simply neutralized, as Šmeral attempted. Even among the agricultural workers, mistakenly regarded as the active agent in the struggle against the Agrarians, conditions were such that part of them were enticed by the prospect of land offered by Švehla. The Left nevertheless looked to them as their natural allies as they were the lowest section of the country community around whom most of the village poor were gathered. These were regarded as more or less analogous to industrial workers in terms of their conditions of social life and their place in the productive process. Yet in contrast to the towns, where the proletariat was more or less organized and led by a distinct class made up of members of a bourgeois and a worker intelligentsia and represented a large minority of the urban population, the agricultural workers had no such advantages. Unions were thin on the ground until 1918 and the village did not play the directly coercive role which for example it did in Russia. Conditions hence were not favourable for a violent seizure of land at a time when most expected to gain something from the reform which was prudently kept hanging in the air. It is no surprise then that the organizations of cottagers' efforts to form groups of the poor in the villages to elect commissions intended to carry out a land reform in their own interests met with little success.[40].

The Left was unable to influence the character of the Land Reform which was determined by the party approximating most closely, at least in the short-term, to the ideals of the majority in the countryside. This was the Agrarians who despite their unpopularity in the later war years accurately read the signs and stole a decisive march on all of their political opponents with the founding of the "Domovina." The rural movement had few if any of the characteristics of an anti-capitalist struggle, which was a prominent feature of the movement in the towns, and was led under the exclusively nationalist slogan of "Redress for the White Mountain." On the other hand, there was a significant strike movement among the landless agricultural workers which in many cases was led by urban proletarians and their representatives.[41] Yet these strikes were in the main directed to achieving increases in wages or protests against usurious prices. The estates of the landed aristocracy were not infrequently attacked and occupied but as often as not these acts were inspired by the need to find some solution to the problem of the wretched supply situation. In addition, neither strikes nor occupations were sustained for any length of time, although those on the former Imperial estates in the Kladno, Kralupy and Slaný regions lasted a month and significantly were supported by the local miners and steelworkers, and tended to follow the seasonal character of agricultural work.

Yet despite an attempt at a general strike in the countryside in April 1920 in support of increased wages and a wave of demonstrations in the Mělník region against the profiteering of the medium and great peasants and the unsatisfactory conditions in the Republic, the countryside stubbornly refused to catch fire. With a vast fund of land available one way or another, it was unrealistic to expect the small peasants and dwarf-holders to rally around the banner of the landless. In general terms, historical conditions in the countryside did not favour the radical socialists' solution to the question of the land. The breakdown of medium-peasant holdings had led to a growth in the number of small peasant cultivators to about 2 million in 1917[42] which was more than twice as many as the landless proletariat. The most unstable social element in the countryside then and one which could be won over given the appropriate policy and an accurate recognition of their conditions of life, were those small peasants at the lower margins of the group. In the sense that many worked in industry, they were semi-proletarian. On the other hand, their thinking was dominated by their commitment to a piece of land and a more or less traditional agrarian way of life which this involved. It was this group and those immediately above them, all of whom were intent on avoiding the pressures to drive them into the class of landless proletarians who were potentially the most radical element. Yet the radical Left's ideological outlook tended to blinker them insofar as they dogmatically asserted the landless to be the revolutionary class on the land. They regarded the struggle in a real sense as more or less an extension of the class struggle in the towns and so welcomed the rash of agrarian strikes though they promised more than they delivered. In reality, they were rarely organized or coordinated by unions, mainly localized and never attained the mass proportions often seen in the industrial centres. Not infrequently they were led by Czech Socialists[43] who often disagreed with the local SDs about strategy.

Perhaps more significant from the viewpoint of the mass struggle was that a significant part of the landless, the day-labourers, cultivated allotments on their own account. Though not dwarf-holders, neither were they purely wage-workers. All they needed to gain something from the land reform was a rudimentary agricultural inventory, which many already had. These then would in all likelihood not fight for the collective or cooperative kind of agriculture the SDs, whether Right or Left, proposed. The interests of the small peasants and dwarf-holders collided with those of the landless, part of whom, as we have seen, were also attracted by the Agrarian slogan of "a free peasant on free land."

Had Šmeral addressed himself to the claims of the small peasantry instead of holding out against the nationalization of the great estates and attempting to delay their distribution, to which incidentally the Agrarians whipped up a storm of opposition,[44] he might have achieved much more. Arguably, he might have been able to mobilize the peasants on a programme for the immediate division of the great estates and, through the link between the industrial towns and the peasants working in industry, might have been able to defend the expropriations. But, unlike the SRs who had been in the Russian countryside for decades before their time came, agrarian organizations of the SDP hardly existed before 1914. Šmeral mistakenly looked to the "agrarian factories," the great estates, where relatively high concentrations of workers were to be found, to provide the basis for a form of collectivization. Yet this attempt to adopt the Bolshevik approach was not appropriate to the conditions. Peasants were alarmed at the prospect of becoming wage workers on cooperative or collective farms and gave their support to the Agrarians which was reflected in the rapid growth of the Domovina. In practice, the struggle was largely pre-empted when the small peasants were given rights to buy their leases. Among other things, this knocked the stratum of peasant–industrial workers out of the struggle. For them, it concerned only an end to the landlord and tenant relation and the ownership of a piece of land rather than an expansion of the holding. Frequently they continued to work in the towns. There were examples of small peasants occupying land, but these were more often than not protests against the considerable delays in dividing or otherwise distributing the lands nationalized in May 1919. These diminished considerably when the pace of the reform quickened in 1920 by which time about 170,000 landless and cottagers had been granted land on interim leases.[45] A combination of the disregard for the peasantry's land hunger and the socialists' traditional almost exclusive preoccupation with urban industrial revolution had effectively prevented them taking advantage of the conditions of at least one numerous section of the peasantry, thereby fatally prejudicing their chances of fostering a genuine revolutionary movement in the countryside.

Plate I. The editorial board of the SDP newspaper "Právo lidu" in 1905.

Plate II. The young Bohumír Šmeral

Plate III. The evening edition of the SDP newspaper "Právo lidu" from December 12, 1917

Plate IV. The First of May celebrations on Václavské Náměšti, Prague, 1918.

Plate V. A contemporary caricature of the editorial board of "Rudé Právo" (1921).

Plate VI. Antonín Janoušek.

Plate VII. Edmund Burian.

Plate IX. XIII Congress of the SDP [Right] – November 1920.

Plate X. Petr Cingr.

Plate XI. Karl Kreibich.

Plate XII. Josef Stivín.

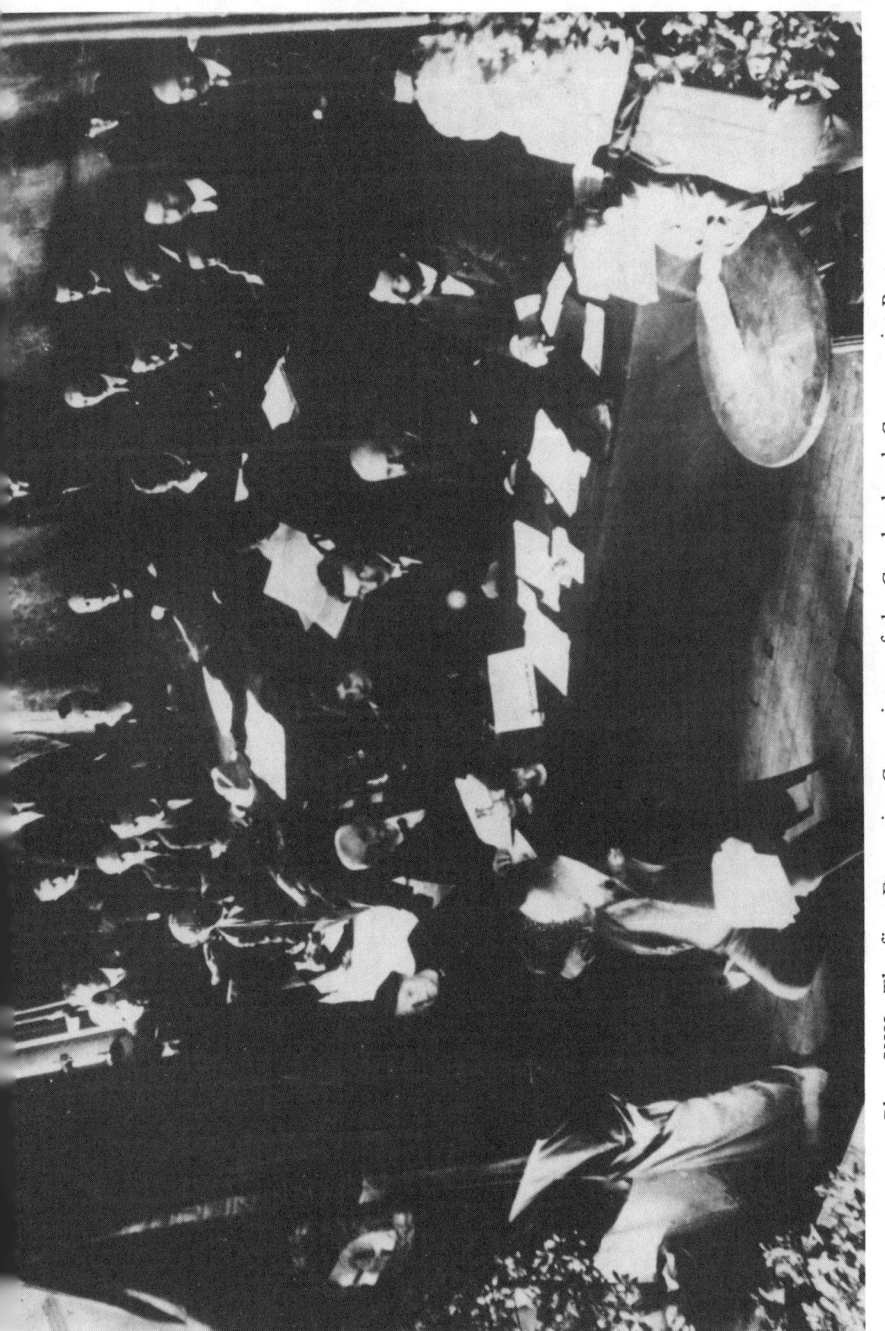

Plate XIII. The first Executive Committee of the Czechoslovak Communist Party.

Plate XV. The December 1920 General Strike in Kladno.

Plate XVI. Alois Muna (1927).

**Part Three**

## The External Environment

Three areas of the external environment most crucially affected Šmeralism. These were the Russian Revolution, the Versailles peace negotiations and the problem of Hungary. Kun's attempt at treaty revisionism had the most direct and striking impact on the radical socialist movement, in that large sections of Šmeral's erstwhile supporters temporarily abandoned him at a critical moment. Versailles and the Revolution, on the other hand, had more oblique and longer lasting effects. The Revolution influenced the attitudes of the governing elite and these were reflected in the political system and the policies derived from it. This aspect in combination with the working out of the pressure from the Allies, which emphasized the need for some form of parliamentary democracy, placed constraints of an indirect nature on Šmeral which for all that were no less powerful than the resurgence of nationalism occasioned by the Hungarian communists. The affects of Kun's initiative have been most extensively documented and for this reason I propose to discuss its impact at some length while restricting myself to more or less brief extrapolations relating the significance the two other external dimensions had for Šmeral.

In general, the Russian Revolution affected individually and severally four areas of Czech society. The constitutional arrangements of the Czech state[2] reflected the fears of the government of Bolshevik emphasis on popular, direct democracy and were designed to inhibit its growth. Further, the programmes of successive coalition governments were to a significant degree based on the publicized social and economic aims of the Bolsheviks. In the conditions of the time, it was a successful ploy suggesting the responsiveness of government to the mass of the people, in whom the Revolution had wrought a change in consciousness, and the inevitability of basic social change. The Orthodox SDs were involved in this in two principal ways. Firstly, their presence was required in the government to make its programme plausible, given the

149

preponderance of socially conservative elements. Secondly, they had to apply themselves to the problem of the Russian Revolution itself which was gaining acceptance as the orthodox model of a socialist revolution and as such was in competition with their own. Finally, there was the group of Czech Bolsheviks around Muna whose experience and perception of it drew them into socialist radicalism.

In conditions of war, the Czech policy reacted well to the Russian October Revolution, insofar as its Decrees on Peace and the self-determination of nations were thought to be capable of helping the national aim. The strikes and demonstrations, like the mutinies in the armed forces, though often of a radical socialist complexion, were welcomed as an essential part of the struggle for a national state. The proletarian socialist aspects of the Revolution were freed by the founding of the Czech state however, and these threatened the political hegemony of those administering it. The Czech state thereafter changed its attitude and sought to build certain safeguards into the framework of the state, and particularly into its political organs, which for all practical purposes restricted or otherwise contained expressions of popular democracy and mass participation. The composition of the National Committee was in part a reaction against direct democracy and a successful attempt to exclude the socialist sections of the labour movement. The threat to its authority implied in the values of the Revolution was made explicit during the action of 14th October. It was met by founding local NCs, not infrequently disabling the local Socialist Councils, which were superior in numbers and organization, by drawing away their members or otherwise dividing their loyalties. Obedience to Prague was enforced and their powers were reduced until the arrangements of state demanded their complete abolition. The fear of revolution too was revealed in the government's response to the local election victory of the SDP. The introduction of financial commissions into local government effectively involved a form of coalition, which constrained the operation of town and village administrations in a majority of which the SDs otherwise had a free hand.

The social environment too felt the impact of Russia which was expressed after 1918 most dramatically in the working class. Even the politically inert peasantry pricked up their ears at its message, though only in response to the land question. More significant for the balance of social forces in the state were the affects it had on the working class. Its aims found a ready echo and its appeal to direct democracy was likewise found to be congenial. These sympathies were mirrored in the movement for the defence of Russia which emerged in response to the efforts of the government to supply its enemies with war-supplies, most marked in the context of the Russo-Polish war. This provided the focus too of the broader movement against intervention which influenced the foreign policy of the Czech state. The Revolution on the other hand brought out the problem of national consciousness in the working class, which collided with their socialist instincts. This contradiction reappeared in a vivid form in the special circumstances of Hungary and I propose therefore to discuss it more fully later in the chapter.

Finally, the October Revolution provided the framework for the debates on the nature of socialism. All of these reactions affected Šmeral in different ways. He agreed with the goals of the Bolshevik Revolution, which was reflected in his formulation of the main party programme, and he won support from many ordinary workers. On the other hand, he disagreed with some of the Bolshevik tactics, in particular, violence and terror,[3] as they were not in accord with modern Czech traditions. This corresponded with the attitudes of large sections of the intelligentsia. Yet this did not mean he condemned the Revolution out of hand nor that he formed a negative view of it as a whole. This balance of the acceptance of goals and rejection of tactics set him apart from the Orthodox SDs who for a time paid lip-service to the aims of the revolution, but in practice quickly threw out the whole idea. The committed Left were attracted by Šmeral's support for revolutionary aims but dissented from his strategy and under the influence of Lenin gradually came to regard him as a Centrist standing on the Left of the Orthodox SDs and sharing their views on parliamentary democracy and political legitimacy. The acceptance of this view internationally strengthened the Bolshevik ascription of him as a national communist and not an internationalist, which came to nudge him into a position between the Comintern and Social Democratic Orthodoxy. His championing of socialization and the other social and economic aims of the Revolution combined with the success of this message in the proletarian constituency and the consequent repercussions for them both in party and government induced the Orthodox SDs to attack him for his assumed agreement with Bolshevik revolutionary tactics. This had an impact in the working class seen most clearly in the neutralization of the unions and the inhibitions of workers otherwise sympathetic to his cause.

Šmeralism arguably failed because he was trapped within his own values. He would not make a revolution without mass support, but lacking the necessary level, he still would not turn to armed rebellion. Although there was a powerful ground-swell of sympathy for the aims of socialism, the working class were not moved sufficiently by Bolshevism to accept unhesitatingly the lead of the radical Left who thereby failed to bolshevize them. On the other hand, the Orthodox SDs failed to turn them away from radical socialist sympathies nor could they conciliate them enough so as to willingly accept the social and economic system as it stood. Yet they did sympathize with the Orthodox SDs' nationalism. Šmeralism then provided at least half of the solution to working class aspirations, Bolshevism considerably less so, in that it added nothing to the social and economic dimension, while the Orthodox SDs satisfied only the proletarian demand for a national state.

The Allies' view of the social situation in the Czech Lands[4] was affected by the October Revolution too and this was reflected in the peace negotiations. Reports of Bolshevism in the Czech Lands were common in Paris and there was concern that the Revolution was beating an uninterrupted path through Central Europe and threatening to provoke a conflagration in the West. The Allied diplomats hence obliged the Czech politicians to address themselves to the problem of restraining the social movement by all possible means. The Czech state was anyway predicated on the Allies' agreement and the Czech government was concerned with presenting it as a good, solid bourgeois state based on political, social and economic institutions congenial to the Entente and therefore likely to gain acceptance as the basis of a viable state. Hence it was built on structures opposed to and limiting socialism. Yet Versailles created permanent problems above those of socio-economic organisation related to the contradiction vis-á-vis national self-determination which the peace represented. Plans were conceived and abandoned, like the one for a Swiss-style federation, which might have corresponded more closely to a solution of the nationalities question. But while in the short run Versailles encouraged the Czech state to form a bulwark against socialism, in the medium- and long-term, it created an environment encouraging the continuing clash of nationalities. The resentment of the national minorities, more or less excluding the Germans, to the Czech state worked itself out through a commitment to radical socialism. In Slovakia, support for this had an ethnic basis and suggested that socialism could provide a vehicle for a nationality struggle, as we shall presently see.

The emergence of Bolshevism in Hungary was in the circumstances of post-war Central Europe ultimately bound to affect political conditions in Czechoslovakia. In doing so, it created severe difficulties for Šmeral. These derived from the reactions of the government, the political parties and the social milieu to the threat posed by Kun's revolution. Hungary highlighted the problem of national identity in its most general sense, the vulnerability of the state in the new Europe and provoked rapid changes in proletarian consciousness which aptly reflected the contradictions in the aspirations of the Czech working-class. The abandonment of Šmeral at the height of the crisis suggests that proletarian class-consciousness was transformed for a time into nationalist consciousness. In the prevailing international conditions, radical socialism created a clash with nationalism which neither Šmeral nor anybody else could avoid. The false identification of Šmeral's internationalism with the activities of Kun's regime enabled the Orthodox SDs to use the nationalist sentiment of the Czech workers generated by the crisis against him. In effect, he was squeezed between the Hungarian revolution and the nationalism of the state.

The Bolshevik government in Budapest represented an extension of Soviet power into Central Europe, which, in the shape of the Slovak Soviet Republic, underlined two major problems of the Czechoslovak Republic. Insofar as it evoked a radical response in sections of Slovak society, it underlined the social problem of the Republic. This however was inextricably linked with the problem of the Hungarian minority in Slovakia to whom it appealed, not only as a radical socialist, but also as a nationalist movement aimed at hindering or preventing the loss of the Slovak territories and a de facto revision of the peace settlement. The reorganization of the territories forming the old Empire entailed political and territorial changes reflecting the change from an Austro-Czech to a Czech-Slovak basis. The elevation of the Czechs to the ruling nationality in a Czechoslovak state caused serious problems of adjustment for both the Slovaks and especially the Hungarians. The latter were unable to accept lightly their loss of power and privilege, particularly in the light of a more or less traditional Czech–Magyar animosity, and accordingly displayed extreme reluctance to relinquish their administrative and political functions in Slovakia. This was marked in the eastern and southern areas of Slovakia[5] where the Hungarian minority lay cheek by jowl with their co-nationals in Hungary proper.

The Slovaks too were apprehensive about their future under a Czech government. Although Kramář stressed the government's wish to show the Slovaks what it meant to live in a free state removed of "political, national and economic oppression,"[6] he still found it necessary to emphasize that the despatch of the Czech army did not represent an invasion.[7] Despite Masaryk's assertion that the Czechs and Slovaks were a nation together,[8] many Slovaks were suspicious, convinced that the Czechs would seek to impose a new form of political domination. The official policy of the government embodied in the theory of Czechoslovakism had a luke-warm reception in Slovakia as Kramář recognized.[9] Czech interest in Slovak autonomy was minimal and despite the thanks Hlinka expressed to "our brother Czechs" for winning the Slovaks their freedom,[10] many voices were raised against them. Indeed within a short time, Hlinka himself complained bitterly that the Czech "Hussites,

Sokols and Progressives" had brought Bolshevism to Slovakia.[11] He demanded also the right for Catholic Slovaks to have their own people in parliament and administration.[12]

Religion was not the only issue on which they expressed their hostility. However, it was the most clear-cut in the sense that it was intimately connected with the preservation of the language and culture of the Slovaks and that a relatively large and homogeneous group of Catholic priests, who made up the backbone of the Slovak intelligentsia, mobilized themselves in its defence. These clerics, like many of the Slovaks in minor positions in local administration, had had to find some way towards rapprochement with the old and oppressive Hungarian regime from which they were pleased to have been liberated. Their gratitude however was not so deep that it could still their fears for the future. Their habits and outlook acquired under the previous regime were transformed in the new conditions in such a way that their ethnic and cultural propinquity to the Czechs often appeared unimportant and, far from treating the Hungarians as national enemies, they discovered a new Madarophile sentiment in themselves.

Resistance to the Czechs however came not only from these *Madărŏn* circles as they were known but from areas of Slovakia where industry had grown up. This of course excluded those more or less purely Hungarian regions where the administrations were under instructions from the government in Budapest to resist the extension and consolidation of the Czech administration.[13] Workers in the small mining towns in Central Slovakia, especially those strung along the valleys of the Váh and Hron rivers, were not at that stage anti-Czech for the same reasons as, for example, Hlinka was. For them, the most compelling reason was hunger. Indeed, food existed, some 15,000 wagons,[14] mainly potatoes and sugar beet. However the setting of the line of demarcation by the Allies, which had completely cut off the roads and railway line to Eastern Slovakia, combined with generally bad communications in the mining regions to render their uninterrupted provisioning impossible. Rail transport anyway was in a parlous state. Of the 800 locomotives running through Slovakia in peace time, only 120 had remained and 70 of these had been sabotaged.[15] In addition, the Polish occupation of Těšín and part of the Košice-Bohumín line had severed the connection with the Ostrava coalfields. As a result, Slovakia could not be supplied with coal, which brought factories to a standstill and led to wholesale unemployment. The flour mills too were put out of action and a danger existed of a complete breakdown in the rail system. Against the background of the food crisis and unemployment, the Slovak workers vented their frustration in anti-state activity, which in certain cases, for example in Topolčany,¹⁶ fused with radical socialist agitation.

Leaving aside the problem of the Hungarian minority, conditions in Slovakia indicated that the Czechs had a nationality and a social problem with their brother Slavs which complicated the internal consolidation of the state and ultimately affected its security internationally. They needed the Slovaks' support at the peace settlement to reinforce their claims to those areas where the Hungary minority demanded the right to be united with the mother country. Yet contrary to the expectations of the Prague government, the Slovaks were not always pro-Czech nor always anti-Magyar. Slovak national opposition weakened the Czech's claim to run a national state and affected their position at the peace conference. Slovak social opposition on the other hand, though small, represented, in the light of changing conditions in Hungary, a danger to the state which was magnified by the potential threat of a link-up with radical socialism in the Czech Lands.

Even before Kun's rise to power in Hungary, the government in Prague feared that a real possibility existed of Czechoslovakia being cut off from the Allied Powers and ultimately strangled by Bolshevik movements in Berlin, Saxony and Bavaria.¹⁷ Before the Hungarians invaded, Beneš regarded the problem of the old Hungarian Ruthenia as more pressing than the activities of the Hungarian minority in Slovakia. Sub-Carpathian Ruthenia provided Czechoslovakia with a border to both Russia and Romania. The Hungarians had abandoned it at the end of the war thereby leaving a free passage to Bolshevik agitators and the Red Army into Slovakia. The Ruthenes, who numbered about half a million,¹⁸ were more or less starving and this helped to make them susceptible to Bolshevik ideas. A Czech administration supported by the army had therefore to be placed in this eastern outpost of the Republic as the most effective counter to the Bolshevik challenge. It was vital to dominate the route providing a passage to Romania which had a problem with the Hungarian minority in Transylvania not dissimilar to the one the Czechs had with the Hungarians in Slovakia. Their community of interests could be expected to make them willing allies. A Czech administration in Užhorod was likewise necessary for the re-organization of the supply situation. In practice, the Allies materially aggravated the problems of the Czechs. The provisional line of demarcation set in Paris effectively severed the connections between the Czech Lands and the eastern parts of the Republic and exacerbated the supply crisis.¹⁹ The absence of a mandate from the Peace Conference to occupy Ruthenia also tied the Czech government's hands. The Allies' stress on the demarcation line as the provisional frontiers of the state was exploited by the Hungarian minority, who insinuated that the Czech occupation of Slovakia was only a temporary arrangement before it was returned to Hungary proper. Yet the failure to shift supplies from the west provided them with other opportunities to incite the Slovak population. Their allegation that the supply situation was attributable to the Czechs' lack of interest in their brothers' plight seemed to be borne out by events. A significant section of society, notably in Central and Eastern Slovakia, gave greater credence to the view that the Czechs' presence amounted to an occupation which would work itself out nationally and socially to their disadvantage.[20]

Official policy was not taken in by Kun's formal recognition of the Czechs' claim to Slovakia.[21] The government indeed had responded before this—to the proclamation of the Hungarian Soviet Republic—with Klofáč's appeal to Beneš for weapons,[22] which showed the Allies that the Czechs were determined to prevent the spread of Bolshevism. The declaration of martial law too was significant. It underlined their resolution and actually prevented the unhindered operation of Bolshevik agents in the different parts of Slovakia. However the Czech cause was hampered by the failure of the Allies to act rapidly enough upon Beneš' recommendation for Ruthenia. This enabled the Hungarian Red Army to enter Užhorod without resistance in early April 1919 which emphasized the vulnerability of Eastern Slovakia. They were not entirely unwelcome for, quite apart from the effect their message had on a famished population, there was clear evidence that the Czech officials were treating the Ruthenes in Prešov in a more disdainful manner than had the old Hungarian administration.[23] This did not encourage pro-Czech sentiment among the Slovaks either and, as Kramář observed, was bound to threaten the Czech position concerning national minorities at the peace conference, unless something was done about it.[24]

The threat posed by the soldiers of the Hungarian Red Army was not purely military, although they numbered among their activities frequent incursions across the demarcation line as a prelude to attacks on Czech patrols and military installations.[25] More often than not they were assisted by the local Hungarian population to whom they distributed weapons. Equally important, however was their agitation and propaganda activity which made skillful use of the social problem in Slovakia and had significant effects on both the military effectiveness of the Czechoslovak armed forces and on the consolidation of the civil administration. Kun's definitive ending of the old regime in Hungary and the erection of a Soviet Republic appeared to contain the germ of a solution to the nationality and social problems of the Slovaks. His promise of a Soviet Republic based on a federation of different nationalities with equal rights[26] was treated as a serious alternative to the solution of the Czechs. In Hungary, he had destroyed the power of capitalism and had thereby taken a step towards the destruction of the type of national domination, regarded as a by-product of the system of economic relations, which had been so strong a feature of Hungarian–Slovak relations. The overthrow of capitalism and the scheme for an international socialist federation was a promise of social and national liberation for the Slovaks and was in direct competition with the Czechoslovakism of the Prague government. By no means did all Slovak resistance to the Czechs turn on this issue. It is scarcely conceivable that, for example, Hlinka would have regarded this as an acceptable solution. Yet there are grounds for believing that it had an impact in the armed forces under the control of the government in Prague and also in the local administrations and offices of the organs of state. Hungarian agitation found a ready response among the rank and file soldiers of the Czech army, most of whom were Slovaks drawn from the countryside.[27] They played on their fears of "Czechification"[28] by pointing out among other things that the numerical preponderance of Czechs in the command structure of the army was the model for the future administration and development of Slovakia under Czech tutelage.

Apart from this nationality dimension, the Hungarians were enabled to exploit a class or social dimension to the unrest in the ranks. This consisted in the burning resentment resulting from the fact that only men from lower social groups were called to serve at the front while the well-situated escaped military service entirely.[29] The effect of these dissatisfactions was visible in generally low morale and desertion on a wide-scale,[30] though not to the Hungarians, which aptly reflects the ambiguity of their position. Desertion was perhaps a national, though individual, act of protest achieved without plan or leadership, which was not intended to offer any material benefit to the Hungarians. On the other hand, they were always kept well-informed about the difficulties and movements of the Czech army one way or another from within its ranks.[31] At the end of the war, all state, local government and church officials, likewise administrators of the Kingdom of Hungary were provisionally left in their posts if they took an oath of obedience to the Czechoslovak Republic.[32] In many cases, the local administrations retained an ethnic Hungarian element. The Slovak officials, whether in town councils, administration or even military offices, despite their promise of obedience, displayed strong anti-Czech sympathies and under the impulse of Hungarian agitation embarked on a campaign of passive resistance linked in places with sabotage.[33] This tendency was visible in other less *Madăron*-inclined areas of Slovak society. The railway workers, for example, frequently disrupted those sections of the rail system affecting the transport of the Czech forces. Post office workers spread rumours along the telegraph system. The gendarmerie responded to Czech instructions more often than not by deserting their posts. Only the police seemed immune to the influence of the Hungarians. It appears to be a great historical paradox that, after their release from bondage, they could so easily forget the centuries of Hungarian domination and turn on the agent of their liberation and turn back towards their former oppressors. The Czech military presence was perceived as an occupation and therefore a de facto abrogation of Slovak claims for national autonomy. National resistance to this fused, in certain sections of society, with support for the aims of radical socialism, which, put another way, meant support for Kun's solution to the social problem as opposed to that of the Czechs. Radical socialist groups emerged in parts of Slovakia quite independently of Hungarian influence, although the most powerful developed in association with the Magyars. For example in Košice, an International Committee of Soviets numbering 60 persons was discovered and broken up.[34] Radical socialists were strong in the purely ethnic Slovak area of Liptovský Mikuláš, where the Czech communist Kříž was active.[35] In addition, the fact that Vrútky, Lieskovec/Zvolen and Ružomberok, the latter more generally associated with clerical conservatism than socialism, sent radical socialist delegates to the Prague parliament in 1920[36] suggests a significantly high level of popular ethnic Slovak support. The annihilation of the right in the Slovak SDP[37] is further evidence of this, albeit in changed conditions. At all events, it is more or less clear that radical socialism in Slovakia in 1919 did not grow up entirely on the bayonets of the Magyar Red Army nor was it a political persuasion exclusively displayed by the Hungarian minority. Conceivably, the form of communism which the Hungarians stood for was not necessarily a thing to be feared by the Slovaks even if it did stand for the return of the lost territories as Burks suggests[38] provided the reconstruction of historic Hungary was undertaken on federalist and socialist principles. Despite the sense of a common historical past reflected in the theory of Czech and Slovak brotherhood, on which events have more than once cast doubt, a significant section of Slovak society was unable to accept that their claims to equal political and economic rights could be realized within a capitalist republic in which the Czechs had an overwhelmingly preponderant influence. The popularity of "economic Bolshevism" to use Šrobár's phrase, could not be doubted, particularly in the countryside.[39] This provides part of the explanation for support for the short-lived Slovak Socialist Republic which was seen as combining the principles of national self-determination within a multi-nationality structure with the socialization of agriculture and industry.

The Czech government then was confronted with both a national and social threat from the Hungarians and to a lesser degree also from the Slovaks. The menace was enhanced after they had fused. Official circles regarded the agitation of the Hungarians and, later, the invasion as part of a wider, more or less revanchist movement echoing the old pan-Germanism of the previous era. The support for Kun in Vienna, the socialist, pro-Austrian and anti-Czech stance of Galicia and the Hungarian attack interpreted as the prelude to a link-up with the invading Poles in Těšín, were regarded as parts of a scheme to incite the defeated populations of the former Central Powers against the Allied peace settlement in general and towards the destruction of the Czechoslovak state in particular.[40] Kramář, the prime-minister, favoured military intervention in Hungary as indeed he did in Russia. Masaryk's view however was on the face of it more circumspect. He accepted that nothing could be done without the agreement of the Entente and declared himself in favour of a defensive neutrality as far as Hungary was concerned. This was a fair reflection of opinion in the Czech Lands where there was a marked distaste for militarism and anything connected with it and also a degree of proletarian support for the social and economic aims of Kun's government. However, while Masaryk preached non-intervention, his Minister of National Defence, Klofáč had in April 1919 been making preparations for a military solution to the problem of Hungary. In early April, he gave the army orders to mobilize[41] and on 26th, under French command crossed the line of demarcation in Slovakia in a push towards Budapest.[42] This was against the official policy of the Czech government which had decided on 1st April not to interfere in the internal affairs of a neighbouring country and called forth a sharp rebuke from the Orthodox SDs and the socialist bloc in parliament reminding Beneš and Kramář of their responsibilities to the coalition government.[43] Šmeral too was completely opposed to intervention. His publication of the secret mobilization and advance of the army and of evidence of munitions earmarked for the war was greeted in silence by the government. The discrepancy between the government's policy statements on Hungary and the activities of the Czech forces who had taken Miskolc as the first stage of their plan to link up with the Romanian army did not provoke much opposition at the time. It is true that both the working class and the intelligentsia were passionately anti-war and anti-militarist. But, until the Czech-Hungarian conflict spilled over into Slovakia in late May 1919, there was little visible reaction. The radical Left indeed warned the Czech government that intervention would only be possible over the dead bodies of the Czech proletariat,[44] while the Czech army was at that very moment encamped in Hungary. In reality, the Left, Šmeral included, did little more than agitate among those workers producing war-materials, as for example in Škoda-Plzeň, in the vain hope that output would slacken or stop altogether. Hauser played a major part in strengthening the anti-militarist mood by playing on the general fear of another conflagration. Yet in practice, nothing very positive was achieved in either preventing attempts at intervention or in defending Kun. There were however two aspects of the domestic situation which overshadowed the conflict with Communist Hungary, at least in its early days. All eyes were concentrated on the food crisis, which in May provoked a series of hunger riots and provided an opportunity for a re-examination of attitudes on the question of popular violence and revolution. This was connected with the second point, even to a degree helping to cause it, the frailty of the coalition which was in the throes of the crisis precipitated by the resignation of the National Democratic ministers. Šmeral had grounds for optimism in thinking that, in conditions of economic and social deprivation and of the government's incapacity, class interest would rally the working class and, to a degree, likewise the intelligentsia, who, more or less proletarianized by the war, were not averse to responding to the economic circumstances besetting them. There was a significant measure of proletarian solidarity with the social and economic aims of Kun but there was a factor constraining the radical Left. There was an unwillingness to follow his path, as socialization, it was argued, would do nothing to alleviate the supply problem.[45] This of course bore the imprint of the Orthodox SDs.

On the whole, the proletarian supporters of what later became the Marxist Left were content with the concerned stance of their representatives in parliament which, with the President's stated opposition to foreign adventures, scarcely allowed the problem to impinge on their consciousness. They were uninterested in the plight of the Slovaks nor in the punitive conditions of martial law in Slovakia. To that extent their sentiments were determined more or less by a sense of national superiority insofar as it manifested itself at all. However the counter-attack of the Hungarians after they had re-captured Miskolc and the drive into Slovakia changed all that. It displayed the military weakness of the Czech army which caused the many proponents of a civilian militia to change their ground. Indeed, it ultimately led to the acceptance of the *Branný zákon* which all SDs had said they would oppose with all their strength. The misleading reports of Hungarian numerical superiority,[46] evidence of atrocities committed on Czech POWs[47] and the publication of Kun's aim to link up with the Soviet Red Army along the Košice-Prešov-Bardějov axis created a climate of national emergency. The government responded by declaring martial law in the Frýdek and Bohumín areas of Eastern Moravia, the gateways through which Bolshevism in one form or another was expected to gain entrance to the Czech Lands.[48] The radical Left felt the full force of the Austrian war laws. The radical newspapers were subjected to a strict censorship and the smaller ones were ruined financially. The correspondence of suspected persons was searched, while they were confined to their native towns and villages. In a few cases, people were interned contra legem and foreign nationals were expelled.[49] The garrison in Kladno as in all other known areas of radical socialism was strengthened[50] and the government attempted to decapitate the organization of the Left by arresting Muna and Zápotocký[51] and sever their connections with Lenin.

Yet these direct affects of the Hungarian crisis did not have such a powerful affect on Šmeral's movement as the fundamental overnight change in consciousness experienced in the great majority of the working class, who in normal conditions supported the aims of socialism he espoused. The problem of national security was brought down to the level of the individual and out of the forum of the Peace Conference or of the association with Romania and Yugoslavia. In the specific conditions of Slovakia, radical socialism was identified with Hungarian irredentism. Despite the radical socialist programme implemented by Kun in Hungary and his plan for a socialist federation of nationalities having equal rights, the nationality relation from the days of the Empire reasserted itself. For the Czech working class, there was the dim recognition that if the Hungarians were allowed to stay in Slovakia, it would make the Czechoslovak Republic impossible. The Czech Lands by themselves could scarcely hope to survive even if the Entente gave them their imprimatur. The origin of the Slovak Soviet Republic also presented a problem. At that time there was no evidence that it was not a Hungarian puppet trying to conceal its aggressive intentions towards the Czech Lands behind an appeal to federalism and socialization.[52] No doubt, the Czech parties distorted and misinformed Janoušek's views on the matter. Yet the fact remained; he was a leading member of the Kladno radicals, an intimate of Kun and involved as the go-between with Muna, who himself, had been implicated in preparations for a rising that had led to his arrest. Faced with a perceived threat to the state, the Czech worker, despite difficult even hardly bearable social conditions, reacted nationalistically. The state was seen to be above party and class interest and the Czech proletariat reacted not according to class interest but according to national identity. In conditions of hard-won freedom, the Czech workers responded enthusiastically to Tomášek's appeal to step up production for the war effort. Tusar was showered with offers from factory workers, the Workers Gymnastic Unions and the Sokols all eager to fight at the front. Yet they did not go to defend

Slovak society from the claimed depredations of Hungarian revanchists. They volunteered because an independent Slovakia was an essential part of the Czech national state without which it would have been hard put to survive. The experience of the Czechs in the actual attainment of the state reflected a certain kind of ideology which regarded the state as being above party interests or at least as an interest basic to all parties, each of which had a duty to help preserve it.[53] This was misleading in the sense that the notion of state was used more or less exclusively to refer to the type of state which actually existed implying that no other was possible. Despite the desperate social and economic conditions of the early days of the republic, the Czech proletariat and their leaders accepted this view. At the same time, they believed it possible to alter its economic and social arrangements without affecting the political form of the state. In effect, the bourgeois parties with the Orthodox SDs had a stranglehold on proletarian consciousness in that few questioned their assertion that the socialist revolution was not only a negation of the then existing Czech state but of all types of national state. Socialist revolution and the national state then were regarded in the conditions of the time as mutually exclusive. This however did not prevent the Czech working class from moderating their attacks on the internal organization of the state as they anyway hardly constituted an attempt at revolution. On the other hand, when an external factor intervened, with the Hungarians' appearance in Slovakia, they regarded it as first and foremost a national and irredentist threat and the socialist dimension of Kun's movement which, at least in parts of Slovakia, appeared to offer a solution was ignored. Kun's initiative was a de facto revision of the peace treaty and an attack on the Czech state. International conditions could not allow this. SD organizations and even families were split on the question of Hungary and attitudes to it became the acid test by which patriots or traitors were recognized. It came as no surprise when even members of the radical Left refused to place the interests of international socialism over those of the bourgeois state. Brodecký and Stivín, both hitherto fervent fighters for socialism, intimates of the Kladno revolutionaries and in the latter case, an honorary member of Kun's government, revealed themselves as nationalists. They jumped to the defence of the state taking for the period of the crisis the majority of the Czech proletariat over to the Othodox SDs.[54]

Šmeral was well aware of the problem deriving from the relationship between radical socialism and nationalism. His reaction to Kun's counterattack was one of dismay. He could have done nothing to prevent it nor indeed anything about it afterwards. Nevertheless he appealed to Kun to evacuate Slovakia[55] hoping thereby to rescue something of the work of the previous six months. Shortly after and fearing for his life, he disappeared. The response of the Kladno radicals was no less muted. Their primary concern was a rapid cessation of hostilities in Slovakia and thereafter to set about the task of picking up the pieces. They attempted to revive the old antimilitarist slogans of the war-years but discovered that in this instance the Czech workers by and large favoured a miliary solution to the conflict. Their accusations that the Orthodox SDs had colluded with the government over the military enterprise which had provoked Kun's counter, though not so wide of the mark, found little response and their calls for a party congress to resolve the matter[56] were in the circumstances hopelessly optimistic. Although the cause of socialism had been dealt a severe blow, there was an element of consolation. In general terms, Hungary marked a stage in the consolidation of the radical Left in that the most significant crypto-nationalists were revealed. On the other hand, there was another aspect which affected Šmeral's plans to maintain a broad radical democratic socialist movement. Sizeable splits appeared in the Moravian organizations and principally in Brno. The neutrality, or rather confusion, of Burian, the leader of the old Brno Centralists, who stood closest to Šmeral on the issues raised by the case of Kun caused Václav Friedrich to secede and found his own radical communist group.[57] Friedrich, an ex-Red Guard who had served under Muraviev, demanded a strictly revolutionary and internationalist approach and his initiative split the radicals in Moravia into the Bolshevik Left and the adherents of a mass radical socialist party. Friedrich with his comrades Rydlo in Třebič, Pergl-Beneš (Ostrava) Knofliček, Pospíšil and Doležal[58] ultimately came to squeeze Šmeral from another direction.

The Hungarian Revolution brought out the contradictions in the aspirations of the Czech working class and exposed the limitations of their class consciousness in a time of danger to the bourgeois state. When the threat receded, nationalist feeling as is to be expected ebbed with it and their response to events was more strongly influenced by class interest once again. Their nationalist reaction however was instructive in that it at least showed Šmeral the importance of leavening the movement with the sections of the intelligentsia who, for one reason or another, tended to be less prone to national feeling and more capable of maintaining an internationalist stance. However, precisely this aspect represented one of Šmeral's major difficulties. The Orthodox SDs' claim that Šmeral supported the aims of the Russian Revolution, which overshadowed his disagreement with its methods, allowed them and the bourgeois parties to manipulate working class opinion against him. His internationalism was frequently interpreted as loyalty to a foreign power whose aims implicit in world revolution included an end to Czech independence. Try as he might to go it alone according to specific national conditions, ultimately he had little choice but to come to rest in the arms of the Comintern. There is perhaps another point worth making. The evidence from Slovakia suggests that certain sections of ethnic Slovakia society were capable of combining nationalist with radical socialist sentiments in contrast to the Czechs. This may conceivably be explained as the Slovaks simply hailing to the ideology of the nation which they regarded as offering a defence against Czech political domination and ignoring the possible consequences of membership of the Hungarian socialist federation. It may on the other hand be legitimate to conclude that in general radical socialism does not create a clash with nationalism when national consciousness is at the level present in a relatively class undifferentiated agrarian society, as Burks suggests.[59] The development of a powerful, clearly defined proletariat tends to produce a growth, not only in class, but also in national identity, which acts in specific conditions as a brake on proletarian revolutionary movements. This tends to affect mass democratic revolutionary socialist movements more strongly than narrow parties dominated by the intelligentsia.

## Conclusion

The foundation of a multi-national Czechoslovak Communist Party in 1921 was a signal that the Czech radical socialist movement had formally abandoned Šmeralism. Many took this as a sufficient ground for believing that the Orthodox SDs had been correct all along in placing Šmeral in the Bolshevik camp. A significant section of the Czech Bolsheviks however agreed with the strictures Kreibich made at the "Unity Congress" which suggested that Šmeral had been and remained a Centrist. It is true that Šmeral played a major role in the founding of the Communist Party. Yet he regarded this as a negation of his road to socialism. From 1921, his career in the labour movement seemed to be essentially a compromise between his wish to distance himself from the changes being initiated in the party, though hardly then visible, and a desire to serve the international communist movement in some way. The Comintern offered opportunities for an intellectual of his standing and this neatly coincided with the Bolshevik centre's desire to remove radical socialists from influential positions and replace them with individuals whose qualifications included the ability to manipulate the party apparatus and adopt unqualified and unquestioning political stances. After the Bubník controversy in 1925, Šmeral had little to do with the party except insofar as it touched his primary activity in the Comintern as an expert on questions of socialism in Manchuria. Šmeralism was defeated in the Czech Lands because some of its aspects proved to be contradicted by the conditions in which they operated. The basis of this conclusion then is a brief appraisal of the common ground Šmeral shared with the Orthodox SDs and the Bolsheviks, if any, and the balance of its failures and successes.

The Orthodox SDs regarded Šmeral as a Bolshevik. Muna and the Czech communists thought of him as standing on the left-wing of the Orthodox SDs. Both viewpoints contain serious weaknesses. Though Šmeral challenged the Orthodox SDs for the leadership of the Party, their differences were not simply based on differing tactics. They clashed over both ends and means. Šmeral's principal aim was, broadly speaking, the socialization of large-scale industry and agriculture, likewise the institutions of finance capital, as the necessary prerequisite for the transformation of society into one more strongly reflecting social equality and justice. The Orthodox SDs were less interested in the kind of rapid and deep social change he envisaged. Though they often expressed their committment to a socially just society and paid lip-service to socialization or nationalization as a principle, they did not in practice go beyond a piecemeal approach which, on the vital questions of the socialization of the mines and the Land Reform, gave the decisive advantage to their coalition partners. The differences in aims were matched by different views of the means of change and party organization. Šmeral did not agree with their assertion that, in the conditions of the time, parliament could meet all the demands placed upon it in this respect. The coalition government which sprang from it was unacceptable in that it was an embodiment of the principle of class reconciliation. His view then did not rule out parliament as such, but was based more explicitly on the mobilizing of the masses which, as we shall presently see, was not fully worked out and constituted, in the final analysis, a source of weakness. Šmeral's party was designed to safeguard class-proletarian aims and attract the participation of the masses. It was intended to be mainly, but not exclusively, proletarian and reflected his democratic conviction that change must come from below. The Orthodox SDs represented a party and a governing elite which made strenuous efforts to exclude the masses and glossed over any special position for the proletariat within the party. In general, however, they were correct in associating Šmeral with the aims of Bolshevism, which in practice were little different from those of any other radical socialists from the time of Marx and before. Yet, they were wide of the mark in ascribing to him support for Bolshevik notions of tactics or party organization. The challenge to them, and ultimately to the state—for the struggle was not simply an inner-party affair—was essentially radical, mass, democratic socialist and not that of an armed and minority revolutionary group.

Lenin too was on shaky ground when he described Šmeral as a Centrist. It may legitimately be doubted if he held this view other than as a polemical statement against an opponent on the same side of the fence who, in the conditions of the Czech Lands, had attracted a mass movement and hence placed himself in competition with Bolshevik orthodoxy. Lenin's penchant for reducing more or less everything into simple, unequivocal and universalistic terms was, on balance, an agitation requirement. But this did not do justice to Šmeral's position. Contra Lenin, he did not want to socialize

## CONCLUSION

all of industry and agriculture. Having regard to the industrial and agricultural composition of the Czech Lands, he allowed a place for small-scale private industry and farming units. We have no evidence to conclude that he might have changed this in the event of a socialist revolution. However this is one area where it is legitimate to suggest that, as small-scale industry employed a majority of workers, the exploitation of labour might well have persisted. Šmeral seems not to have addressed himself to this aspect which would certainly have required more working out. Leaving this aside, Lenin was concerned more with Šmeral's resistance to centralism. This sprang from his conviction of the need for an open-party in which the working masses were to have representation at all levels, from the Executive Committee, to the smallest branch organization. This was an important part of the radical socialists' plans for the reform of the SDP which reflected their agreement that the shape of the future party would follow the class composition of the leading organ elected at the XIII Congress of the SDP (Left), "the party within a party," half of whose members were full-time industrial workers. Though Lenin objected to the preponderance of the intelligentsia among the leaders of the Czech radical socialists, there were significantly more in the leading organs of the Bolshevik party. The Czech working masses were at the level of development which gave them a legitimate claim to be recognized and the right to elect party functionaries and similarly to vote them out if they did not endeavour to work for the reflection of proletarian opinion in the decisions of the party. In Russian conditions, "hard-centralism" might have been an appropriate way, but it was related to a different revolutionary tactic and had only a deleterious affect on the Czech workers. Laying down narrow lines of obedience, erecting the party organization on the basis of hierarchy and elitism was essential to a conspiracy theory of revolution but unhelpful to a tactic based on a mass, democratic revolution. The struggle against the Orthodox SDs had been initiated partly because they had trampled all over inner-party democracy. It was therefore unlikely to accept similar restrictions even though they might be directed to the achievement of radical socialist ends. Lenin too was chary about Šmeral's notion of party composition. Although it kept the leading role for the industrial proletariat, it allowed a place for others of a non-proletarian complexion, which he thought likely to affect the dictatorship of the proletariat. Yet the intelligentsia were not inherently petty-bourgeois by inclination. They were an important part of the mass movement, who shared some of the disadvantages and exploitation implicit in their wage-relations and, in the period of revolutionary transition, had an important role to play in organization and administration. Possibly, Lenin regarded them as of doubtful quality insofar as they were attracted by Šmeral's decision to abstain from cold-blooded revolutionary violence and terror. Šmeral perhaps was on more dangerous ground in respect of his wish to involve the small peasants and producers, likewise the petty-traders. Their instincts in specific situations might for a time lead them to go along with the revolution, but their size as a social group could well prove to be an obstruction to the proletarian plans of the movement afterwards. As has already been referred to, this point was more or less glossed over.

Šmeralism was a success in a number of ways. It was a type of radical socialism which applied well to the conditions of the Czech Lands. It respected the norms of political legitimacy and democracy more faithfully than either the Orthodox SDs or the Czech Bolsheviks and it gained a mass following, especially among the working class. The rank and file were not excluded from active participation in the movement but were to an extent encouraged to imprint their wishes, subject to the democratic process, on its leading figures. In this respect, Šmeralism arguably made more effort to achieve a degree of genuinely working class representation than the practice of either the Orthodox SDs or the Czech Socialists. In addition, its tactics made it acceptable to a section of the intelligentsia, though Šmeral was concerned to guard against their domination of the movement. His conception of what the future party would be like gave them no privileged position, but rather sought to integrate them into the working class on the basis of their capacity to remedy some of the deficiencies in proletarian education.

Šmeralism did not address itself to all problems. Yet it competed more or less successfully against rival ideologies which had the advantage of claiming to represent a universalistic or unqualified philosophy. Though Šmeral's solution to the nationalities question was logically coherent, in conditions of intense national conflict, it was not popular. It was based on a compromise between the need for internationalism, which reflected the proletariat's real relation to the means of production, and a recognition of the power and attraction of nationalism. However in the prevailing conditions, there were only two viable options; one was a simplistic form of internationalism and the other, the solution of the Czech nationalists. The Czechoslovak state claimed to have solved the problem of the minorities, or at least to have laid the basis for a solution. The ruling Czech nationality was in a more or less close ethnic and language relation with the Slovaks who were officially regarded as their brothers. The Hungarians, for one reason or another, were dismissed. The problem of the Germans remained, but this did not affect the majority of Czechs coming out in favour of a more or less simplistic notion of Czechoslovak nationalist orthodoxy. A minority on the other hand supported the internationalism of the Czechoslovak CP. Šmeral came to be regarded as associated with the Bolsheviks, though his internationalism was significantly different. His stance was interpreted as essentially anti-nationalist and this seriously affected his popularity.

Šmeralism failed, but this was less a failure of its rational and constructive solutions than the failure of its strategy which conflicted with some short- and long-term conditions making it at that time impossible. As an alternative model of socialism, it reflected more closely the predispositions embedded in some aspects of Czech historical culture and the economic and social conditions of the Czech Lands than the Orthodox SDs. Its solution to the nationalities question took account of their claims to equal rights and also of the problems related to them posed by the position of the state in Central Europe, without however acquiring the inward-looking character of the Orthodox SDs. Though it failed as a strategy in the early post-war years, it emerged again after the Second War as an alternative when the expulsion of the German minority more or less removed the conditions of national conflict which had proved to be the major source of constraint in 1919-1920. It emerged once more in the late 1960s when the Bolshevik model of socialism was held to be a conspicuous failure in meeting the conditions and traditions of the Czechoslovak state.

However, Šmeralism as a strategy ran into enormous constraints. These lie not least in the contradictions in the relation between his strategy and the conditions in which he operated which indicated the fundamental problem to be one of timing. His revolutionary strategy was built on winning over SDP institutions and, in association with the popular movement of radical socialist sympathizers, to exert overwhelming pressure, first in the regions and after having won control there, in the centres of government. It was a tactic devised as most appropriate to conditions of fluidity and one designed to achieve its ends in a relatively short space of time. The fluid conditions themselves tended to rule out long-term solutions. In all likelihood, other kinds of constraints would have interposed if he had taken ten years to build up his movement. However he was locked in a contradiction, in that his strategy aimed at a rapid shift in proletarian opinion in favour of a socialist revolution, when in practice the incidence of proletarian nationalism negated or neutralized permanent and unambiguous support for the kind of mass and democratic revolution Šmeral envisaged. His strategy ran up against Czech nationalism which could not be overcome quickly and hence contradicted it. The short-term internal conditions and the international position of the Czechoslovak state were the principal sources of his weakness. The failure to develop alternative institutions or to find an antidote to parliamentary restrictions and the underestimation of the Orthodox SDs were mistakes connected with the nature of his strategy, while his ideology was at least partially responsible for the error in respect of the peasantry. These contributed to his failure, but were of a more or less secondary significance to the constraints imposed by conditions which ultimately made his strategy unviable.

Šmeral had no realistic answer to the question of the land and the problem of the peasantry. The socialist ideology of the pre-war years more or less overlooked these questions and this was reflected in the practise of the SDP. Its legacy was the concentration on the industrial proletariat as the agent of change which was translated more or less uncritically in conditions of the countryside into a reliance on the imagined revolutionary instincts and interests of the landless workers. But they did not represent the largest coherent social force in the countryside and, insofar as their primary interest was the maintenance of their jobs on collectivized or cooperatively organized great estates, they were conservatively inclined. Šmeral was looking for allies for his mass, urban revolutionary movement and he overlooked the potential basis for support in the small peasants and those cultivating the so-called dwarf-holdings. This may well have reflected his scepticism that little help could be expected from a social group whose consciousness was dominated by small-scale agricultural production, no matter how uncertain. In all likelihood, there was too a significant lack of knowledge of the conditions of the peasantry. The fact remained that this group was numerically the most powerful in the countryside and indispensable for a mass, democratic revolution. However instead of trying to actively engage this potentially revolutionary group, for example by advocating the parcelling of land, Šmeral stuck to the conventions of socialist thinking and missed an opportunity to pre-empt the drive of the Agrarians to achieve a dominant position in the countryside. In so doing, he lost too a valuable potential ally in the shape of the small peasants working in light industry in the small towns and villages of the Czech Lands. These could have provided a vital link between town and country, but, placed as they were, became a likely target of the Czech Socialists with the result that they were lost to the revolutionary socialist movement.

Šmeral made other mistakes relating to the institutions of parliament and party, and likewise the relation between them. His strategy was based on winning a majority of the rank and file supporters of the SDP, thereafter winning the leading organs of the party in a democratic manner. Yet he overestimated the democratic morality of the Orthodox SDs who refused to

# CONCLUSION 171

accept the result. But he had no effective answer to their response. He needed party institutions to mobilize the working class and he had no feasible institutional alternative to them. Secondly, he counted on the SDs resigning from the coalition, or at least being abandoned by it—thereby opening up the system. He did not quite realize that the Orthodox SDs were at that stage vital to the functioning of the state and hence had to be defended at almost any cost. To break down the restrictions placed on him by the political and parliamentary system, he proposed to gain control of the party. Despite a majority within it, this was seen not to be open to him. A revolutionary armed attempt to change this situation was no part of his strategy. Perhaps the only way he could have worked himself out of this predicament was to have enlarged the time-scale he had given himself. Yet he was operating under constraints from another side and between them, he became the subject of a squeeze. Both Orthodox SDs and Bolsheviks claimed the support of the working class in that they both gave direct, straightforward answers as the solutions to social and economic problems. They both appealed as a universalistic type of socialism. Šmeralism was unable to emulate them in this regard and his modifications of both positions ultimately could not survive in those conditions. The December General Strike was the culmination of the squeeze in that afterwards, the lines were drawn more clearly between nationalists and internationalists. Šmeral recognized the difficulty of working outside the two power blocs and the fact that he could not by himself cope with the difficulties presented by the international situation. His joining the Bolshevik camp was based on his hope that the Comintern could provide the necessary dimension of support internationally. However, he was soon disabused of the idea that, in the internal organization and conduct of the party, his values, and not Lenin's, would play the decisive role. He maintained some freedom to manoeuvre for a time, but he was unwilling to alter his opinions on the role of the party in the revolution and socialist democracy and not unwillingly gave way to the new breed of party functionaries.

Šmeral found it impossible to achieve his democratic aims within the SDP and likewise his economic aims within Czech society as a whole. The political system smothered his efforts and induced him to preserve his economic aims in the company of the Czech Bolsheviks. Had the SDP and the system been sensitive to change which the scale of Šmeral's movement suggested it should have been, then its affect might have been felt in at least two significant areas. Šmeral would no doubt have attempted to achieve a better deal for the minorities, especially the Germans. His success in breaking into the system of government, without scaling down or losing either democratic or economic aims would have provided a model of radical socialist orthodoxy to all advanced industrial societies superior to that of Bolshevism. As it was, he had the option of accepting the limitations of the system and losing sight of his aims; or, as he was in the event forced into the position of doing, of maintaining his economic aims and accepting the consequences of embracing a democratically objectionable principle which would ultimately work itself out in fulfilling the demands of the centre of Bolshevik orthodoxy. The socialization of the means of production would hence be paid for in the adoption of Soviet institutions, which practice later showed to be a partial negation of democratic worker participation in their administration. For radical socialists to wait until democratic norms are abided by involves the postponement of the realization of economic aims. They are typically forced to scale them down, which plays into the hands of capitalism by allowing the elements of the system time to re-group. Šmeral's experience seems to show that it is not always true that a democratic majority can impress its will on the minority and also that it is not only in non-parliamentary democratic states that the will of a party minority can prevail. His specific contribution to the history of socialism lies in his attempt to combine radical socialist aims with a radical, mass, democratic party, without accepting compromise on the aims at the price of the means, nor vice versa. His defeat is another example of the apparent intractability of this problem, but elements of Šmeralism survived into the changed circumstances of the post-war period where it reflected Czech aspirations strongly enough to pose a significant threat to Bolshevism once again.

# NOTES

## Introduction

1. Právo lidu, 11.2.1898.
2. Protokol IX. sjezdu československé sociálně demokratické strany ve dnech 4.-8. září 1909, v Praze, Praha 1909.
3. See his Československá sociální demokracie a další možností a cíle vývoje Rakousko-Uherska - Protokol XI. řádného sjezdu československé sociálně demokratické strany dělnické, konaného ve dnech 7., 8. a 9. prosince 1913 na Žofině v Praze, 120.
4. The great majority of Šmeral's writings are listed in: Bibliografie Bohumíra Šmerala, ÚV KSČ, Praha 1971.
5. Šmeral, Bohumír, Pravda o sovětovém Rusku, Praha 1920.
6. Národní shromáždění "revoluční", Těsnopisecké zprávy. Zasedání Národního shromáždění.

## PART ONE
## Šmeralism

1. Galandauer, Jan, Bohumír Šmeral, Blok Brno, 1978, 102f.
2. See Part Two: Chapter 1, 56-57 and 62f.
3. Quoted in: Šolle, Zdeněk, Socialistické hnutí dělnické a česká otázka [1848-1918], Praha 1968, 43.
4. Kreibich, Karl, Dějiny českého dělnického hnutí, Praha 1949, 32.
5. Šmeral, Bohumír, Národností otázka a sociální demokracie-Referát na IX. sjezdu československé sociálně demokratické strany dělnické konaném v Praze 5.-8. září 1909, Zář 1909, 116-151. [Hereafter: Národností otázka]
6. December 1913 at the XI SDP Congress. See his speech: Československá sociální demokracie a další moznosti a cíle vývoje Rakousko-Uherska; Protokol XI. řádného sjezdu československanské sociálně demokratické strany dělnické, Praha, ÚDKN 1913, 114.

173

7. Šmeral, Bohumír, Národností otázka..., 134.
8. See Part Two: Chapter 1, 74f.
9. Kramář, Karel, Poznámka o české politice, Praha 1907. Beneš was also recorded as saying in 1908 that the ties joining the Austrian nationalities were too strong to allow their splitting into national states. Quoted: Tobolka, Zdeněk, Politické dějiny českého národa, Praha 1915, IV, 103.
10. Sec Part Two: Chapter 5, 163f.
11. Galandauer, Jan, Ibid, 54.
12. Urban, Ota, F. Modráček a B. Šmeral jako představitele dvou ideologických linií, Československý časopis historický, VII, 1963, č. 4, 436. [Hereafter: ČČH]
13. Protokol VI. sjezdu československé sociální demokratické strany dělnické, Praha 1904.
14. AÚML, F55, sg. 70, zápis ze schůze výkonného výboru, 16. srpna 1906.
15. Šmeral, B., Naše stanovisko k náboženství, církvi, klerikalismu a "Volné myšlence". Právo lidu, 30. května 1908; 7. června 1908; 14. června 1908; 15. července 1908.
16. Krejčí. F. V., K monistické akci, Akademie XVII, 1913, 145f.
17. See Part Two: Chapter 1, 57-58.
18. Šmeral, Bohumír, Národností otázka..., 125-127.
19. See Šmeral's polemic with Winter in: Právo lidu, 17. ledna 1902– Mnoho povyku pro nic za nic.
20. Archiv ÚD KSČ, fond. 55-56, A. Němec B. Šmeralovi, 16.1 L 903.
21. Modráček contributed many articles to "Akademie", the theoretical organ of the party, of which he was co-editor. The outline of his views is visible in the following: Modráček, František, Eduard Bernstein proti Marxismu, Akademie, III, 1899, 294f. Modráček, František, H. Spencer, Akademie, IV, 1900, 280f. Modráček, František, Socialistické kapitoly, Akademie, IX, 1905, 49f. Modráček, František, Ideové základy socialismu, Akademie, X, 1906, 447f.
22. Šmeral, B., Na prahu nové éry, Akademie XI, 1907, 35.
23. Ibid.
24. Modráček, František, Studie o Proudhonovi, Akademie, VII, 1903.
25. The aims of the SDP at this time are set out in detail in: Šmeral, Bohumír, Kdo jsou a co chtějí sociální demokraté, brožura, Praha, Září 1906.
26. Ibid.
27. Šmeral, B., Komuniskický manifest a naše státoprávní deklarace - Historické práce, Praha 1961, SNPL, 129.
28. Šmeral, B., Protokol XII řádného sjezdu sociálně demokratické strany dělnické, konaného ve dnech 27., 28., 29. a 30. prosince 1918 v Praze, 1919.
29. See Part Two: Chapter 2 - esp. 86f.
30. See Modráček's speech at the XII Party Congress. Protokol XII řádného sjezdu, 193f.
31. Právo lidu, 10. prosince 1918.
32. See Part Two: Chapter 2, 85f.

# NOTES 175

33. See Švehla's instructions to the police in Prague, Plzeň, Ostrava and Brno in: SAB, Okresní hejtmanství, Brno-Venkov, čj. 71-18.
34. Právo lidu, 3. listopadu 1918.
35. Právo lidu, 19. listopadu 1918.
36. Šmeral, B., Taktika a příští postup strany - Referát na XIII. sjezdu československé sociálně demokratické strany dělnické, konaném v Praze 25.28. září 1920, 105.
37. Protokoly ze sjezdu KSČ, I. sv., SNPL, Praha 1958, 133.
38. See Part Two: Chapter 5, esp. 166f and 178f.
39. Protokoly ze sjezdu KSČ, loc. cit.
40. Odstavec 1, Organizáční řád: Protokol XIII, řádného sjezdu československé sociálně demokratické strany dělnické [levice], jenž se konal 25.-28. září 1920 v Praze, Praha 1920, 232.
41. Odstavec 1, Organizáční řád schvalený slučovacím sjezdem KSČ; Slučovací sjezd komunistických stran Československa, konaný na Smichově ve dnech od 30. října do 4. listopadu roku 1921, Praha 1922, 270.
42. See Part Two: Chapter Three - 115f.
43. SAB Brno. Okresní soud trestní Brno, zn. U III 605/1919: "Organisace bývalých vojínů".
44. See Part Three passim.
45. Protokol XII. řádného sjezdu . . . , Organizáční řád, odstavec 6-8, Praha 1920, 42-50.
46. The Comintern's objections are to be found in: Dopis III Internacionály k návrhu organizačního řádu, Slučovací sjezd komunistických stran Československa, Praha 1922, 59-68. The rules of organization of the CPC are in the same work: 270-280
47. Protokol XIII. řádného sjezdu . . . , odstavec 2, 3.
48. Slučovací sjezd . . . , odstavec 2.
49. Ibid, odstavec 5, 6, 8.
50. Dopis III Internacionály. . . . . , 60.
51. Ibid, 59.
52. See Part Three, 199-200.
53. Prohlášení poslanců a senátorů Marxistické levice, Sociální demokrat, 27. května 1920.
54. Protokol XIII. řádného sjezdu. . . . . . , 119.

# PART TWO

## Chapter 1: Nationalism in the Czech Lands

1. See Part Three - 190f.

2. Šolle, Zdeněk, Socialistické hnutí a česká otázka [1848–1918], Praha 1968, 31f.
3. See Gladding-Whiteside, Andrew, Austrian National Socialism before 1918, Martinus Nijhoff, The Hague 1961, esp. Chapter 3 "The migration in Bohemia".
4. See Part Two: Chapter 5 - Table 3, 172, 178.
5. Gladding-Whiteside, Andrew, Ibid, quoted 79.
6. Kreibich, Karel, Ibid., 10f.
7. For example, the strike of Czech, German and Polish miners in January 1900. Autorský kolektiv, Nástin dějin československého odborového hnutí, Práce Praha 1963, 78.
8. Přítomnost, roč. 1927, esp. 724, 742, 759, 787, 800, 822.
9. Venkov, 14. února 1919 reported the change in the National Socialists' policy when they accepted the principle of private property in the context of the struggle over the Land Reform.
10. Nástin. . . .81.
11. Gladding-Whiteside, Andrew, Ibid, 32.
12. Nástin . . . , 94.
13. Quoted Gladding-Whiteside, Andrew, Ibid, 79.
14. Quoted Hošek, Josef, Československá strana socialistická ve vládě a v Národním shromáždění 1918–1922, ČČH, 3, 1972, 285.
15. Statistisches Handbuch des Königreichs Böhmen, Prague 1913, 56.
16. Nástin. . . . , 75.
17. See Part Two: Chapter 5 - 172, 178.
18. Šolle, Zdeněk, Dělnické hnutí v českých zemich, 1887–1897, Praha 1951, 220.
19. 256, 369 votes were cast for them. PM 1891-L900: 8/1/17/1/4525/1897 Quoted Šolle, Dělnické hnutí v českých zemích 1887–1897, Praha 1951, 303.
20. Mommsen, Hans, Die Sozialdemokratie und die Nationalitätenfrage im habsburgischen Vielvölkerstaat. I. Das Ringen um die supranationale Integration der zisleithanischen Arbeiterbewegung [1867–1907], Wien 1963, 202-203.
22. Kodedová, O., a kolektiv, Ohlas první ruské revoluce v českých zemích v letech 1905–1907, I, II, Praha 1959, 1962. Especially documents: I, 541, 545; II, 98, 108, 292, 309, 456.
21. Šolle, Zdeněk, Dopis Sigmunda Reise V. Adlerovi, Archiv für Sozialgeschichte, IX, red. prof. dr. Georg Eckert, Hanover 1970, 147.
23. Quoted Rosdolsky, Roman, Friedrich Engels und das Problem der "Geschichtslosen" Völker, Archiv für Sozialgeschichte, red. prof. dr. Georg Eckert, IV, Hanover 1964, 147.
24. Dělnické listy, 3.7. 1910.
25. Šolle, Zdeněk, Socialistické hnutí dělnické. . . . , Ibid., 30.
26. Šolle, Zdeněk, Tří dopisy A. Babela o počátcích "Práva lidu", ČČH, XV, 1967, r. 3, 439-488.
27. Adler, Victor, Briefwechsel mit August Bebel und Karl Kautsky. Gesammelt und erläutert von Friedrich Adler, Wien 1954, 379, 383, 386.

# NOTES 177

28. See Part One - 24f.
29. Dopis Náhlíka Adlerovi; quoted Šolle, Zdeněk, Socialistické hnutí dělnické a česká otázka, Praha 1968, 38.
30. Statistisches Handbuch des Königreiches Böhmen, Prague 1913, 56.
31. Quoted Hošek, Ibid., 285.
32. Chmelář, Josef, Politické rozvrstvení Československa, Praha 1926, 35.
33. In 1907, 71, 773; in 1911, 101, 214. Hošek, loc. cit; Chmelář, loc. cit.
34. Nástin. . . . , 87f.
35. Hlášení c.k. policejního ředitelství v Praze presidiu místodržitelství, čj. 1491, 2184 ze dne 22. července 1911.
36. AMV, 9. dubna 1915, PM 1911-1920, 8/1/13/2 - 18433/1915.
37. Tobolka, Zdeněk, Ibid., IV, 120.
38. Zápisy o jednání tiskového odboru československé sociální demokracie v Praze, AÚV KSČ, fond. 70, sign. 48.
39. Kašík, Vladimír, Snahy o jednotnou reformistickou stranu v letech 1917-1918 a jejich porážka, Rozpravy Československé academie věd, 1961, sešit 9, roč. 71, 29.
40. For the movement of wages, see Part Two: Chapter 4, Table 3, 145.
41. Nástin. . . . 96.
42. Protokol XII. sjezdu Československé sociálně demokratické strany dělnické, Praha 1919, 40f.
43. Tobolka, Zdeněk, Ibid, IV, 230.
44. Soukup František, 28, říjen 1918, Orbis Praha 1928, 426f.
45. SAB, B 40, 312, 2300.
46. SÚA, PM 1911-1920, 8/1/65/59/14099/1917.
47. Hajšman, J., Mafie v rozmachu, Praha 1934, 91.
48. Preisse, for example, spoke of the nationalizing of the mines and foreign-owned land. Peroutka, Ferdinand, Budování státu, Praha 1933-1936, I, 24. Večerník Práva lidu, 13. prosince 1917: Zástupce českých agrárníků prohlašuje se pro rozdělení pudy po vzoru ruském.
49. Nová doba, 23 srpna 1917.
50. Šmeral, B., Historické práce, Praha, 1956, 17, 38.
51. For example: Modráček, František, Zásady směru radikálně socialistického v československé sociální demokracii, Praha 1917. Modráček, František, Česká sociální demokracie a státní socialismus Akademie XXII, 1917, č 2. Modráček, František, Právo lidu 26. listopadu 1917.
52. Lenin, V. I., Questions of National Policy and Proletarian Internationalism, Progress Publishers Moscow,1964 edition, 110f - The Socialist Revolution and the Right of Nations to Self-determination. Bolshevik ortodoxy here is equal to the Leninist position which prevailed over Bukharin's position and became the established view of the Soviet government.
53. See Note 45.
54. Na zdar, 20. března 1918.

55. For Hodonín, see Slovácko, 18. srpna 1918; Prostějov - Hlas lidu, 3. května 1918; Brno - Dělnický deník, 8, května 1918; Kladno - Svoboda 7. května 918.
56. Reproduced in: Veselý, Jindřich, O vzniku a záložení KSČ, Praha 1952 30-31.
57. See Part Three - 199.
58. See Part Two - Chapter 1, 77.
59. Šmeral, Bohumír, Komunistický manifest a naše statoprávní deklarace Historické práce, 128-136.
60. See Part Two - Chapter 4, 142.
61. SÚA PMV, Praha, S 63, 1548/19.
62. SÚA Praha, PM, 1911-1920, sign. 8/1/75.13 - čj. 31019/19.
63. Svoboda, 30 října 1918.
64. Rovnost, 24. května 1919.
65. Právo lidu, 7. června 1919.
66. See Part Three - 190f.
67. SÚA PMV, M 48, čj. 6098/20, zn. 235-127-9.
68. AMZV Praha. Telegram., č 4825-4290.
69. Kratochvil, Jaroslav, Cesta revoluce, Praha 1928, 153-155.
70. Kratochvil, Jaroslav, Ibid., 410f.
71. AMZV Praha, Pařížský archiv, sv. 8, č 963. Tasker H. Bliss to Beneš.
72. In the absence of documentary evidence, I have used: Veselý, Jindřich, Češí a slovácí v revolučním Rusku [1917-1920], Praha 1954, 148.
73. Veselý, Jindřich, Ibid., 147.
74. Veselý, Ibid., 183. This writer makes no reference to documentary evidence nor to sources of any kind and it would therefore seem to be in order to exercise a degree of caution in respect of these figures.
75. Kratochvil, Ibid., 535-536.
76. SÚA Praha PMV, E-1, 225-46-1, čj. 22546.19. For the trial of Jelinek, VÚA Praha MNO Varia, čs. divis. soud Praha čj. Dtr. 2702/19.
77. SÚA Praha PMV odd. N, 225-1372-1, čj. 8I75/19; odd. N, 225-1373-1, čj. 6808/19. VÚA Praha, MNO, pres. 1918-1923, kart. 76, č. 27, čj. 31875.
78. AMZV Pařížský archiv, sv. 85, č. 1848.
79. See Part Two - Chapter 2, passim.
80. See Part Two - Chapter 2, 86f.
81. See Part Two - Chapter 3, 131 and Chapter 2, 98.
82. See Part One - 40-41..
83. See Part Two - Chapter 2,121.
84. Kotek, J., Odborové hnutí zaměstnanců, Praha 1930, 173.
85. Nástin . . . , 130.
86. See Part Three 196.

… 179

## Chapter 2: The Challenge from the Political Environment

1. See Part Three, 190f.
2. Provolání předsednictva Národního výboru k lidu o vyhlášení samostatného statu. Lidové noviny, 29. října 1918.
3. See Part Two - Chapter 3, 105.
4. Soukup, Ibid., II, 953. Wiskemann, Elizabeth, Czechs and Germans, OUP 1938, 52.
5. See Part Two - Chapter 1, 81.
6. Peroutka, Ibid., I, 19f.
7. Právo lidu, 28. října 1918 Naše revoluce, Praha 1924, 360.
8. SÚA Praha, Národní výbor 1918, čj. 3955/18.
9. SÚA Praha, Národní výbor 1918, b. čj. Koncept.
10. SÚA PMV, N 3, čj. 434/18.
11. See for example: SÚA Praha, Národní výbor, 1918. Bez čj. Koncept.
12. See: Lipscher, Ladislav, Zur allgemeinen Analyse des politischen Mechanismusin den ersten Tschechoslowakischen Republik in: Bosl, Karl [ed] - Die "Burg". Einflussreiche politische Kräfte um Masaryk und Beneš, Munich and Vienna, 1973–1974, 150, 152.
13. See Part Two - Chapter 3, 126.
14. Peroutka, Ibid., III, 1961.
15. Šedivý, K. Cesty československé vnitřní politiky, 1918–1925, Praha 1925, 9f.
16. Sociální demokrat, 27. května 1920.
17. Peroutka, Ibid., I, 667f.
18. NSR TZ o 18. schůzi Národního shromáždění v Praze, dne 21. ledna 1919, 459. The SDP should have been allotted 74 mandates, not 54 as was the case.
19. Ibid. 14. schůze, 9.1. 1919, 342-344.
20. Šmeral, Bohumír, Kdo jsou a co chtějí sociální demokraté, část II, Sociální demokracie a všeobecné rovné právo hlasovácí, Zář v Praze, 1906.
21. Protokol XII sjezdu . . . . . . předběžná zpráva, Praha 1919, 119-120.
22. Právo lidu, 3. listopadu 1918.
23. Večerník Práva lidu, 13. března 1919.
24. Československá statistika, sv. 1, řada 1, sešit 1. SDP-32·52 CSP-17·32
25. Večerník Práva lidu, 16. června 1919. This source suggests that they had "the lion's share" in the victory.
26. Kašík, Vladimír, Ibid., passim.
27. Šedivý, K., Ibid., 9f.
28. Peroutka, Ibid., I, 674f.
29. Šedivý, Loc. cit.
30. Československá statistika, Loc. cit.
31. KPR, Praha. Kramář, spis "Hlásit do Lán". Opis.
32. See Part Two - Chapter 5.
33. Sbírka zákonů a nařízení 1918, č. 37, 30.

34. Kolektiv autorů, 50 let: 1918-1968: k některým otázkám politickým předmnichovské republiky, Praha 1968, quoted 32-33.
35. AMZV Praha. Pařížský archiv, č. 3313. Kramář Benešovi.
36. Lidové noviny, 10. června 1928.
37. Atlas československých dějin, Praha 1965, 35-36. Šedivý, Ibid., 26f.
38. See: Malá, Irena a Štěpán, František [eds], Prosincová generální stávka. Praha 1961, esp. docs. 2-9 inc. Bechyně, R., Pero mi zůstalo, Praha 1947.
39. See Part Three - 200.
40. Lidové noviny, 25.9. 1920.
41. Měsičník služba. Letáky "Služby". č. 2. Tisk.
42. VÚA Praha. MNO generál inspektor 1920, ksrt 18/27 1/29-2, čj. 961·370, 757.
43. NS TZ, 85. schůze 28.10. 1919, 2554-2560.
44. These are the "Sisson Papers" on the "German-Bolshevik conspiracy" and are mentioned in: Ve víru povalečném - Em V. Voska, Praha 1922, 10. I would like here to express my thanks to Prof. Zbyněk Zeman for drawing my attention to this and also for supplying me with a photocopy of the relevant reference.
45. Kolektiv, 50 let, Ibid., 36.
46. Čas, 5. až 23. zaří 1920, Naše otázky a Sovětské Rusko.
47. See esp.: Masaryk, T. G., O Bolševictví; O diktatuře proletariátu, Knihovnička služba: Svazek 1 a 2, v Praze, v Dubnu 1921.
48. Lidové noviny, 25.9. 1920.
49. See Part Three - 201.
50. Lidové noviny, 6.6. 1928.
51. See Part Two - Chapter 3, 129.
52. Rudé právo, 29.9. 1920.
53. Loc. cit.

**Chapter 3: The Challenge of the Radical Socialists**

1. There were many of these. See i.e. Vrbenský, who spoke of him as "an imperialist non-socialist" Česká demokracie, 14. a 21. září 1917.
2. Stivín, J., Akademie, r. 1918, č. 12, 409-412.
3. Kárník, Zdeněk, Socialisté na rozcesti: Habsburk, Masaryk či Šmeral?, Praha 1968, 273f.
4. Skorkovský, J., Právo lidu, 16. srpna 1918.
5. Kašík, Ibid., gives an account of the process of convergence in the SDP and the CSP.
6. Právo lidu, 17. srpna 1918. Večerník Práva lidu, 23. srpna 1918.
7. Rovnost, 9. září 1918.
8. Právo lidu, 6.-8. října 1918.
9. Archiv ÚV KSČ, fond 1918, č. dok, 13, 5.

# NOTES

10. Loc. cit.
11. Naše revoluce, r. 1924, 386-389.
12. Dělnický deník, 22. října 1918. The censored republican constitution was reprinted in full on 7th. Nov. 1918.
13. Loc. cit.
14. Kárník, Zdeněk, Ibid., 276.
15. See Part Two - Chapter 1, 78.
16. See Part Three, 186f.
17. AMZV Praha. Pařížský archiv, č. 6784.
18. Večerník Práva lidu, 13. prosince 1917 for example carried a report of the Agrarians' acceptance of a "Bolshevik agrarian programme".
19. AMZV Praha. Pařížský archiv, č. 3313. Kramář Benešovi.
20. See Part Two - Chapter 2, 89-90.
21. AMZV Praha. Pařížský archiv, č. 3313. Kramář Benešovi.
22. Právo lidu, 2. listopadu 1918.
23. Hlas lidu, 27. listopadu 1918.
24. SÚA Praha. MVP, čj. 251/1918.
25. SAB Policejní ředitelství, Brno, čj. Pr. 7064/18
26. The eight-hour day, for example, was introduced in Hrádek-Nová Huť by a joint action of the Socialist Council, the Metalworkers Union and the local National Committee who forced it on the unwilling foundry owners before the law had been passed. SÚA Praha. Národní výbor 1918. čj. 3350.
27. See for example: Šikyř, K., Dělnická tělocvičná jednota pří tvoření republiky, Praha 1938, 15, 30.
28. SAB, Okresní hejtmanství Brno-Venkov, čj. 71/18.
29. Dr. Fr. Bk., Sociální otázka v českém státě, Akademie, r. XXIII, 7f.
30. SAB. Národní výbor 1918, čj. 1959.
31. Právo lidu, 19. listopadu 1918.
32. Loc. cit.
33. Loc. cit.
34. Šteidler, František, Československé hnutí na Rusi, Praha 1922, 48. Kratochvil, Ibid., 34.
35. The Commission for Mandates reported that 30 to 40 of the 763 delegates were in this position. Stivín, Josef, Po sjezdu strany, Akademie, roč. XXIII, 123f.
36. Protokol XII sjezdu . . . . . . , 170f.
37. Stivín Josef, Po sjezdu strany, Ibid., 81f.
38. Svoboda [kijevská], 28. prosince 1917.
39. 1500 is the figure estimated by Štvrtečký, Štefan, Sjazd československých komunistov v Moskve v mají 1918, Příspěvek k dějinám KSČ,1958, č. 5, 131f. [Slovak]
40. Československý deník, 23. července 1918.
41. Seidlová, Božena, Přes bolševické fronty, Praha 1922, 87f.
42. See Part Two - Chapter One, 78.

43. Peroutka, Ibid., I, 567f.
44. Peroutka, Ibid., I, 579.
45. Československý deník, 11. prosince 1918.
46. Rovnost 5.2. 1919.
47. SÚA Praha. PMV. S 4, čj. 3139/19.
48. Právo lidu, 8. ledna 1919.
49. SÚA Praha. PMR, protokoly vlády, č. 14.
50. Quoted Peroutka, I, 579.
51. See Part Three, 201-202.
52. VÚA Praha. MNO Varia zn. III, 219/2, čj. 2694/19.
53. The resolution against the communists was carried by 25 votes to 20. Právo lidu, 16. ledna 1919.
54. SÚA PM 1911-1920, 8/1/11/42, č. 625/19 contains Svozil's assessment of the Orthodox SDs' view of the role of the party.
55. Slánské rozhledy, l. února 1919.
56. Dělnický deník, 31. prosince 1918.
57. Právo lidu, 14. ledna 1919.
58. SÚA Praha, PMV, sign. K44, čj. 6155/19.
59. Sociální demokrat, 28. února 1919.
60. Pravda, 4 března 1919. Laštovka, Vojtěch, Vznik a formování Marxistické levice, Praha 1960, 258.
61. MZA, I-K-6376499/21.
62. See i.e. Jiskra [třebičská], 18.1. 1919 which printed many of the speeches Lenin made at the Moscow Soviet.
63. SAB. Vrchní státní zástupitelství, sign. C 1,356/19.
64. SÚA Praha. PM 1911-1920, sign. 8/1/11/5, čj. 8139/19.
65. SÚA PP 1916-1920, A - 15/1, č. 6181/19.
66. Právo lidu, 10. března 1919.
67. SAB, Okresní soud trestní Brno, zn. U III, 605/1919.
68. Sociální demokrat, 14. března 1919.
69. See Part Three - 202.
70. See Part Two - Chapter 1, 74f.
71. See Part Three.
72. Duše Prahy a duše Kladna, Sociální demokrat, 14. března 1919.
73. Svoboda, 27. Března 1919.
74. They were held six weeks before the first municipal elections. From a possible 660, 150 workers took part. Pondělník, 12. května 1919.
75. The Eight Conditions are in: Kárník, Zdeněk, Počátky Marxistické levice, ČČH, 1959, č.4.
76. SÚA Praha PMV, odd. N, čj. 5724/19.
77. SÚA Praha PM 1911-1920, sign. 8/5/121/161, čj. 15957/19.
78. Svoboda, 10. dubna 1919.
79. VÚA Praha, generální inspektor., kart. 2, 1919, č. 162.

# NOTES

80. Sociální demokrat, 10. října 1919.
81. Programové prohlášení Marxistické levice schválené na její první konference, 7. prosince 1919. Sociální demokrat, 21. ledna 1920. Archiv ÚD KSČ, č. 1919/90.
82. Sociální demokrat, 18. března 1920.
83. The most important were Alpári, Hamburger, Sallai, Revai, Munnich, Pór and Seidler. Pór, Erno, Vyslanie Alpáriho na územie Československa, Videň, n.d. Svoboda, 8. dubna, 1920.
84. Červen, 13. března 1920. SÚA, pres. MV, IV/K/44, čj. 10363/20.
85. Právo lidu, 30. dubna 1920.
86. Sociální demokrat, 27. května 1920.
87. KPR. Praha T 423/21.
88. Právo lidu, 20. května 1920.
89. SAB, B 40, 19, 8273, 8378.
90. SÚA PMV, IV, S/5 Morava 1920, 11051.
91. Rovnost, 29. června 1920.
92. Duch času, 20. srpna 1920.
93. Peroutka, Ibid., II, 1961.
94. ÚD KSČ, Archiv TGM, Kommunisté 1919-1921.
95. The Orthodox SDs drew up a rule that Congress delegates had to be party members of at least three year standing. Peroutka, Ibid., III, 1963-4.
96. Protokol XIII. řádného sjezdu Československé sociálně demokratické strany dělnické [levice], jenž se konal 25.-28-září 1920 v Smetanově síně Obecního domu v Praze, Praha 1920, 295-6.
97. Ibid, 275, Odstavec D.
98. See Part Two - Chapter 2, 92-93.
99. SAB, B 40, 24, 14474.
100. "Nothing is being done, we are all waiting but we do not know what for." SAB, B 40, Karton 17, čj. 6392/20.
101. The government estimate is in: SÚA Praha, Pres. M R 702/137.
102. AMZV Praha. Politické zpávy Videň 1920, č. 128.

## Chapter 4: The Economic Demands

1. Statistické příručky republiky československé, Praha 1920, 47-48.
2. See Part Two - Chapter 5, 173f.
3. Honzík, Miroslav, Praha 1921: Vzpominky, Fakta, Dokumenty, Svoboda Praha 1981, 92.
4. Venkov, 1. listopadu 1918.
5. Peroutka, Ibid., II, 928f.
6. Reproduced in: Přehled hospodářského vývoje Československa v letech 1918-1945, Praha 1961, 132f.

7. Věstník ministerstva pro zásobování lidu v československé republice roč. 1920, roč. 1921.
8. Přítomnost, roč. 1927-724, 742, 759, 787.
9. Maiwald, K., Index průmyslové výroby v ČSR, Obzor národohospodářský, č. 6, roč. 1934.
10. SÚA PM 1911-1920, 8/1/LL/18, čj. 2512/19.
11. Věstník, Ibid., roč. 1920, 2-4; roč. 1921, 26.
12. Statistická příručka československé republiky, dil. II, Praha 1925, 199-201.
13. Statistika úrazového pojištění za rok 1923, 4-5. Zprávy SÚS, roč. 1924, 941-949.
14. Přehled, Ibid., 137.
15. Frankenberger, O., Pracovní a mzdové poměry zemědělského dělnictva v Republice československé, Praha 1928, 48-78.
16. Křen, J., Československo v obdobi dočasné a relativní stabilisace kapitalismu 1924-1929, Praha 1957, 60.
17. Teichová, A., O výdělečné činnosti členů poslanecké sněmovny ve volebním obdobi 1929-1935, ČČH, roč. 1955, 114-128.
18. SÚA Praha. MSP, III/5/6, čj. 1847/19.
19. Statistická příručka, dil. II, 455.
20. Odborové sdružení československé, roč. 1918, 278-9.
21. TZ RNS., 11.února 1919.
22. Statistická příručka, Ibid., dil. II, 457.
23. SÚA Praha. MVP, čj. 129/19.
24. SÚA MSP III/5/71, čj. 23931/19.
25. SAB, B 40, kart. 26, 390.
26. SÚA Praha MSP, čj. 16601/111/19-28.7. 1919.
27. Chmelář, J., Ibid., 36f.
28. Nástin. . . . , Ibid., 100, 123, 129-130.
29. Nástin . . . , 130. To 348, 349 in 1920.
30. See for example the protests of the Brandys nad Labem workers in: SÚA Praha. PM: 1911-1920, Sign. 8/1/55.11, čj. 18263/19.
31. SÚA Praha. PM 1911-1920, Sign. 8/1/92/19; čj. 181619, 18162.19, 18901/19, 18902/19.
32. Statistická příručka, Ibid., dil. II, 468.
33. Zprávy SÚS, roč. 1934, č. 135-137.
34. Printed in: Právo lidu, 2. listopadu 1918.
35. The Brno workers' demands are in: SAB, Policejní ředitelství-Brno, čj. Pr. 7064/18. For those of the Olomouc workers, see: Hlas lidu, 27. listopadu 1918; for Poldiná hutí, SÚA Praha, MVP, čj. 251/1918. The resolution of the Kladno-Slany SDP is in: Ohlas Velké říjnové socialistické revoluce v Československu, Sborník dokumentů z let 1917-1918, Praha 1957, 88-89.
36. SÚA Praha. Národní výbor, 1918, čj. 3350.

# NOTES

37. See: O pozemkové, stavební a bytové politice v Československé republice, Praha 1928.
38. TZ NSČ "revoluční", 54. schůze, 23/5/1919, 1581–1587.
39. Loc.cit.
40. Loc. cit.
41. Večerník Práva lidu, 22. května 1919.
42. Protokol XII řádného sjezdu, Ibid., 209.
43. Národní shromážděni Republiky československé v prvém desitiletí, Praha 1928, 24.
44. Peroutka, Ibid., I, 796.
45. AMZV Praha. Pařížský archiv, č. 2586. Národní shromáždění 1918–1919, č. 321, 383.
46. See Dr. Englšš speech: TZ RNS "revoluční", schůze 15, 364.
47. See Part Two - Chapter 5, 180f.
48. Svoboda, 22. ledna 1919 carries a statement of their views on socialization.
49. Kolektiv, Přehled . . . , 31.
50. Ibid., 32.
51. See Part Three, 189.
52. Usnesení konference Marxistické levice, konané 5. zaří in: Za revoluční stranu, Dokumenty ke vzníku KSČ, 1919–1921, Praha 1972, 71f.
53. Přehled, 183. This is based on the figure for 1930.
54. Loc. cit.
55. This figure was supplied to me by the Institute of Marxism-Leninism in Prague. I have not been in a position to check it. There is a second figure for 1924 - 99,700.
56. As per note 55.

## Chapter 5: The Social Problem—Town and Country

1. Statistická přírucka Republiky československé, IV, 112-113, Praha 1932 [1930 figure].
2. See Part Two - Chapter 1, 53-54.
3. Ibid.
4. Österreichische Statistik, Band LVI - 4. Heft, Ergebnisse der Landwirtschaftlichen Betriebszählung vom 3. Juni 1902, Wien 1907 [hereafter ÖS].
5. Loc. cit.
6. I am not happy with this term as the notion of the bourgeoisie is most appropriate to the towns. But the other possibilities are even less appropriate, so we are more or less stuck with it. I have encountered the same problem with "velký rolník", for which I use the expression "rich peasant".
7. ÖS, Loc. cit.
8. ÖS, Band LXXXIII, 4. Heft, Ibid.

9. Statistická příručka království českého, Praha 1913, 416-417. Debts on land [zemské desky] rose from 3 million crowns in 1908 to 8 million in 1910, similarly for those of the "gruntovné desky" from 64 to 87 million.
10. See Table One this chapter.
11. ÖS, Loc. cit.
12. ÖS, Loc. cit.
13. ÖS, Loc. cit.
14. See Part Two - Chapter 4, 139-140 and Table 1, 141.
15. ÖS LXXXIII, Ibid.
16. From 1900 to 1913, 769,000 persons emigrated from the lands which later formed the Republic, an average of 60,000 per annum, a figure which represented one-third of the natural growth of population. A majority of these were Slovak. Sborník Dvacet let československého zemědělství, 1918-1938, Praha 1938, 34.
17. Venkov, 4.6. 1911 - Pachtovní družstva.
18. Venkov, 9.7. 1911.
19. 10 let republikanské strany československého venkova, Praha 1929, 10.
20. Právo lidu, 13. srpna 1918.
21. In July 1917, Agrarian MPs demanded a rise in prices for requisition goods and a stop to the requisitioning of cows and oxen. Venkov, 14.7. 1917.
22. Almanach okresní hospodářské záložny 1882-1932, 574.
23. Loc. cit. 1914 - 15.6 million 1918 - 496·3 million
24. Venkov z roku 1915, Ernstová sbírka, č. 42, SÚA, Zem. lensí odd.
25. Právo lidu, 15.10. 1917 - Bouřlivou poptávku po šlechtické pudě.
26. Denkscrift über die von der k.k. Regierung aus Anlass des Krieges getroffenen Massnahmen, Zweiter Teil, Wien 1916, 4-8.
27. See Part Two - Chapter 4, Table Four for the general movement of wages.
28. Statistický přehled, Ibid., 21, 25.
29. Loc. cit. 956, 306 including apprentices and day-labourers.
30. Nástin . . . ,Ibid., 129.
31. Reich, E., Základy organisace zemědělství ČSR, Praha 1934, 70.
32. Mimořádné zprávy SÚS RČS, roč. 1931, Zemědělské závody podle stavu z května 1921.
33. Peasant riots took place in protest against their influence in the administration of the requisitions. See: César, J., Otáhal, M., Hnutí venkovského lidu v českých zemích v letech 1918-1922, Praha 1958, Dok. 622, 625. César, Otáhal, Ibid., contains evidence of their support for the centres [ústředny] and likewise opposition to high prices [Dok. 621, 626 and 638 respectively], but while this constituted an opposition movement in the countryside, it had nothing in common with the aims of the landless. Peasant unrest broke out again in 1921 in the Domovina as a reaction against the bias of the Land Reform towards the rich peasants.
34. Právo lidu, 29. listopadu 1918, Socializace zemědělské výroby.
35. Akční program - Socialismu a zásady pro přechod k němu-Odstavec D: Protokol XIII, řádného sjezdu, Ibid, Praha 1920, 270-277.

# NOTES 187

36. Sociální demokrat, 9. září 1920. Usnesení konference Marxistické levice - Odstavec 2.
37. Rudé právo, 29.9. 1920; Svoboda, 19. listopadu 1920.
38. Zemědělec, 5.8. 1920.
39. Náš venkov, 27.2. 1920.
40. Sociální demokrat, 28. března 1919.
41. See: César, J., Otáhal, M., Ibid, dok. č. 213, 214.
42. Večerník Práva lidu, Pozemková držba v českých zemich, 13. prosince 1917.
43. César, J., Otáhal, M., Ibid. 423.
44. Večer, 5.4. 1919. Bolševické pikle proti vyvlástnění velkostatků.
45. Pozemková reforma, roč. 2/1920, 3-5.

## PART THREE

### The External Environment

1. This passage is a summary of the connections made by several writers. The literature in this area is large and I have set out in my bibliography a few of these.
2. See Part Two - Chapter 2, 85-86.
3. See Part One - 45f.
4. AMZV especially the Beneš' section of the Pařížský archiv is a good source of evidence for the Allies view of the Czech Lands. See for example his reports for January 1919 for their reaction to the social programme of the Kramář government; April-June 1919 for the Hungarian crisis and February 1920 for Russia.
5. Boháč, Antonín, Ze slovenské statistiky; výběr úvah politických, Praha 1919, 125.
6. TZ RNS 1918–1919, 314.
7. Dr. Karel Kramář, Život-dílo-práce, Praha 1936.
8. Masaryk, T. G., Cesta demoracie, soubor projevů za republiky, Praha 1933, 61-64.
9. KPR Praha. T 317/22.
10. TZ, RNS, č. 24, 30.1. 1919.
11. Slovák, 1.11. 1919.
12. Sidor, K., Andrej Hlinka 1864–1926, Bratislava 1934, 329.
13. AMZV Praha. Pařížský archiv, č. 4859.
14. Ibid.
15. Ibid.
16. Ibid.
17. Beneš to Clemenceau: AMZV Praha, Pařížský archiv, č. 364, kopie.
18. Ibid.
19. VUA Praha. MNO pres. 1918–1922, k. 155, čj. 6314/1, čj. 12868.
20. AMZV Praha. Pařížský archiv, č. 179.

21. AMZV Praha, Telegramy došlé, č. 478/1919. Kopie telegramu [German]
22. AMZV Praha, Telegramy odeslané, č. 485/1919. Kopie radiogramu.
23. AMZV Praha, Pařížský archiv, č. 12320, Telegramy došlé, č. 450/1919.
24. Ibid.
25. AMZV Praha, Presidium, čj. 1079/1919.
26. Reimann, Pavel, Dějiny KSČ, Praha 1930, 140.
27. VÚA Praha. MNO Presidium, čj. 28755/19.
28. Ibid.
29. SÚA PMV, N kart. 1401, sv. 4, fol. 177.
30. Ibid.
31. Ibid.
32. Zákon o mimořádných opatřeních na Slovensku: odstavec 2: Sbírka zákonů a nařizení státu československého, č. 64/1918, 55 [Tisk]
33. AMZV Praha. Pařížský archiv, č. 4859.
34. AMZV Praha, Presidiální registratura, čj. 982/19.
35. VÚA Praha, MNO Presidium, čj. 28755/19.
36. Sociální demokrat, 27. května, 3. června 1920.
37. See: Za revoluční stranu-Dokumenty ke vzniku KSČ 1919–1921, Praha 1971, note 5,397.
38. Burks, R. V., The Dynamics of Communism in Eastern Europe, Princeton UP, 1961, 192.
39. Šrobár, V., Osvobodené Slovensko, Praha 1928, 423.
40. AMZV Praha. Pařížský archiv, č. 4875. Masaryk-Benešovi: 14. června 1919.
41. VÚA Praha MNO. Pres. 1918–1923, k. 323/13, čj. 10807.
42. VÚA Praha MNO, III. Odb. č. 345/3.
43. KPR Praha. Sign. D 457/19. Opis.
44. Peroutka, Ferdinand, Ibid., II, 1019f.
45. See for example the radical Moravian newspaper "Svornost" [22 května 1919]
46. AMZV Praha. Politické zprávy Budapešť, 1919, č. 177. Telegramy došlé 1919 č. 615. Reported to have 100,000 troops, the Magyars in fact had three divisions to the Czechs' six.
47. AMZV Praha. Pářížský archiv, č. 724.
48. SÚA Praha, PMV, odd. N. čj. 5724/19.
49. SÚA PMV, Sign. K 44, čj. 6155/19.
50. SÚA PMV, Sign. N, čj. 4731.
51. SÚA PMV, Sign. M5, čj. 453/19. For the drive against Moravian and Saxon communists see: SAB, Presidium zemského úřadu, K.16, čj. 5067/20. For the cooperation of the Czech and Prussian police in Silesia: SÚA Praha PMV 1920, č. 2/1, čj. 6240/20.
52. AMZV Praha. Telegramy došlé, č. 768/19.
53. See i.e. Lidové noviny, 11. června 1919.
54. See Stivín's article: Slovensko je a bude naše - Právo lidu, 7. června 1919.
55. Peroutka, Ferdinand, Ibid., II, 1021.

56. Svoboda, 12. června 1919.
57. AMV PMV, IV/F.36, č. 3588 N/19. SAB B 40/1/3, č. 6688/19.
58. SÚA Praha. PMV, K 44, čj. 6155/19.
59. Burks, R. V., Ibid., esp. 187-201.

# LIST OF WORKS CONSULTED

## Unpublished Sources

Archiv Ministerstva vnitra, PM 1911-1920
Archiv Ministerstva zahraníčních věci, Pařížský archiv
Archiv Národního Shromáždění, Praha
Archiv Ústavu Marxismu-Leninismu.
Kancelář presidenta republiky
Státní archiv Brno
    Brněnské policejní ředitelství [B 26] 1910–1921
    Moravské místodržitelství [B 13-14] 1910–1918
    Okresní hejtmanství Brno-Venkov
    Vrchní státní zástupitelství
Státní ústřední archiv
    Národní výbor - 1918
    Presidium Ministerské Rady
    Presidium Místodržitelství 1911–1920
    Zemský soud trestní - Praha
    Presidium Ministerstva vnitra
    Presidium Zemského Úřadu
Ústřední vojenský archiv Praha-Karlín
    generální stávka 1920, pres. 1920, sign. 47-7/20
Vojenský ústřední archiv, Ministerstvo národní obrany
    generální inspektor

## Newspapers and Journals

Akademie, Praha
Dělnický deník, Brno
Hlas lidu, Prostějov
Jiskra, Třebíč
Lidové noviny
Náš venkov

# Newspapers and Journals (cont'd.)

Náše revoluce
Na zdar
Právo lidu
Průkopník svobody
Rovnost
Rudé právo
Slanské rozhledy
Slovácko, Hodonín

Socialistické listy
Sociální demokrat
Stráž lidu
Svoboda
Svornost
Večerník Práva lidu
Zemědělec

## Printed Sources

*Party Congress Protocols:*

Protokol IX. sjezdu čsl, sociálně demokratické strany dělnické ve dnech 4. až 8. září 1909 v Praze, Praha 1909.
Protokol X. sjezdu čsl. sociálně demokratické strany dělnické ve dnech 23. až 27. prosince 1911 v Národním domě na Smichově, Praha 1912.
Protokol XII. sjezdu čsl. sociálnědemokratické strany dělnické konaného ve dnech 27., 28., 29.a 30. prosince 1918 v Representačním domě v Praze, Praha 1919.
Protokol XIII. řádného sjezdu čsl. sociálně demokratické strany dělnické [levice], jenž se konal 25.-28.září 1920 v Obecním domě v Praze, Praha 1920.
Protokol XIII. řádného sjezdu čsl. sociálně demokratické strany dělnické [pravice], konaného ve dnech 27.-29. listopadu 1920, Praha 1921.
Protokol Ustavujícího sjezdu Komunistické strany československé který se konal v Karlině 14.-16. května 1921, Praha 1921.
Slučovací sjezd komunistických stran Československa, konaný na Smíchově ve dnech od 30. října do 4. listopadu roku 1921, Praha 1922.

*Collections of Documents:*

Boj o směr československého státu-Svazek 1, Praha 1965; Svazek 2 Praha 1969-ed. Kocman, A., Pletka, V., Radimský, J., Trantirek, M., Urbanková, L.
Československá statistika.
Hnutí venkovského lidu v českých zemích v letech 1918–1920, Praha 1959-ed. César, J., Otáhal, M.
Národní shromáždění československé "revoluční", těsnopisecké zprávy.
Národní shromáždění republiky československé v privém desitiletí Praha 1928.
Prosincová generální stávka 1920, Praha 1961, -ed. Malá, I., Štěpán F. Sbirka zákonů a zářizení 1918.

# WORKS CONSULTED 193

Sborník dokumentů ÚD KSČ, Praha 1955.
Souhrnná hlášení pražského místodržitelství o protistátní, protirakouské a protiválečné činnosti v Čechach 1915-1918, Praha 1957-ed. Otáhalová, Libuše.
Souhrnná týdenní hlášení presidia zemské správy politické v Praze o situaci v Čechách 1919-1920, Praha 1959-ed. Kocman, A.
Za revoluční stranu: Dokumenty ke vzniku KSČ: Praha 1971.
Založení KSČ, Praha 1954.
Zásedání Národního shromáždění 1919.

## Bibliographies

Bibliografie Bohumíra Šmerala [ÚV KSČ, Praha 1971]
Bibliografie KSČ [ÚV KSČ, Praha 1971] - 4 svazky

## Printed Books

Baerlein, Henry, The March of the Eighty Thousand, London 1926.
Bartošová, Š, Bieberle, J, O boji přerovských železničářů v roce 1920, Časopis Matice Moravské, 75/1956.
Bauer, Otto, Die österreichische Revolution, 2. vyd., Wien 1965.
Bechyně, Rudolf, Pero mi zůstalo, Praha 1947.
Beneš, Edvard, Stětová válka a naše revoluce, Praha 1928, sv. 1-3.
Böhm, Vilem, Im Kreuzfeuer zweier Revolutionen, München 1924.
Boros Ferenc, K vzťahom maďarskej komunistickej emigrácie a československej marxistekej l'avice, Historický časopis, VII, 4.
Borský, Lev, Před válkou o válce, Minulost a přítomnost, Praha 1920.
Brugel, L., Geschichte der österreichischen Demokratie, Wien 1925.
César, J., Černý, B., Od sudetoněmeckého seperatismu k plánům odvety, Liberec 1960.
César, J., Černý, B., Politika německých buržoazních stran v Československu v letech 1918-1938, Praha 1962. sv. 1.
Červinka, K., Na cestách naše revoluce, Praha 1920.
Dubský, Vladimír, KSČ a odborové hnutí v Československu na počátku dvacátých let, Praha 1966.
Dyk, V., Vzpominky a komentáře, Praha 1937, sv. 1-2.
Falta, Jose, Dějinný vývoj sociální demokracie československé, Praha 1927.
Gajan, K., Příspěvek ke vzniku KSČ, Praha 1954.
Gajan, K., Příspěvek k založení KSČ, Praha 1954.
Gajan, K., Marxistická levice a boj československého lidu na obranu a za uznání Sovětského Ruska [1919-1920], Sovětská historie, r. 4, 1954, č. 6.
Gajda, Rudolf, Pamětí, Praha 1920.

Grimmichová, M., Proces s oslavanskými velezrádci, Brno 1921.
Hajšman, J., Česká mafie, Praha 1932.
Hudec, J., Revolucionism a reformismus v sociální demokracií, Akademie XII, 1908.
Hudec, J., Sklon k revisionismu a reformismu, Akademie XV, 1911.
Chmelář, J., Politické rozvrstvení Československa, Praha 1926.
Chyba, A., Postavení dělnické třidy v kapitalistickém Československu, Praha 1961.
Kapras, Jan, O českém státě za války a po válce, Praha 1926.
Kašík, Vl., Snahy o jednotnou reformistickou stranu v letech 1917-1918 a jejich porážka, Praha 1961.
Kárník, Zd., Počátky marxistické levice, Československý časopis historický, 1959, č 4.
Kárník, Zd., Socialisté na rozcestí: Habsburk, Masaryk čili Šmeral? Praha 1968.
Kárník, Zd., Za československou republiku rad, Praha 1963.
Kárník, Zd., Založení KSČ v severovychodnich Čechach, Havlíckuv Brod 1961.
Ke vzníku ČSR: Sborník státí k ohlasu Řijnové revoluce a ke vzniku ČSR, Praha 1958.
Klevanskij, A. Ch., Čechoslovackije internacionalisty i prodajnyj korpus, Moskva 1965.
Klír, M., Úloha B. Šmerala pří výpracovávání strategickotactické orientaci KSČ [1921-1924], Příspěvky k dějinám KSČ, č. 1, 1965.
Klíma, A., Počátky českého dělnického hnutí, Praha 1949.
Klofáč, Václav, Odkaz naše revoluce, Praha 1923.
Kolejka, Josef, Konec a počátek I. Rozpad habsburské monarchie. Sborník Matice Moravské, r. 86, Brno 1967.
Kolejka, Josef, Revoluční dělnické hnutí na Moravě a ve Slezsku [1917-1921], Praha 1957.
Kolektiv, Komunistická internacionála a čs. dělnické hnutí, Praha 1959.
Kosík, Karel, Česká radikální demokracie, Praha 1958.
Kotek, M., Česká sociální demokracie za války, Praha 1920.
Koudelka, J., Sociální demokracie v československé revoluci, Plzeň 1920.
Kratochvil, J., Cesta revoluce, Praha 1922.
Kreibich, Karel, Dějiny českého dělnického hnutí, Praha 1949.
Kreibich, Karel, 60 let dělnického hnutí, Praha 1946.
Kreibich, Karel, Těsný domov, širý svět, Liberec 1968.
Krejčí, F. V., Naše osvobození, Praha 1920.
Křížek, Jaroslav, Čeští a slovenští rudoarmejci v sovětském Rusku [1917-1920], Praha 1955.
Křížek, Jaroslav, Dvacátý transport čs. legie, Praha 1955.
Křížek, Jaroslav, K boji čsl. levice o čs. legie v Rusku počátkem roku 1918, Historie a vojenství, 1964.
Křížek, Jaroslav, T. G. Masaryk a vystoupení čs. legie na jaře 1918, Československy časopis historický, r. 14, 1966, č. 5.

# WORKS CONSULTED 195

Křížek, Jurij, Příspěvek k dějinám rozpadu Rakousko-Uherska a vzniku ČSR, Příspěvek k dějinám KSČ, 1958, č. 5.
Kudela, J., Státní převrat v Brně v roce 1918, Brno 1928.
Kvasnička, J., Československé legie v Rusku [1917-1920], Bratislava 1963.
Laštovka, Vojtěch, Vznik KSČ na Plzeňsku, Plzeň 1962.
Lenin, V. I., Spisy, sv. 32, Praha 1955.
Leser, Norbert, Zwischen Reformismus und Bolschewismus. Der Austromarxismus als Teorie und Praxis, Wien 1968.
Masaryk, T. G., Světová revoluce, Praha 1925.
Maxa, P., V boji za samostatnost, Praha 1927.
Mendl, Bedřich, Československý dějepis 1918-1928, Praha 1929.
Merhaut, Cyr., Dokumenty naseho osvobození, Praha 1919.
Modráček, Frantíšek, Několik myšlenek ku diferenciálnimu názoru dejinnému, Akademie, I, 1897.
Modráček, František, Iluze moderního socialismu, Akademie II, 1898.
Modráček, František, Eduard Bernstein proti marxismu, Akademie III, 1899.
Modráček, František, H. Spencer, Akademie IV, 1900.
Modráček, František, Studie o Proudhonovi, Akademie VII, 1903.
Modráček, František, Socialistické kapitoly, Akademie IX, 1905.
Modráček, František, Ideové základy socialismu, Akademie X, 1906.
Modráček, František, Zásady směru radikálně socialistického v československé sociální demokracii, Praha 1917.
Modráček, František, Kniha na oslavu jeho šedesátých narozenin, Praha 1931.
Molisch, P., Geschichte der deutschnationale Bewegung in Österreich, Jena 1926.
Na ochranu sociálně demokratických zásad, Praha 1920. Naše revoluce roč. 1-15.
Nejedlý, Zdeněk, Z prvních dvou let republiky, Praha 1921.
Olbracht, Ivan, Obrazy ze soudobého Ruska, Praha 1920.
Olivová, V., Z dělnických bojů v letech 1921-1923, Praha 1960.
Opočenský, Jan, Konec monarchie rakousko-uherské, Praha 1928.
Opočenský, Jan, Vznik národních států v řijnu, Praha 1927.
Olšovský, B. a kolektiv, Přehled hospodářského vývoje Československa v letech 1918-1945, Praha 1961.
Otáhal, Milan, Dělnické hnutí na Ostravsku [1917-1921], Ostrava 1957.
Otáhal, Milan, Zápas o pozemkovou reformu v ČSR, Praha 1963.
Otáhalová, L., Příspěvek k národně osvobozenskému boji lidu v českých zemích [srpen 1914 až březen 1917], Praha 1964.
Paulová, Mil., Dějiny Maffie, Praha 1937 a 1946[?], sv. I-II/1.
Pekař, Josef, K českému boji státopravnímu za války, Praha 1930.
Pekař, Josef, Říjen 1918, Praha 1924.
Pekař, Josef, Světová válka, Praha 1921.
Peroutka, Ferdinand, Budování státu 1918-1921, 4 svazky, Praha 1933-1936.
Peša, V., Národní výbory v českých zemích roku 1918, Praha 1962.

Peša, V., Příspěvek k řešení agrárně rolnické otázky v českých zemích na počátku 20. století, SMM, sv. č. 78. 1959.
Pichlík, K., Vzpoury navrátilců z ruského zajetí na jaře 1918, Praha 1964.
Pichlík, K., Vávra, V., Křížek Jar., Červenobílá a rudá: vojáci ve válce a revoluci 1914-1918, Praha 1967.
Pór, František Desiderius, Maďarská sovětská republika 1919 a její ohlas na Slovensku, Praha 1959.
Pospichal, Miloslav, Vznik ČSR a cesta k založení KSČ v Olomouci Olomouc MNV, 1965.
Přehled československých dějin, díl III, Praha 1961.
Reimann, Pavel, Dějiny komunistické strany Československa, Praha 1930.
Scheiner, J., Sokoly, Praha 1920.
Seidlová, Božena, Přes bolševické fronty, Praha 1925.
Sicha, R., Český vojín a říjový převrat v Brně, Brno 1933.
Skála, J., Stručné dějiny čs. dělnického hnutí až do roztržky sociálně demokratické strany v září 1920, Praha 1920.
Skála, Jan, Šmeralova idea státu rakouského, Dějiny a současnost, r. 7, 1965, č. 12.
Soukup, František, 28. říjen 1918, Praha 1928, sv. 1-2.
Soukup, František, Revoluce práce, Praha 1938.
Stein, V., Po drážďánském sjezdu, Akademie VIII, 1904.
Stivín, Josef, Několik poznámek ke sjezdu strany, Akademie XXIII, 1918.
Stivín, Josef, Po sjezdu strany, Akademie XXII, 1919.
Sychova, L., Werstadt, J., Československý odboj, Praha 1923.
Šafář,?, Marxistická levice, Praha 1923.
Šantrůček, B., Václav Klofáč, Praha 1918.
Šedivý, K., Cesty československé vnitřní politiky 1918-1925, Praha 1925.
Šmeral, Bohumír, Historické práce, Praha 1943.
Šmeral, Bohumír, Národnostní otázka v sociální demokracii v Rakousku až do sjezdu hainfeldského, Praha 1909.
Šmeral, Bohumír, Pravda o sovětovém Rusku, Praha 1920.
Šolle, Zdeněk, Internacionála a Rakousko. Internacionála a počátky socialistického hnutí v zemích bývalé habsburské monarchie, Praha 1966.
Šolle, Zdeněk, ie Sozialdemokratie in der habsburgischen Monarchie und die tschechische Frage. Archiv für Sozialgeschichte, sv. VI-VII, red. prof. dr. Georg Eckert, Hannover 1967.
Šolle, Zdeněk, Die tschechische Sozialdemokratie zwischen Nationalismus und Internationalismus. Archiv für Sozialgeschichte, sv. IX, red. prof. dr. Georg Eckert, Hannover 1970.
Šolle, Zdeněk, Gajanová, Alena, Po stopě dějin. Češi a Slováci v letech 1848-1938, Praha 1969.
Štern, E., Deset let naší sociální politiky, Praha 1929.
Šťastný, Ferdinand, České delnictvo v revoluci, Praha 1924.

# WORKS CONSULTED 197

Štvrtecký, Štefan, Českoslovenkí komunisti v Turkestane v rokoch 1917-1920, Příspěvky k dějinám KSČ, r. 3, 1963, č. 3.
Štvrtecký, Štefan, Sjazd čs. kommunistov v Moskve v máji 1918, Příspěvky k dějinám KSČ, 1958, č. 5.
Štvrtecký, Štefan, Vznik a činnost československého oddelenia pri Ludovem komisariate pre národnostné otázky v Sovětskom Rusku, Příspěvky k dějinám KSČ, r. 2, 1962, č. 2.
Tobolka, Zdeněk, Česká politika za světové války, Praha 1922.
Tobolka, Zdeněk, Dějiny sociální demokracie od jejich počátků až po sjezd hainfeldský, Praha 1923.
Tobolka, Zdeněk, Počátky dělnického hnutí v Čechách, Praha 1923.
Tobolka, Zdeněk, Politika, co má vědět o československé republice každý občan, Praha 1925.
Tobolka, Zdeněk, Politické dějiny československého národa, 4 svazk, Praha 1937.
Tomáš, J., Provádění zákona o podporách v nezaměstnanosti, Sociáln revue, Praha 1920.
Tomášek, František, Vývojové předpoklady československé revoluce, Praha 1923.
Urban, Ota, Bohumír Šmeral a František Modráček jako představitele dvou ideologických linii, Československý časopis historický, r.11, 1963, č. 4.
Vavrdová, Jaromíra, První pozemková reforma na státcích olomouckého arcibiskupství, Olomouc 1967.
Verunáč, Václav, Dělnická otázka a naš průmysl, Praha 1923.
Veselý, A. P., Omladina a pokrokové hnutí, Praha 1902.
Veselý, Jindřich, O vzniku a založení KSČ, Praha 1952.
Veselý, Jindřich, Jak se zrodila naše strana, Praha 1961.
Veselý, Jindřich, Češi a slováci v revolučním Rusku 1917-1920, Praha 1954.
Veselý, Ludvík, Rozhodujicí rok, 1921, Praha 1960.
Vlach, M., Sobotecký anarchokomunista, Ort 1959.
Voženílek, J., Pozemková reforma v ČSR, Praha 1924.
Voženílek, J., Předběžné výsledky pozemkové reformy, Praha 1931.
Wiskemann, Elizabeth, Czechs and Germans, London 1938.

## Memoirs

Habrmann, Gustav, Mé vzpominky z války, Praha 1928.
Hartl, Antonín, Knihy navrátů, Praha n.d.
Klofáč, Václav, 25 let práce československé strany socialistické, Praha 1927.
Landová-Štychová, Historický vyznam 14. října 1918, Praha 1919.
Leonier-Pavlík, M., Říjnový převrat královéhradecký roku 1918, Hradec Kralové 1918.
Licht, Antonín, Váleční vzpominky z doby perzekuce, Praha 1925.
Medek, R., Za svobodu, Praha 1926-1929.

Muna, Alois, Ruská revoluce a čcskoslovenské hnutí na Rusi, Kladno 1919.
Robl, Rudolf, Taganrog, Brno 1924.
Reimann, Pavel, Ve dvacátých letech: vzpominky, Praha 1966.
Soukup, František, Pamětnimu listu čs. soc. dem. strany dělnické 1872, 1922, Praha 1927.
Stehlik, C., Modráček, F., Česká sociální demokracie v boji s republikou, České Budějovice, 1920.
Synek, Jan, Vzpominka na leta 1917–1921 v Rusku, Časopis Matice moravské, r. 75, 1956, č. 3-4.
Synek, Jan, Vzpominky na léta 1917–1921 - Návrat z Ruska, Časopis Matice moravské, r. 77, 1958, č. 1-2.

**Additional Works**

In German

**Printed Sources**

Denkscrift über die von der k. und k. Regierung aus Anlass des Krieges getroffenen Massnahmen, Zweiter Teil, Wien 1916
Österrichische Statistik, Band LXXXIII, 4. Heft, Ergebnisse der Landwirtschaftlichen Betriebszählung vom 3. Juni 1902, Wien 1907
Statistiches Handbuch des Königreiches Böhmen, Prague 1913

**Printed Books**

Adler, Victor, Briefwechsel mit August Bebel und Karl Kautsky. Gesammelt und erlautert von Friedrich Adler, Wien 1954.
Lipscher, Ladislav, Zur allgemeinen Analyse des politischen Mechanismus in der ersten Tschechoslowakischen Republik in: Bosl, Karl [Ed.], Die Burg-Einflussreiche politische Kräfte um Masaryk und Beneš, Munich and Vienna, 1973–1974, 150, 152.
Mommsen, Hans, Die Sozialdemokratie und die Nationalitätenfrage im habsburgischen Vielvölkerstaat: I. Das Ringen um die supranationale Integration der zisleithanischen Arbeiterbewegung [1867–1907], Wien 1963.

# WORKS CONSULTED

## In English

### Printed Books

Burks, R. V., The Dynamics of Communism in Eastern Europe, Princeton UP 1961.
Gladding-Whiteside, Andrew, Austrian National Socialism before 1918, Nijhoff, The Hague, 1961.
Lenin, V. I., Questions of National Policy and Proletarian Internationalism, Progress Publishers, 1964 edition.
Suda, Zdeněk, Zealots and Rebels, Harvard UP 1981.

## In Czech

### Official Publications

Almanach okresní hospodářské záložny, 1882–1932, Praha 1932
Mimořádné zprávy Státního úřadu statistického, ročník I, Praha 1931
Statístický přehled Republiky československé, Praha 1930
Statistická příručka Republiky československé, Praha 1932
Statistická příručka království českého, Praha 1913

# NAME INDEX

Adler, Alfred, 37, 39, 40, 41

Bechyně, Rudolf, 15, 68, 87, 97, 141
Beneš, Edvard, 69, 155
Bergmann, Rudolf, 136
Bernstein, Eduard, xiii
Brodecký, Vilém, 50, 70, 92, 96, 162
Burian, Edmund, 83, 163

Cingr, Petr, 83

Frankenberger, Otakar, 136
Friedrich, Václav, 163

Habrmann, Gustav, 43, 88, 89
Hais, Arno, 83, 89
Hlinka, Andrej, 153-4
Houser, Václav, xiii, 160
Hybeš, Josef, xiii

Kautský, Karl, 15, 45
Klofáč, Václav, 29, 33f., 37, 42, 159
Kohn, [Archbishop], 9
Koníček, 83
Kostyál, Bedřich, 20, 90
Kotek, 42
Koutný, Tomaš, 63
Kramář, Karel, 67, 80, 81, 120, 153, 159
Kreibich, Karl, xix, 165
Kříž, Josef, 158
Kun, Bela, 149, 156, 162

Landová-Stychová, Loisa, 78
Lenin and Leninism: see introduction and conclusion; also 15, 18, 20, 22, 24, 45-6, 90, 101

Martov, Julius, xxvi, 23, 24
Masaryk, Tomaš, 51-2, 65, 66f, 153, 159
Meissner, Alfred, 40, 41, 43, 82
Modráček, František, xiii, xiv, 9, 11, 13, 47, 141
Muna, Alois, 19, 46, 52, 54, 70, 72, 80, 89, 91-4, 116, 122, 123, 161

Náhlík, 40
Němec, Antonín, xvii, 39, 40, 96
Němec, Franta, 90
Neumann, S. K., 53-4, 90

Pergl, Josef, 89, 92
Pik, Luděk, 83, 89

Rydlo, Otto, 89, 92

Šmeral, Bohumír, Part 1, passim et al
Soukup, František, 96, 114
Staněk, František, 77
Štefánik, Milan, 51
Stivín, Josef, 50, 70, 77, 87, 90, 92, 96, 97, 99, 162
Stych, 10
Švehla, Antonín, 20, 65, 67, 80, 119, 143

Tomášek, František, 65, 161
Tusar, Vlastimil, 62, 65, 92, 95, 161

Vácek, Václav, xiii
Vajtauer, Emil, 20
Viškovský, Karel, 136
Vrbenský, Bohuslav, 44, 54, 120

Winter, Lev, 11

Zápotocký, Antonín, 88, 89, 93, 94, 161

201

# SUBJECT INDEX

Agrarian Bank, 129, 137
Agrarian Party, 52, 65, 67-8, 86, 87, 127, 129, 132, 135, 137, 140, 143, 145
Agricultural holdings, 133 [Table 7]
Agricultural labour-composition, 134 [Table 9]
Anarchists, 34, 44, 53-4, 95

Březové hory, 69
Brno, 38, 41, 68, 79, 81, 101, 117, 125
Brno Centralists, 78f, 83, 96, 100, 163
Brno Nationalities Programme, 37, 40

Čas, 69
Central Council for the Union of Communist Groups, 97
České slovo, 42, 69
Český dělník, 42
Československá obec dělníká [CSP unions], 34, 42, 54
Committee for Defence against the White Terror, 89
Controlled economy, 106, 119
Copenhagen Congress [1910], 39
Czech communists, 83, 84f, 90, 92, 98, 150, 163
Czech countryside, 128f
Czech Legion and Legionnaires, 50, 51, 69, 90
Czechoslovakism, 157
Czech Social Democrats before 1914, 33, 34, 36, 39, 41, 42
Czech Socialist Party [CSP], see NCSP
Czech Union, 43, 75

Dělnické listy, 38
Domovina, 65-6, 139, 143, 145

Duchcov, 34
Dwarfholders of land, 130, 132, 139

Eight Conditions, The, 93

Fideikomis, 128, 132
Fixed voting lists, 61-2

Gesellen, 31

Hungarian Communists, 95, 149
Hungary, 57, 149, 152-3

Impact of Russian Revolution, 149-151
Inflation, 105
International Committee of Soviets, 158
Invasion of Slovakia, 92

Karlín, 144
Key system, The, 16, 59
Kladno, 31, 49, 52, 68, 85, 89, 90, 93, 101, 114, 117, 144
Kolín, 90
Králupy, 144

Land: ratio of rented to owned, 134 [Table 9]
Land Reform, 121, 127
Landless proletariat, 126, 132, 137, 138, 148
Latifundiae, 128, 132, 135

Martial Law, 160-1
Marxist Left, 62, 94, 95, 96-7, 98
Mělník, 144
Minimum Demands of the Škoda workers, 83, 117

203

## SUBJECT INDEX

Most, 34
MPs' mandates, 61

National Committee, 75, 77, 81, 150; local NCs in 1918, 60
National Democrats, 52, 60, 61, 65, 122
NCSP [later CSP], 29, 33, 34, 35, 37, 41, 42, 80, 145

Odborové sdružení československé [SD unions], 101, 105
Olomouc, 81
Orthodox SDs, 13, 15, 16, 17, 24, 46, 52, 70, 81, 82, 95-6, 97-8, 100, 151-2, 163; also Introduction, Part One and Conclusion-Passim
Ostrava, 33, 41, 47, 72, 79, 81, 88-9, 125

Pardubice, 72
Peasant supply quotas, 106
Peasantry, 129, 131, 139, 140
Political system of the Republic, 58f
Prague (and the Red Ring), 31, 35, 44, 68, 92, 117
Pravda [plzeňská], 89
Právo lidu, xix, 38, 99
Proletarian internationalism and nationalism, 30f, 36, 39, 48-9
Přerov, 90, 97, 125

Radical socialism in Slovakia, 158
Reichenberg, 33
Retail prices, 109 [Table 2], 111 [Table 3]

Slovak Soviet Republic, 156-7
Slovakia, 153, 155
Šmeral, Bohumír, 3, 4, 5f, 6-8, 9, 10, 11, 16, 19, 20f, 24, 25, 29f, 40, 70f, 77f, 79f, 85, 122f, 126f, 142, 151, 159, 162; and especially Introduction, Part One and Conclusion-Passim
Social composition of CPC [1924], 123
Socialist Councils in 1918, 53, 76, 78f
Socialization of production, 119-122
Spravedlnost, 89
Stráž svobody, 90
Strikes, 32, 116, 118 [Table 6]
Svaz zemědělských dělníku [Union of Agricultural Workers], 115, 116, 127, 139

Těšín, 154
Topolčany, 154
Trhové Sviny, 114

Unemployment, 114
Unemployment Benefits, 114, 119
Universal Suffrage, 63-4
Užhorod, 155-6

Wartime agricultural production, 104
Wartime requisitions of food, 104, 136-7
Wealth-shifts in wartime, 107-8, 107 [Table 1]
Workers Councils, 93, 101

Železná ruda revolt, 51
Žižkov, 116

DUE DATE

MAY 0 7 1991

SEMST
SEMST JUN
GL OCT 1 1 199
NOV 3 1989
DEC 8 1989
FEB 2 0 1990
MAR 2 6 1990
APR 3 0 REC'D
GLX FEB 1 5 1996
FEB 0 6 1996
201-6503
GL/Rec

Printed in USA